The Handbook for Apartment Living

The Handbook for Apartment Living

Joan Bingham

Chilton Book Company RADNOR, PENNSYLVANIA

Published in Radnor, Pennsylvania, by Chilton Book Company
and simultaneously in Don Mills, Ontario, Canada,
by Nelson Canada Limited

Library of Congress Catalog Card No. 80-70350
ISBN 0-8019-6987-5 *hardcover*
ISBN 0-8019-6988-3 *paperback*

Manufactured in the United States of America

1 2 3 4 5 6 7 8 9 0 0 9 8 7 6 5 4 3 2 1

To
ARDETH BINGHAM;
JASON, SALLY, *and* GARY BATCHELDER;
PETER, WENDY, *and* STEPHANIE GORMAN;
and to DON, *who suggested*
I write this book.

Contents

The Handbook for Apartment Living

Chapter 1

Finding the Ideal Apartment

The number of apartment dwellers is increasing rapidly. New complexes are springing up all over the country, and people with an eye for profit are converting everything from row homes to old barns into apartments. Construction costs have escalated so dramatically that soon only the wealthy may be able to afford a single house. Consequently, more and more people will be calling an apartment "home." This can be a delightful way to live or a disheartening experience, depending on what the apartment dweller finds out before he signs a lease, and how much he knows about adapting his surroundings to his own way of life. The person who knows what he's getting into before he signs a lease has a good chance of getting maximum enjoyment from apartment living.

If you are about to become an apartment dweller, this chapter is for you. If you already have your apartment, you may want to give the chapter a cursory look before reading the rest of the book.

Getting Started

Where do you look for your apartment? The telephone book? The newspaper? A real estate broker? A fee-paid rental agent? That depends on the type of apartment you're looking for and how long you can wait to get it.

If you want to live in a large complex, you'll find most of them listed under "Apartments" in the telephone book. You can go through the Yellow Pages, calling those that appeal to you and asking the questions at the end of this chapter. You won't actually find your apartment this way, but you will eliminate a lot of places and may come up with some possibilities. There isn't always an opening in the complexes (people may wait for years to get into a particular complex), but you may have better luck with newer places or those where there's still construction going on. They generally offer a good choice and often, in an effort to get all the apartments rented, there will be a pretty good introductory special, such as a month or two free occupancy. This is an enticing bonus, but don't count on its being at the start of your lease. It's almost always the last month or two.

The daily newspaper is also an excellent source of information for apartment hunters. Privately owned buildings, small complexes, apartments in out-of-the-way places are usually advertised in the paper. They aren't always as glorious as the ads make them sound; but that's part of the fun of looking, and every once in a while you'll find one that's under-advertised. An ad that reads "four rooms and bath" could lead you to a real palace!

Real estate brokers usually don't like to bother with apartment rentals. The profits they make on them are slim. But occasionally brokers will take listings for friends, and many brokers own rental buildings. So don't eliminate them in your search. Just don't be surprised at the number of brokers who say, "Sorry, we don't handle any rentals."

Fee-paid rental agencies provide a relatively new way of renting apartments and houses. There are drawbacks, though, for the prospective tenant. First, before you can even find out the address of that cozy three bedroom place with a fireplace, and a yard, in a quiet neighborhood (exactly the kind of place you've been searching for) and for only $150 a month including utilities . . . you may have to plunk down a fee. The fee will be at least $20 and will probably not be refundable if you fail to find an apartment. You are paying just to look at the agency's listings. There is no guarantee that they'll find anything for you or that they will even look. These lists almost never have pictures, just brief descriptions and addresses or telephone numbers—like the ads in the paper.

After paying the fee, you're apt to find out that your dream house: a) has been rented already (some agencies have even been known to advertise real estate that is nonexistent); b) is too far from where you want to live; c) does exist in the right location for you and at the stipulated $150 a month—it has a fireplace, and three bedrooms, and the utilities are paid by the landlord. But wait! On closer inspection you discover that the fireplace happens to be the only heat. The plumbing is outdoors in a building with a crescent on the door. There isn't any electricity. And the reason the neighborhood is quiet is because every other house has been condemned. This is, of course, an exaggeration, but it illustrates a point. Not all fee-paid rental agencies are dishonest or shifty. But don't be too anxious to part with your money. They've had a great many dissatisfied customers.

Many of these agencies get their listings right out of the classified section of the newspaper, the same way you can. They see an ad, call the owner and ask if they may list the apartment at no charge to the owner. Most owners say "yes." And why not? It's no loss for them one way or the other. And they may get the apartment rented, which is, after all, what they want.

Sometimes, if you read ads carefully, you can find the same apartment listed both by the owner and the fee-paid rental agency. The wording is different but the description and area often give it away.

Are you looking for a city apartment or a country place? A city apartment, in a good neighborhood, usually costs more than a comparable one in the country. If you work in the city and must commute daily, that commuting cost should be considered, especially these days when transportation is so expensive. But if you're a devotee of country living, chances are the commuting costs won't matter to you.

Apartments in the country aren't as easy to come by and there are far fewer complexes. But don't let that keep you from looking. In recent years some luxurious complexes have been built well outside the city limits. Take a look at the bulletin board in the local grocery store or supermarket. It often bears intriguing ads for rural places to rent.

It's essential to know the neighborhood in which you're contemplating making your home. A beautiful apartment that's inexpensive is suspect. Check out that neighborhood thoroughly. This is especially important if you're a woman living alone. It's no fun to be afraid to go home at night.

What to Look For

Once you've decided on location, and you're actually looking at an apartment, listen while you look. Do you hear the patter of feet overhead? If so, the floors and ceilings are probably not thick enough. Can you hear the stereo next door? You may like the sonata your prospective neighbor is playing—until you hear it at two o'clock in the morning. And remember that if you can hear him, he can hear you. That means keeping your stereo, your TV, and your voice at a low pitch. Is it worth it?

Many good complexes have 3½-inch concrete slabs between floors. These make the apartments virtually soundproof. Pressed wood floors and ceilings with 6 inches of insulation are also quite effective in combating noise, and are more common since concrete slabs require steel beam construction. For best soundproofing, walls should be made of cinder block filled with pearlite or a comparable insulating material. The building inspector in the city or town where you are looking should be able to supply you with construction facts about the building in which you're interested. These desirable features aren't always found in the more expensive places so don't be fooled by the trimmings. Costly doesn't always mean good or even soundproof.

Don't be afraid to ask questions of the person who's showing you around the apartment. And don't take evasive answers. When you're inquiring about noise level, "I don't know of anyone who has complained" is an evasive answer. So is, "Not too high," when you're asking how much the heat or utilities bills run. These people should be able to give you concrete answers and figures backed up by previous bills. If the place is new, the local gas or electric company will gladly give you a rough estimate of what they think it will cost to power it.

Many apartments, both old and new, have wall-to-wall carpeting. If you don't own rugs, this can provide a major savings. And carpeting is a big help in soundproofing. But examine the carpet well. In many buildings it is very cheap and looks very cheap, especially if the apartment has been tenanted before and the carpet has had a chance to show wear. Even if the carpet is new, you may find that it will show wear quickly. Only the poshest apartments provide posh carpeting.

If you rent an apartment that lacks adequate soundproofing, you'll be a captive audience and you may not like the "apartment symphony."

If you have rugs of your own, wall-to-wall carpeting can actually be a disadvantage. When your rugs lie on top of it, they tend to wrinkle in the center and get waves along the edges when you walk on them. Often the color the landlord supplies (usually gold or green) won't blend with your own rugs and furnishings.

Some places give you the option of using their carpet or supplying your own. There is, of course, an additional rental charge if the landlord supplies carpet. In my opinion, it's seldom worth it. For the money you're paying to rent a carpet that is not just what you want, you can probably purchase your own. If you have no further use for it when you vacate the apartment, sell it.

If the apartment is carpeted, find out what's underneath. Is there a good thick pad, and most important, is there flooring or just a concrete slab? A rug placed directly on concrete without a thick padding in between produces a chillingly cold walking surface. I lived in an apartment one entire winter where I was never warm below the knees, no matter how high I turned the thermostat. The damp cold that radiates from this type of floor is especially damaging for anyone who has arthritis, rheumatism, or circulatory difficulties. It's terrible for a small baby who's learning how to crawl, or for a child who spends a great deal of time playing on the floor. If you rent an apartment like this, you'll be better off if you do have carpeting of your own to put over the wall-to-wall. It helps, but by no means eliminates, that cold, damp feeling.

Apartments with outside entrances of their own are not nearly as inviting to burglars as those with entrances from corridors which afford the thief a much better chance of breaking in without detection. He can listen and watch for approaching people. But an entrance which leaves him visible to passers-by is far more risky for him, and usually not worth the chance.

The problem of cleanliness is easier to solve with your own entrance, too. Many complexes don't take proper care of corridors. It is a good idea to ask the landlord how often the corridors are vacuumed. Don't accept an uncertain answer. Get specifics! Once a week is generally not enough. Twice a week isn't too often. If you have an outside entrance of your own, you don't encounter this problem.

While you're finding out about corridors and entrances, check the lighting. Are there enough lights in the halls and outside the doors? How late are they left on at night? Do they go out at midnight? If you work the late shift, you may object to groping around to get your key in the lock. Or you may feel uncomfortable coming home and not being able to see if someone is lurking in the corridor or outside your private entrance. If the apartment has corridors, are the outside doors left unlocked so that anyone can enter the building, or do you need a key to get in? Some buildings have a doorman. Supposedly no one gets by him without permission from a tenant. This is a great comfort in a big city. Other complexes have television scanners that cover the halls in the building, monitoring any suspicious activity. Precautions of this type discourage all but the most determined burglar.

Check to see if there is sufficient light on staircases. While you're on the staircase, notice whether or not it is carpeted. If not, you might hear the footsteps of every person who goes up and down, day or night.

Does the owner live in the building or complex? This has its advantages and disadvantages. When things go wrong, it's easy to find a resident landlord. Since he lives there too, he's usually a caring landlord. This is his home, not just an income property. The noisy neighbor that's driving you up a wall is driving him up a wall too, and chances are that he won't put up with it. But if you're the noisy neighbor, you may not be so enchanted with a resident landlord, nor he with you. If you live anything but a quiet life, you may be better off if the landlord lives across town or is just another big faceless corporation to whom you pay a monthly check. But it can be catastrophic if something goes wrong and the faceless corporation hasn't left anyone in charge.

Large apartment buildings and complexes often have resident managers. These people don't usually care as much what goes on in the buildings as the owners do, but it's still their job to deal with your complaints swiftly. If you forget your key, the resident manager should have one; if the neighbors are loud, you have someone to whom you can complain. If the plumbing leaks, the resident manager is supposed to see that it's fixed. Many of these people are Johnny-on-the-spot fix-it types. They'll repair the refrigerator, the leak in the roof, the short circuit, and the dishwasher quickly and efficiently, and usually with a smile. They may even fill you in on the latest gossip.

But the resident manager doesn't replace a maintenance crew. If your apartment building has a lawn, someone has to mow it. If there's a walk someone has to shovel it when it snows. Ask who that someone is. And also take a good look around to see if whoever is supposed to be doing it is actually taking care of the job. Is the lawn freshly mowed or does it look like a hay field? Don't hesitate to ask other tenants how often these things are done.

What about window washing? Of course, the inside is going to be your responsibility, but what about the outside? If the apartment is on the tenth floor, you may have second thoughts about trying to get the outside of your windows sparkling. Many well-run apartments have a maintenance crew to take care of this twice a year.

That brings us to the question of which floor best suits your needs. High-rise buildings will be discussed later. For now, let's consider the buildings with three floors. Many older buildings and a number of newer complexes fall into this category.

A basement apartment is usually a few dollars cheaper per month than apartments on the upper floors. Often the natural light is considerably less because a good portion of the place is underground. And these apartments tend to be damp. You have, in addition, the potential problem of noisy neighbors overhead. These places, in real estate vernacular, are known as "garden apartments"—in most cases a misnomer.

Let's move up to the first floor, which is really the middle floor. While you don't encounter a problem with dampness, you usually do pay more rent than you would for the "garden apartment" in the same complex. If the floors and ceilings aren't soundproof, you're going to get noise from above and below. You'll still have the herds overhead and you'll have to try to avoid disturbing your neighbors underneath you. You're the filling in the sandwich.

The top floor costs still more but it gives you the heavenly advantage of not having anyone overhead to bother you. But, like everything else, it also has built-in disadvantages. If the building has no elevator, and few of these three-story buildings do, think of making that climb with heavy bags every time you shop. On the bright side, exercise is good for you!

Another drawback is heat in summer. Since heat rises, so does the bill for air conditioning a third floor apartment. And if you don't have air conditioning you'll probably swelter. If there's an attic or a good-sized storage space over your top floor apartment, some of the heat will go there, but if the building has a flat roof or just a crawl space, that apartment will get the full brunt of the summer sun.

Unless it's air-conditioned, the top floor of a building that has a flat roof is no place to live on a scorching hot day.

Heating and Air Conditioning

While the presence of heat is a problem in summer, its absence can be a problem in winter. You should look into this before signing a lease on any apartment. The big questions are: Who controls the heat? And who pays for it? As the cost of fuels for heating soars, more and more apartment owners are leaving this cost to the tenant. In years past, most apartments were heated at the owner's expense even though the tenants controlled the heat. And in cases where there is only one heating unit to take care of two or more apartments, the landlords still pay the heating bills.

Before you heave a sigh of relief and start a search for an apartment where you won't have to pay for heat, take heed! Many of the landlords who pay for heat also control it. This means that you may roast all winter or you may freeze. The landlord, if he's not heartless, is going to try to keep everyone in his apartments reasonably warm. In order to do this, he may have to jack the heat up fairly high to accommodate some of his tenants. Since heat rises, the people on the third floor may be extremely warm, while the people on the first floor may be freezing.

With the trend toward keeping the heat down for the good of the nation, many a landlord has become a flag waver, keeping his apartments at 65 degrees in the name of patriotism. So if the apartment in which you're interested comes heat paid, ask who controls it. If it's the landlord, ask at what temperature he sets the thermostat. Then, if that suits your comfort range, get it in writing. After the lease is signed and you're freezing, it's easy for him to swear he never told you he'd keep the temperature at 70 degrees.

If you're expected to pay for the heat, find out what kind of fuel is required. Electric is enormously expensive. But many of the apartments heated this way have thermostats in every room, making it possible to shut off a room that's not in use, thus considerably lowering the heating costs.

Oil is no longer cheap but it is efficient, providing the oil man can make it through the snow drifts. It isn't as clean as electricity or gas heat, although it's infinitely cleaner than coal. Because of the fuel shortage, some oil dealers won't take on any new customers; be sure you have someone lined up to service your burner and supply you with oil, before you sign the lease.

Natural gas is used to heat many apartments. It's very efficient and, in many parts of the country, slightly less expensive than oil. Coal is still used to heat some apartments. Don't rule it out. It's far cheaper than other types of heat even though it's more work for someone.

You also need to know who maintains the burner and sees that it's kept clean and running. If you assume that the landlord does, in most cases you're right. There are exceptions, however. Be sure that the facts about this are clearly understood before you sign the lease. Ask when the burner was last cleaned. For safety as well as efficiency, it should be done every year no matter what kind of fuel is used.

That takes care of keeping warm in winter. What about keeping cool in summer? Is the apartment air conditioned? Does it need it? Central air is lovely, but not perfect. The cost of running a central unit that will cool a five-room apartment, for instance, is high and still going up. Individual room units on the other hand, give you the option of shutting off rooms and only cooling the portion of the apartment that's in use.

Some apartments have sleeves, through the walls, for the air conditioners. These enable you to enjoy the benefit of the cool air and the benefit of the light and view at the same time. Inquire whether the apartment owner or the tenant provides the units for these sleeves.

If neither air conditioners nor sleeves are in evidence and you want to provide your own units, ask about wiring. Some large units need a 220 line, and any air conditioner needs a line of its own. No other appliance or light should run off the same fuse. In many places this is a law.

If there's central air conditioning, find out who pays. Just because the landlord pays for the heat doesn't mean he pays for the air conditioning.

Other Concerns

WIRING

Whether you're going to put in air conditioning units or not, you should check the wiring in the place you're considering. Some cities have passed ordinances requiring property owners to update the wiring in their buildings to meet certain standards. Even if this ordinance exists in your area, the enforcement is generally slow. For adequate service with all of today's modern conveniences, a house should be wired for at least 100 amp service. The more electrical appliances you have, the higher amp service you'll need. You don't want to move into a place only to discover that you can't run your hair dryer without blowing a fuse, or that you can't use the vacuum cleaner while the refrigerator motor is on.

While you're finding out about the wiring, don't forget to check the wall outlets. How many are there in each room? Many areas require a minimum of one double outlet on every wall. Having more than that is a real bonus and fewer means trouble with dangerous extension cords and multiple plugs. Outlets on the floor are outdated and in most places they don't meet with the wiring code. If you find them, chances are that the wiring in the apartment is ancient, inadequate, and unsafe. Furthermore, such outlets collect dust, attract children with pointed objects, and are easy to trip over.

PLUMBING

Although not easy to check visually, in an older building ask about the plumbing. Modern fixtures may be connected to old pipes subject to leaking at any time. Although most apartment owners are quick to fix plumbing problems because they can be damaging to their property, you'll find it inconvenient if the sink or toilet gets stopped up when you have company. In one case I know of where the pipes were old, water started running out of an overhead electrical fixture—a scary experience.

CABLE TELEVISION

Cable television is popular in many areas. Some places provide a cable hookup, and the price will be included in the rent. In others you must get the cable yourself, make all the arrangements with the cable company, and pay an installation fee as well as the monthly rate. It sounds like cable paid for by the landlord is the better deal. But that's not always true.

Some complexes have contracts with cable companies to hook up all their apartments. The catch is you may find the cable hookup for your television set also services many of the other tenants in the building. This makes for a weak signal and poor reception. In one apartment I had, the new color set was fuzzy much of the time. I called in a repairman who explained to me that eight other apartments were hooked to the same line. At peak watching hours, none of us was getting adequate power from the cable. So, you may be better off supplying your own.

Whether cable is supplied or you pay for it, find out how many hookups you're allowed to have. If you're a four television family with a two hookup limit, you may be unhappy in your new home. Some landlords only allow a cable connection in one room because they don't want the floor, ceiling, or walls marked from the installation of further cables. A clause to this effect may even appear in the lease.

LAUNDRY FACILITIES

Many apartment complexes provide laundry facilities. These are often coin-operated concessions owned by an outside firm. Take a look at the laundry room. Some of them are pretty grim—dingy, dirty, no place to fold or hang clothes, seldom serviced. If the laundry room looks bright and shiny, ask how many families use each washer and dryer, and what hours the laundry room is open. About eight families per washer and dryer gives you a good chance of getting a crack at the machines on a regular basis, providing the families aren't too big. But if there are more than that, chances are the machines won't be available when you want them, and you shouldn't let their presence influence your decision about the apartment.

If there is no laundry room, or if the facilities don't look appealing or are overcrowded, find out how far it is to the nearest laundromat. Is it a convenient distance, considering the mode of transportation you have to use to get there? And what hours is it open?

Some apartments have washers and dryers right in the apartment. This is great if you wash frequently. It's great anyway, but in some cases it's an unnecessary luxury. These apartments do cost more than similar ones without laundry facilities. Is it worth the extra money per month? This depends on how often you wash clothes and what your other options are for doing laundry.

Other apartments have hookups for laundry facilities but you must provide the washer and dryer. For some people this is the best solution. Instead of paying extra rent to use the landlord's machines, they can put the same money into payments on a washer and dryer of their own.

A large, clean laundry room with enough washers and dryers and a table for folding is a large plus for any apartment building.

Still other landlords won't allow you to wash clothes on the premises at all. This is often because of the water bill. So if you're planning to put in your own small apartment-sized washer and hang your clothes in the back yard, find out if you'll be allowed to do it.

MAJOR APPLIANCES

For all of us who hate oven cleaning the self-cleaning oven is one of the greatest inventions since fire. Some modern apartments have these wonders. Surprisingly, they don't run up your electric bill much more than a regular range does.

The frost-free or self-defrosting refrigerator-freezers are another matter. These work-savers can cost up to twice as much to run as a conventional refrigerator.

Two-door refrigerators (those with a separate, outside door for the freezer compartment) are vastly superior to the models which have only one outside door. Frost doesn't build up as fast, and freezer units operate more efficiently with the protection of that outside door. Many one-door models don't even keep ice cream adequately, so you can imagine what happens to your frozen food, which should be stored at 0 degrees.

Is a dishwasher really necessary? To some people it is, to others it's an energy-burning nuisance. If there isn't one in the apartment you have your heart set on, and you also have your heart set on a dishwasher, ask the landlord if you will be allowed to have a portable one. The installation of these is negligible, they can go with you when you move, and they provide a bit more counter space—something that's short in many apartments. Portable dishwashers can be converted to under-the-counter models.

STORAGE

Some of the most luxurious apartments are shy of storage space. Is there a safe place for you to store your snow tires? Your suitcases? Your lawn chairs and patio furniture? Is it dry, or are your possessions going to get mildewed and musty? Is there an adequate lock on the door? Is the storage bin in a basement? Is it made of chicken wire? That's a thief's delight because it's easy to see what's worth stealing, and it's a cinch to cut through. Or is the bin constructed of good sturdy wood? Is the room that contains the storage units open to anyone or is it kept locked, accessible only to tenants with keys?

TRASH

Who pays for trash pickup? How often is the trash collected? Do you have to provide trash barrels or does the landlord supply them? Perhaps the trash facilities are in the basement of the building. If so, it's essential that the barrels are clean and tightly covered. Is there a trash pickup at all or must you make a trip to the local dump?

If you're looking in a complex, where are the dumpsters located? Is there one near the apartment in which you're interested? Is it so

A trash bin that's overflowing indicates a sloppy attitude on the part of management.

close that you may be bothered by a constant stream of people coming and going? Take a look at the dumpster. Is it brimming full? This is a sign of inadequate service. It's also an invitation to undesirable rodents.

If the trash situation or any other condition in the building leads you to suspect that there may be a problem with cockroaches or other pests, ask. (Naturally, it's better to ask someone who lives there, if you can, rather than the landlord.) Some owners provide free exterminating service on a regular basis. Find out about this before signing a lease.

FLOOR PLANS

Study the floor plan of an apartment carefully! Different floor plans lend themselves to different styles of living. This is the reason some complexes offer many alternate plans. Is the floor plan of the apartment going to help make living pleasant for you and your family? There are many things to consider.

If you have teenage children or a resident in-law, you might prefer a plan that offers bedrooms separated by closets or a bathroom. These provide noise buffers and afford each person a degree of privacy not present when bedrooms have common walls. On the other hand, if you have an infant, you might want the closeness provided by a common wall.

Where do you enter the apartment? Is it a kitchen entrance? If you entertain a great deal, are you going be satisfied having your guests come in this way? Are there two entrances? What is the traffic pattern? Does everything go off of the living room? Are you going to be happy with this? Do you want an entry hall, or do you feel that's just wasted space?

If you have small children, an eat-in kitchen may be preferable to a dining room. But if the boss comes to dinner often, you may feel a formal dining room is essential.

Check out the wall space and size of the rooms. Will your king-sized bed fit into the master bedroom? Is there enough wall for that nine-foot sectional sofa? If you have a piano, are you going to have space for it? Large oversized pieces of furniture can turn a nice little apartment into an obstacle course, ruining the fun of your new home.

Among life's disheartening experiences is finding out on moving day that a prized piece of furniture won't fit through any of the doors of your new apartment, or at least not through the door to the only room in which you want it. Measure! Measure! Measure! And do it when you're in the looking stage—not when you're in the moving stage, or after the lease has been signed. During one move I made—this was before I started using a tape measure—I had to saw the legs off my desk in order to fit it into the room that was to be my office. It was a drastic thing to do but it was absolutely the only way my desk was going to fit into that apartment and the one-year lease was already signed. If I had thought to measure beforehand, I never would have rented that apartment.

Measure your closets, too. Be certain they will hold all of your clothes. Clothes look rumpled all the time if they're jammed into inadequate space. While you're checking the closets, measure the height of the clothes rods. I lived in one apartment where the rods weren't high enough to hang long gowns without their dragging on the floor. Since this was during the time when women wore long dresses to all evening functions, it presented a real problem. I solved it by putting racks for my gowns on the insides of the closet doors. These served the purpose admirably. I probably would have taken the apartment even if I'd measured the rods ahead of time. But it was inconvenient and, to someone else, might have been intolerable.

Walk-in closets should have lights; otherwise you'll stumble around in the dark trying to pick out the outfit for the day. There should be at least one closet for every bedroom. In some of the older apartments, you'll find a closet in the hall instead of in a bedroom. Would this be a problem for you?

Linen closets are handy and, unless you have some other place to keep your sheets and towels, they are essential. A broom closet is also a plus, especially if it's big enough to store your vacuum cleaner.

Cabinet space is another important consideration. I like lots and lots of it, but I've also found that a dining room china cabinet takes care of the overflow and displays my good dishes at the same time. Check and see that the cabinets are well placed so they'll be accessible when you're cooking or putting away dishes. While you're counting cabinets, take a look at the counter space. Is there enough work space? If not, will adding a table take care of the problem?

While you're in the kitchen, try the burners on the stove and turn on the oven to be sure everything works. If it doesn't, ask if it will be fixed before you move in. Many landlords want their properties in top condition and are most willing to correct things if they're pointed out. Others will do the minimum. If a landlord won't replace a dying burner on a stove for you, chances are he won't fix anything that may go wrong during your tenancy. You're better off to keep looking.

CHILDREN

You may love children, but not when they're crying over your head at three in the morning. Some landlords won't allow children. Others will allow them only on the first floor. In a well sound-

"A place for everything and everything in its place" is a necessity in the average apartment.

conditioned building, you shouldn't hear children on the floor below you. Some complexes have buildings where families with children may live and others that are restricted to adults. But before you decide on the building without children, check the landlord's definition of children. In some places they are defined as anyone under 18 or even 21, while in other places children are people under 12. If the landlord says there are no children but the family living in the apartment you want to rent does have two teenagers, you may want to reconsider. If rock and roll is your bag, you may not mind. However, if you're a fan of the classics, you may find that you'd prefer a screaming baby to a couple of stereo-playing teens.

PARKING

There has been a great deal of hassle in some pretty posh places over the problem of parking. When you pay an exorbitant rent and have to drive around the block five times before you find a parking spot, your patience can wear thin.

Many complexes assign reserved spaces to their tenants. It's advisable, however, to find out how many. You may have two cars, and only one space. There may be a garage or carport that can be rented for an additional monthly charge. In some instances it's mandatory to rent one of these if you have more than a prescribed number of cars. For instance, if you have three cars, you may be allowed two spaces and for any additional car you'll have to rent a carport or garage. And you still may have trouble. When space is scarce, someone may take your spot. And in complexes with parking problems, guest parking can be miserable. So find out about parking. If it looks a bit tight to you, but the landlord gives a glowing report, ask another tenant. Irate tenants are usually glad to unload their woes, and you'll end up with an answer that is closer to the truth.

Apartments in the country usually don't have parking difficulties. There is adequate curb space even when there aren't reserved spaces. But city apartments without offstreet parking can be a real challenge for the car owner. And beware of the parking meter. You may work all of the hours those meters are running, but have you considered the day you may be home sick? Do you really want to get out of bed and feed the meter every hour or two? And don't forget about vacations and weekends.

An increasing number of cities are requiring people who divide houses into apartments or build new apartments to provide at least one parking space per unit. This helps, but it doesn't take care of the apartments built or converted before these laws were enacted, nor does it help much if you're a two-car family.

RECREATION

Does the complex you're contemplating offer any recreational facilities—swimming pool, tennis courts, golf? If so, find out your obligations and rights as a tenant. Is the cost of their maintenance included in your rent? If you use the pool often you'll probably prefer this. The cost is then divided among all of the tenants. But if you don't plan to use the facilities, you may be happier in a complex that charges a membership fee to those who do use them. That way you have the option of using the pool and courts, for a stipulated fee, or passing.

If you're an enthusiastic sportsman, ask what hours these facilities are open. Some are available just a few short hours each day and open for a short season. It's disappointing to come home from a hard day's work, looking forward to a dip in the pool, and find that it's closed for the day.

Important Extras

When you're doing your apartment hunting in the dead of winter, the question of screens might not occur to you. Don't just ask about screens—ask to see them, especially if the apartment is an older one, to determine their condition. Any screens that fit properly are better than no screens at all. If the screening needs to be replaced, the time to dicker with the landlord is now, before you rent his property. If he won't agree, you can have the screening replaced yourself, providing you like the apartment enough to feel it's worth it. If there are no screens, however, you'll find that having frames made is costly and you may prefer to look for another apartment.

Conversely, storm windows seem to diminish in importance on a hot summer day. But find out about them, too, especially if you'll be paying the heating costs. Even if the landlord pays for the heat, it's surprising the number of landlords who don't make the investment in storm windows or thermal pane windows, even though it will save them money in the long run. And no matter who's paying for the heat, a drafty apartment is a drafty apartment, not a cozy home.

Do the walls in your prospective home need painting? Who is going to do it? If the landlord says you can paint if you don't like the color, will he supply the paint? Ask if there are any color restrictions like light colors only. Or if you have to cover the walls with white before you leave, ponder a bit before you decide to paint the wall dark green, black or red. You will probably be too busy, when it's time to move out, to cover a dark color with five coats of white.

Are you allowed to wallpaper? If so, must it be strippable paper? Of course, all wallpaper can be stripped off, but what is called "strippable" in the wallpaper trade comes off with a minimum of effort. Sometimes just a tug at the corner will pull off the whole piece. It's also generally washable, a nice bonus in a grimy city apartment.

If you're apartment hunting in a large city, chances are you'll want to be near public transportation, especially if you don't own a car. Don't take someone's vague assurance that the bus leaves from just down the street. "Just down the street" might be ten blocks. Investigate and find out the schedules for trains, buses, subways, or whatever, and the exact stops that they make.

Even the small cities and suburbs have fallen into a high-rise craze. Places that never had a building over four stories now suddenly boast apartments that sit majestically fifteen floors or more above the landscape. The view is magnificent from some of them, but these buildings aren't for everyone. One city that I know of has two fifteen-story, high-rise apartment buildings and the city's most sophisticated piece of fire equipment has a ladder that reaches six stories high. I'd think a long time before I'd rent an apartment on the seventh floor or higher of either one of those buildings.

Yet people do rent apartments that are higher than the local fire department can reach, despite recent scandals about the construction of some high-rise buildings. For example, it has been claimed that in some modern buildings improperly engineered air conditioning ducts will act like pipes, drawing fire throughout the building. So before you fall in love with the tenth floor, check on the local fire equipment.

Apartment Hunter's Checklist

If you've read this chapter thoroughly, you should be able to avoid some of the pitfalls of apartment hunting. The following questionnaire should help you evaluate any apartment you're considering. It's so much easier to fill it in than try to remember later which apartment had which feature. In no way would I presume to tell you how to score this questionnaire. That's up to you. After all, one person's dream home is another's nightmare. But it does help to remember that you're not apt to find everything for which you're looking in one apartment. Rate the items in order of their importance to you.

Total number of rooms___
Dimensions of rooms: Living room__________
 Dining room__________ Kitchen__________
 Bathroom 1__________ Bathroom 2__________
 Master Bedroom__________ Bedroom 2__________
 Bedroom 3__________ Bedroom 4__________
 Family room__________
 Total amount of living space__________
Is there a maximum occupancy per apartment? Yes___ No___
How does floor plan suit your needs? Excellent___ Good___ Fair___
 Poor___
Will your furniture fit? Well___ Fairly well___ Poorly___ No___
Closets: Total number of closets___
 Number of walk-in closets___ Linen closets___ Broom closets___
 Coat closets___ Bedroom closets___ Storage closets___ Others___
Windows: Number of windows___
 Exposure of windows: North___ South___ East___ West___
 Storm windows: Yes___ No___ Some___
 Thermal windows: Yes___ No___ Some___
 Screens: Yes___ No___ Some___
 Condition of screens: Excellent___ Fair___ Poor___
Kitchen Questions:
 Number of cabinets___
 How do they meet your needs? Excellent___ Good___ Fair___
 Poor___
 Counterspace: Excellent___ Good___ Fair___ Poor___
 Dishwasher: Yes___ No___
 Garbage disposal: Yes___ No___
 Trash compactor: Yes___ No___
 Refrigerator: Yes___ No___
 Self-defrosting: Yes___ No___ Two-door: Yes___ No___
 Stove: New___ Old___ Gas___ Electric___

Self-cleaning: Yes__ No__
Kitchen fan: Yes__ No__ To outside: Yes__ No__
Plumbing: Modern__ Semi-modern__ Old__
Who pays for water? Tenant__ Landlord__
Wiring: Amps__ Number of outlets per room__
220 line: Yes__ No__
Separate lines for air conditioners: Yes__ No__
Heat: What kind of heat? Oil__ Gas__ Electric__ Other__
Who pays for heat? Tenant__ Landlord__
Who controls heat? Tenant__ Landlord__
Air conditioning: Central__ Window__ Just sleeves__ None__
Laundry: Laundry room: Yes__ No__ Hours open: __ to __
Separate washers and dryers in apartment: Yes__ No__
Hookups for washers and dryers in apartments: Yes__ No__
Are you allowed to wash clothes on premises? Yes__ No__
Distance to laundromat: Very near__ Fairly near__ Too far__
What size water heater?__ Is it a quick recovery? Yes__ No__
How is soundproofing? Excellent__ Good__ Fair__ Poor__
Is there a:
Patio? Yes__ No__
Yard? Yes__ No__
Porch? Yes__ No__ Garage? Yes__ No__ Carport? Yes__ No__
Reserved parking space? Yes__ No__ How many?__
Parking meters? Yes__ No__
A place to wash your car? Yes__ No__
Location of apartment:
Neighborhood: Excellent__ Good__ Fair__ Poor__
What floor is apartment on?____
Distance to transportation: Very near__ Fairly near__ Distant__
Level of neighborhood noise: High__ Medium__ Low__
Is there a fireplace? Yes__ No__
Fireplace: Electric__ Gas__ Wood burning__
Is carpeting supplied? Yes__ No__
How many cable hookups are allowed per apartment?__
How many apartments are on a cable hookup?__
Is there an outside antenna? Yes__ No__
Is there an outside entrance right into apartment? Yes__ No__

Are corridors cleaned more than once a week? Yes___ No___

Are corridors well-lighted? Yes___ No___

Is there a resident landlord? Yes___ No___

Is there a resident manager? Yes___ No___

Is there a maintenance crew? Yes___ No___

Is there a play area for children? Yes___ No___

Is apartment near schools? Yes___ No___

Are you allowed to have pets?

Dogs: Yes___ No___ Cats: Yes___ No___ Other: Yes___ No___

Is trash pickup included in rent? Yes___ No___

How often is trash picked up?___________

Chapter 2

Legal Ins and Outs

This chapter will acquaint you with legal options and restrictions which may apply to renters in your region and of which you may be unaware. The legal aspects of renting are many, and they vary widely from state to state, from county to county, and even from city to city. Because laws are constantly changing, it's impossible to list here which parts of the country are covered by what statutes (with a few exceptions where the type of legislation in force is unlikely to change).

There are several ways to learn what laws apply. If there is a human relations board or committee in your city or town, they will have free pamphlets explaining some of the renter's rights. Laws are, of course, a matter of public record. A call to the clerk of your local courthouse or city hall should be all it takes to find out where you can unearth the statutes that cover renting in your area. Legal documents, however, are not always easy to understand. You may require the services of a lawyer to unravel the legal jargon. Most cities have a lawyer referral service. (If you live in the country, inquire in the city nearest you.) For a nominal fee, this agency will put you in touch with the type of lawyer you need for your particular problem. The fee you pay the referral service generally includes your first visit to the lawyer; for this purpose, one visit should do it.

Legal aid societies also operate in almost every city, but their waiting lists are long, and your income must be very low in order to qualify for their services.

If you try these sources unsuccessfully, a letter to your state representative should result in help and information.

Leases in General

A lease tells you how you're permitted to live and often says how many people may occupy the premises, which you'll call "home." In most instances, the lease protects you from having the landlord raise the rent during the period of the lease although this isn't always the case, as you will see later in this chapter. Leases are definitely slanted for the landlord's benefit, not for the comfort of the renter. If there is to be a victim, you are likely to be it.

Most leases are written in legalese that few people would understand even if they took time to read them. And not many tenants do read a lease before signing it. Leases are long and complicated. You may just want to get the key to your new apartment and move in, but I can't urge you strongly enough not to sign a lease until you have gone over it thoroughly. If you don't understand a clause, go to a lawyer for clarification. And don't be placated when the landlord tells you that a clause with which you're displeased is standard in all his leases but he never enforces it. If he never enforces it, he doesn't need it in the lease and should be willing to cross it out (and initial this correction) before the lease is signed. If he insists on leaving it in, he has a reason—be careful! A bad lease can be harder to get out of than a bad marriage.

Many landlords won't change anything in the lease, and you may be willing to go along with whatever it says just to get the apartment you like. But do try for the changes and do be aware of the sacrifice you're making if the landlord won't budge.

There are certain clauses you may want inserted in a lease. A sublet clause gives you the right to rent your apartment to another party if at some time during the period of your lease you should find it undesirable or not feasible to continue to tenant the apartment. A transfer clause also works in the tenant's favor. This gives you the right to terminate the lease, usually without penalty, if you're transferred by your company to another area from which it would be impossible to commute.

Try for a clause that doesn't limit, at least not severely, the number of people who may reside in your apartment. The lease might state that the premises can be tenanted only by you and your spouse. What happens if you have a baby? You could be evicted!

Apartment Lease Agreement

1. Parties

This Agreement, MADE THE .... day of ....
one thousand nine hundred and .... (19..........), by and between ....
...................., *Agent,* (hereinafter called "Lessor"), of the one part, and
....
....
....
.... (hereinafter called "Lessee"), of the other part.

2. Premises

WITNESSETH THAT: Lessor does hereby demise and let unto Lessee the apartment or flat of .... rooms and .... bath(s), being No. .... on the .... floor of the building known as ....
....
...................., State of Pennsylvania, to

3. Term

be used and occupied as living apartment only for .... persons and for no other purpose, for the term of ....
beginning the .... day of ....
one thousand nine hundred and .... (19..........) and ending the ....
day of ...., one thousand nine hundred and .... (19..........) for the

4. Minimum Rent

minimum .... rental of .... Dollars ($..........) lawful money of the United States of America, payable in monthly installments in advance during the said term of this lease, or any renewal hereof, in sums of .... Dollars ($..........) on the .... day of each month, rent to begin from the .... day of ...., 19..........,
the first installment to be paid at the time of signing this lease. The first rental payment to be made during the occupancy of the premises shall be adjusted to pro-rate a partial month of occupancy, if any, at the inception of this lease.

5. Inability to give Possession

If Lessor is unable to give Lessee possession of the demised premises, as herein provided, by reason of the holding over of a previous occupant, or by reason of any cause beyond the control of the Lessor, the Lessor shall not be liable in damages to the Lessee therefor, and during the period that the Lessor is unable to give possession, all rights and remedies of both parties hereunder shall be suspended, and if Lessor is unable for any reason to give possession of the demised premises within 5 days of Lessee's demand therefor following commencement of the term hereof Lessee shall have the option, by notice to Lessor, to cancel this lease agreement and receive return of any prepaid rents and security deposit in full and final settlement of any and all claims against Lessor.

6. Additional Rent

Lessee agrees to pay as additional rent any and all sums which may become due by reason of the failure of Lessee to comply with any of the covenants of this lease and any and all damages, costs and expenses which the Lessor may suffer or incur by reason of any default of the Lessee or failure on his part to comply with the covenants of this lease, and also any and all damages to the demised premises caused by any act or neglect of the Lessee, his guests, agents, employees or other occupants of the demised premises.

7. Place of Payment

All rent shall be payable without prior notice or demand at the office of or at such other place as Lessor may from time to time designate by notice in writing.

8. Affirmative Covenants of Lessor

(*a*) Lessor agrees to furnish a reasonable amount of heat commencing not before the first day of October, and continuing not later than the first day of May, following, and to furnish hot and cold water during the continuance of this lease or any renewal thereof, without extra charge. In consideration that no extra charge is made therefor, should Lessor fail to supply same for any reason, Lessor shall not be liable for any damage caused by any such failure not due to Lessor's gross negligence, nor for any damage to property of Lessee caused in any manner by fire, water, heat or steam, or the lack thereof.

(*b*) If Lessee so desires, Lessor, if possible, will make available to Lessee, without charge, a space in the building for the storage of miscellaneous personal property of Lessee. In consideration of the fact that no extra charge is made for the furnishing of such space by the Lessor, it is understood that Lessor shall not be liable for loss or damage to any goods stored, from or by fire or theft or from any cause whatever; and Lessee expressly releases Lessor as bailee or otherwise from all claims for any such loss or damage. It is further understood that the use of storage space by Lessee shall be limited to the time of Lessee's occupancy of the demised premises, and goods left after the expiration of Lessee's occupancy shall be deemed abandoned by Lessee and may be disposed of by Lessor after ten days' notice to Lessee.

9. Affirmative Covenants of Lessee (a) Payment of Rent

Lessee covenants and agrees that he will without demand:

(*a*) Pay the rent and all other charges herein reserved as rent at the times and at the place that the same are payable, without fail; and if Lessor shall at any time or times accept said rent or rent charges after the same shall have become delinquent, such acceptance shall not excuse delay upon subsequent occasions, or constitute or be construed as a waiver of any of Lessor's rights. Lessee agrees that any charge or payment herein reserved, included, or agreed to be treated or collected as rent and/or any other charges, expenses, or costs herein agreed to be paid by Lessee may be proceeded for and recovered by Lessor by legal process in the same manner as rent due and in arrears.

(b) [illegible]

~~(*b*) Keep the demised premises clean and free from all ashes, dirt and other refuse matter; replace all glass windows, doors, etc., broken; keep all waste and drain pipes open; repair all damages to plumbing and to the demised premises; in general, keep the same in as good order and repair as they are at the beginning of the term of this lease, reasonable wear and tear and damage by accidental fire or other casualty not occurring through negligence of Lessee or those employed by or acting for Lessee alone excepted. The Lessee agrees to surrender the demised premises in the same condition in which Lessee has herein agreed to keep the same during the continuance of this lease.~~

(c) Requirements of Public Authorities

(*c*) Comply with any requirements of any of the constituted public authorities, and with the terms of any State or Federal statute or local ordinance or regulation applicable to Lessee or his use of the demised premises, and save Lessor harmless from penalties, fines, costs or damages resulting from failure so to do.

(d) Fire

(*d*) Use every reasonable precaution against fire.

(e) Surrender of Possession

(*e*) Peaceably deliver up and surrender possession of the demised premises to the Lessor at the expiration or sooner termination of this lease, promptly delivering to Lessor at its office all keys for the demised premises.

(f) Notice of Fire, etc.

(*f*) Give to Lessor prompt written notice of any accident, fire or damage occurring on or to the demised premises.

(g) Pay for Gas and Electricity

(*g*) Promptly pay for all gas and electricity consumed in the herein demised premises during the continuance of this lease; and should Lessee fail to make these payments when due, Lessor shall have the right to settle therefor. Such sums shall be considered additional rent and collectible from Lessee, as such, by legal process, and to have all the priorities given by law to claims for rent.

(h) Agency on Removal

(*h*) The Lessee agrees that if, with the permission in writing of Lessor, Lessee shall vacate or decide at any time during the term of this lease, or any renewal thereof, to vacate the herein demised premises, prior to the expiration of this lease, or any renewal hereof, Lessee will not cause or allow any agent to represent Lessee in any sub-letting or reletting of the demised premises other than an agent approved by the Lessor, and that should Lessee do so, or attempt to do so, the Lessor may remove any signs that may be placed on or about the demised premises by such other agent without any liability to Lessee or to said agent, the Lessee assuming all responsibility for such action.

(i) Indemnification

(*i*) Indemnify and save Lessor harmless from any and all loss occasioned by Lessee's breach of any of the covenants, terms and conditions of this lease, or caused by his family, guests, visitors, agents and employees.

10. Rules and Regulations

The Rules and Regulations in regard to the building wherein the said demised premises are located, printed upon the fourth page of this lease, and marked Schedule "A," and such alterations, additions and modifications thereof as may from time to time be made by the Lessor shall be considered a part of this lease with the same effect as though written herein; and the Lessee covenants and agrees that said Rules and Regulations and all alterations, additions and modifications thereof shall be faithfully observed by the Lessee, the employees of Lessee, and all persons invited by Lessee into said building.

11. Negative Covenants of Lessee (a) Use of Premises (b) Assignment and Subletting

Lessee convenants and agrees that he will do none of the following things without first obtaining the consent, in writing of Lessor, which consent Lessor shall not unreasonably withhold, and without providing Lessor with reimbursement for any expenses incurred or incidental to Lessee's proposed action:

(*a*) Occupy the demised premises in any other manner or for any other purpose than as above set forth.

(*b*) Assign, mortgage or pledge this lease or under-let or sub-lease the demised premises, or any part thereof, or permit any other person, firm or corporation to occupy the demised premises, or any part thereof; nor shall any assignee or sub-lessee assign, mortgage or pledge this lease or such sub-lease without an additional written consent by the Lessor, and without such consent no such assignment, mortgage or pledge shall be valid. If the Lessee becomes embarrassed or insolvent, or makes an assignment for the benefit of creditors, or if a petition in bankruptcy is filed by or against the Lessee or a bill in equity or other proceeding for the appointment of a receiver for the Lessee is filed, or if proceeding for reorganization or for composition with creditors under any State or Federal law be instituted by or against Lessee, or if the real or personal property of the Lessee shall be sold or levied upon by any Sheriff, Marshal or Constable, the same shall be a violation of this covenant.

(c) Signs

(*c*) Place or allow to be placed any stand, booth, sign or show case upon the doorsteps, vestibules, corridors, passage ways or outside walls or pavements of said premises, or the building of which the said premises form a part, or paint, place, erect, or cause to be painted, placed or erected any signs, projection or device on or in any part of the premises. Lessee shall remove any sign, projection or device painted, placed or erected, if permission has been granted, and restore the walls, etc., to their former conditions, at or prior to the expiration of this lease. In case of the breach of this covenant (in addition to all other remedies given to Lessor in case of the breach of any conditions or covenants of this lease) Lessor shall have the privilege of removing said stand, booth, sign, show case, projection or device, and restoring said walls, etc., to their former condition, and Lessee, at Lessor's option, shall be liable to Lessor for any and all expenses so incurred by Lessor.

(d) Alterations, Improvements

(*d*) Make any alterations, improvements or additions to the demised premises. All alterations, improvements, additions or fixtures, whether installed before or after the execution of this lease, shall remain upon the premises at the expiration or sooner determination of this lease and become the property of Lessor, unless Lessor shall, prior to the determination of this lease, have given written notice to Lessee to remove the same, in which event Lessee will remove such alterations, improvements and additions and restore the premises to the same good order and condition in which they now are. Should Lessee fail so to do, Lessor may do so, collecting, at Lessor's option, the cost and expense thereof from Lessee as additional rent.

---

ful to the building or disturbing to other tenants occupying other parts

nd the safe carrying capacity of the structure.
to insurance companies, whereby the fire insurance or any other insur-
any part thereof, or on the building of which the demised premises may
be rated as a more hazardous risk than at the date of execution of this
ompanies or carry or have any benzine or explosive matter of any kind
(in addition to all other remedies given to Lessor in case of the breach
Lessor as additional rent any and all increase or increases of premiums
rt thereof, or on the building of which the demised premises may be a

Lessee's goods or property from or out of the demised premises other-
rm of this lease, without having first paid and satisfied Lessor for all
aining term of this lease.
permit the same to be empty and unoccupied.
the following things and matters in and about the demised premises.
to go upon and inspect the demised premises and every part thereof
mised premises or the building of which the demised premises is a part.
le rules and regulations as may be necessary or desirable for the safety,
which the demised premises is a part and of real and personal property
d regulations shall, when communicated in writing to Lessee, form a

ce from either party of intention to determine this lease, or at anytime
' sign, or both "For Rent" and "For Sale" signs; and all of said signs
d may contain such matter as Lessor shall require. Persons authorized
l periods.
nished and services rendered by Lessor not expressly convenanted for
ood that they constitute no part of the consideration for this lease.

all liability by reason of any injury or damage to any person or
any other person, caused by any fire, breakage, or leakage in any part
from water, rain or snow that may leak into, issue or flow from any
mises is a part, from the drains, pipes, or plumbing work of the same,
damage be caused by or result from the negligence of Lessor or its

all liability by reason of any damage or injury to any property or to
or be due to the use, misuse or abuse of all or any of the elevators,
may exist or hereafter be erected or constructed on the said premises
defective construction, failure of water supply, light, power, electric
cause whatsoever on the said premises or the building of which the
abuse be caused by or result from the negligence of Lessor, its servants

maged by fire or other casualty that, in the opinion of a licensed architect
ety days from the happening of such injury this lease shall absolutely
term, at option of Lessor.
be restored, in the opinion of a licensed architect retained by Lessor, to
of the casualty loss, Lessor may, at Lessor's option, restore the same with
mises for that purpose. Lessor also reserves the right to enter upon the
other casualty to the building of which the demised premises is a part,
or a part thereof untenantable. In either event the rent shall be appor-
o account the proportion of the demised premises rendered untenantable
ount of rent due under this clause, Lessee agrees to pay the full amount
recover the excess payment, if any.
liable for any damage, compensation, or claim by reason of the necessity
premises, any inconvenience or annoyance arising as a result of such
ge to or destruction of the premises.
ondition and without any representations, other than those specifically
l/or agents. It is understood and agreed that Lessor is under no duty
e or at any time thereafter unless such duty of Lessor shall be set forth

d into by Lessor with Lessee relative to any alterations, additions, im-
s, additions, improvements, or repairs as required by any such contract,
ns, additions, improvements or repairs shall in any way affect the pay-
except to the extent and in the manner hereinbefore provided.
to the contrary notwithstanding, the Lessor shall have the right at all
ordance with the terms hereof, notwithstanding any conduct or custom
s, and further, that the failure of Lessor at any time or times to enforce
ith the same shall not be construed as having created a custom in any
of this lease or as having in any way or manner modified the same.
l/or the occupants of the premises herein leased shall not conduct them-
ne during the term of this lease or any extension or continuation thereof
in a manner which is improper or objectionable, Lessee shall be taken
be entitled to all of the rights and remedies granted and reserved herein,
of this lease.
venants of Section 9 (*b*) hereof, Lessor may go upon the demised prem-
Lessor to be charged to Lessee as additional and delinquent rent.
is acting
to Lessee for the fulfillment or nonfulfillment of any of the terms and
aken by the owner against Lessee, or by Lessee against the owner.
each of them shall carry to insure the demised premises and the contents
rry pertaining to the use and occupancy of the demised premises shall
rein, their heirs, administrators, successors, and assigns.
niform Commercial Code in all of Lessee's goods and property in, on, or
for the payment of all rent (and charges collectible or reserved as rent)
ssee hereby agrees to execute, upon request of Lessor, such financing
Commercial Code to perfect a security interest in Lessee's said goods

nd/or any other charge or payment herein reserved, included, or agreed
r costs herein agreed to be paid by the Lessee; or
r agreement herein contained; or
e or manifests an intention to remove any goods or property therefrom
other charges then due or that may thereafter become due until the full

for the benefit of creditors, or if a petition in bankruptcy is filed by or
ointment of a receiver for Lessee is filed, or if proceedings for reorgani-
be instituted by or against Lessee, or if the real or personal property of
shall, in good faith, believe that Lessee's ability to comply with the
r, is or may become impaired,
thereupon:

(1) The whole balance of rent and other charges, payments, costs, and expenses herein agreed to be paid by Lessee, or any part thereof, and also all costs and officers' commissions including watchmen's wages shall be taken to be due and payable and in arrears as if by the terms and provisions of this lease said balance of rent and other charges, payment, taxes, costs and expenses were on that date, payable in advance. Further, if this lease or any part thereof is assigned, or if the premises, or any part thereof is sub-let, Lessee hereby irrevocably constitutes and appoints Lessor as Lessee's agent to collect the rents due from such assignee or sub-lessee and apply the same to the rent due hereunder without in any way affecting Lessee's obligation to pay any unpaid balance of rent due hereunder; or

(2) At the option of Lessor, this lease and the terms hereby created shall determine and become absolutely void without any right on the part of Lessee to reinstate this lease by payment of any sum due or by other performance of any condition, term, or covenant broken; whereupon, Lessor shall be entitled to recover damages for such breach in an amount equal to the amount of rent reserved for the balance of the term of this lease, less the fair rental value of the said demised premises for the remainder of the lease term.

17. Further Remedies of Lessor

In the event of any default as above set forth in Section 16, Lessor, or anyone acting on Lessor's behalf, at Lessor's option:

(*a*) May let said premises or any part or parts thereof to such person or persons as may, in Lessor's discretion, be best; and Lessee shall be liable for any loss of rent for the balance of the then current term. Any such re-entry or re-letting by Lessor under the terms hereof shall be without prejudice to Lessor's claim for actual damages, and shall under no circumstances, release Lessee from liability for such damages arising out of the breach of any of the covenants, terms, and conditions of this lease, and

(*b*) May proceed as a secured party under the provisions of the Uniform Commercial Code against the goods in which Lessor has been granted a security interest pursuant to Section 15 (*g*) hereof; and

(*c*) May have and exercise any and all other rights and/or remedies, granted or allowed landlords by any existing or future Statute, Act of Assembly, or other law of this state in cases where a landlord seeks to enforce rights arising under a lease agreement against a tenant who has defaulted or otherwise breached the terms of such lease agreement; subject, however, to all of the rights granted or created by any such Statute, Act of Assembly, or other law of this state existing for the protection and benefit of tenants; and

(*d*) May have and exercise any and all other rights and remedies contained in this lease agreement, including the rights and remedies provided by Sections 18 and 19 hereof.

In Witness Whereof, the parties hereto have executed these presents the day and year first above written, and intend to be legally bound hereby.

SEALED AND DELIVERED IN THE PRESENCE OF:

.... (SEAL)

.... (SEAL)

.... (SEAL)

.... (SEAL)

.... (SEAL)

.... (SEAL)

This Lease is approved with all the covenants contained herein.

By....................................

RULES AND REGULATIONS

SCHEDULE "A"

The public halls and stairways shall not be obstructed or used for any other purpose than for ingress to and egress from the apartments.

No Lessee shall make or permit any disturbing noises to be made in the building by himself, members of his family, guests, his agents, servants or licensees; nor do or permit anything to be done that will interfere with the rights, comforts or convenience of other tenants. No Lessee shall play or suffer to be played any musical instrument, television or radio, in the demised premises between the hours of ten-thirty o'clock P. M. and the following eight-thirty o'clock, A. M., if the same shall disturb or annoy other occupants of the building. All cooking equipment must be used in such a way as to prevent noxious odors from permeating the building.

The Lessee shall not throw or permit to be thrown anything whatever out of the windows or doors, or into the halls of the building.

The delivery of kitchen supplies, market goods, towels, ice, water, newspapers, other supplies and packages of every kind will be permitted only at the entrance provided therefor, and under the direction, control and supervision of the Lessor, and the Lessor will not be held responsible for the loss or damage of any such property, notwithstanding such loss or damage may occur through the carelessness or negligence of the employees of the building. The Lessor will not be responsible for any article left with any employee or in any part of the building.

No baby carriages, velocipedes, bicycles or other large articles will be allowed in passenger elevators, or in the halls, passageways, areas or courts of the building.

The Lessee shall keep the premises leased in good state of preservation and cleanliness, and shall not sweep or throw or permit to be swept or thrown from the premises leased, any dirt or other substance into any of the corridors or halls, elevators or stairways of said building.

The fire escape shall not be obstructed.

No ash can, garbage can, woodbox, kitchen supplies, ice or other articles shall be placed in the halls or on the staircase landings, nor shall anything be hung from the windows, or balconies, or placed upon the window sills. Neither shall any tablecloths, clothing, curtains, rugs or other articles, be shaken or hung from any of the windows or doors.

The water-closets and other water apparatus shall not be used for any other purpose other than that for which they were constructed, nor shall any sweepings, rubbish, rags or any other improper articles be thrown into the same; and any damage resulting from misuse thereof shall be borne by the tenant by whom or upon whose premises it shall have been caused.

Children shall not play in the public halls, entrances, stairways, or elevators.

Each tenant shall use the laundry and drying apparatus, if any, only on such days and hours as the Lessor shall designate.

No animals shall be carried on the elevators or kept in or about the premises, except on written consent of the Lessor.

No window shades or awnings shall be placed on any of the windows excepting those approved by Lessor or the manager of the building, and no awning shall be placed on any window prior to May 1st or allowed to remain on any window after October 1st in any year.

The Lessee acknowledge receipt of notice from the Lessor of the provisions of the Philadelphia Housing Code, effective January 1, 1955, and amendments thereto, providing that the demised apartment shall not be occupied by more than occupants.

APARTMENT LEASE

TO

Apartment No....................

Rent....................

Dated....................

Term....................

FOR VALUE RECEIVED....................hereby assign, transfer and set over unto....................

....................Executors, Administrators and assigns all....................right, title and interest in the within lease and all benefit and advantages to be derived therefrom.

WITNESS....................hand and seal this....................day of....................A. D. 19..........

SEALED IN THE PRESENCE OF

....

FOR VALUE RECEIVED....................hereby assign, transfer and set over unto....................

....................Executors, Administrators and assigns all....................right, title and interest in the within lease and all benefit and advantages to be derived therefrom.

WITNESS....................hand and seal this....................day of....................A. D. 19..........

SEALED IN THE PRESENCE OF

....

18. Confession of Judgment for Money

Lessee covenants and agrees that if the re
under the provisions of this lease) shall remai
cause Judgment to be entered against Lessee,
of Court or Attorney of any Court of Record t
pursuant to Pennsylvania Rules of Civil Proc
tions of rent permissible under the provisions c
and Attorney's commission, for which authoriz
Such Judgment may be confessed against Les
provisions of this lease) and/or for all char
commission of five percent (5%) of the full
Pennsylvania Rules of Civil Procedure No. 29
exercises thereof, but successive complaints m
after they become due as well as after the exp
lease.

19. Confession of Judgment for Possession of Real Property

Lessee covenants and agrees that if this le
renewal or extension thereof and/or when th
may cause a judgment in ejectment to be ent
authorizes and empowers any Prothonotary,
against Lessee in Ejectment for possession of
sylvania Rules of Procedure No. 2970 et seq.
agrees that a Writ of Possession pursuant the
writ or writs of possession pursuant thereto, t
and agrees, that if for any reason whatsoeve
premises demised hereunder shall remain in or
the termination of this lease as above set forth
judgments by confession in Ejectment for pos

20. Copies

In any procedure or action to enter Judgm
in Ejectment for possession of real property
or averment of the facts constituting the def
rence, or event authorizes and empowers Less
evidence of such facts, defaults, occurrences,
affidavit or averment shall be sufficient eviden
of Attorney, any rule of court, custom, or pr

21. Waivers by Lessee of Errors, Right of Appeal, Stay Exemption Inquisition

Lessee hereby releases to Lessor and to
Judgment by Confession by virtue of the wa
Prothonotary or any Clerk of any Court of R
sold on a Writ of Execution or other process.
of the term or sooner termination of this leas
three (3) months' notice to quit and/or the
amended, and agrees that five (5) days' notic

22. Right of Assignee of Lessor

The right to enter judgment against Less
the option of any assignee of this lease, be ex
name, any statute, rule of court, custom, or pra

23. Remedies Cumulative

All of the remedies hereinbefore given to
current. No determination of this lease or the t
against the Lessee for rent due at the time or
tion, nor shall the bringing of any action for
of rent be construed as a waiver of the right

24. Condemnation

In the event that the premises demised he
as to the part so taken, terminate as of the dat
space taken or condemned or shall cease if th
reason of the complete or partial taking of the

25. Subordination

This Agreement of Lease and all of its t
other arrangement or right to possession, un
of the demised premises and of the land or
any and all mortgages and other encumbranc
taining the same; and Lessee expressly agrees
feiture or otherwise, then this lease shall the
Lessee hereby waives any and all claims for d

26. Termination of Lease

It is hereby mutually agreed that either p
notice thereof at least
upon the same terms and conditions in force i
of and so on from
other days' written notice of ter
have given such written notice prior to the e
lease, and Lessee shall hold over after the exp
and conditions mentioned in such notice for a
Lessee shall give notice, as stipulated in this
or extension thereof, and shall fail or refuse so
shall have the option either (*a*) to disregard
shall continue thereafter with full force precis
the present term or any renewal or extension
the said lease; whereupon the Lessee expressl
notice. All powers granted to Lessor by this
by Lessee as well during any extension of the

27. Notices

All notices must be given by certified mail,

28. Lease Contains all Agreements

It is expressly understood and agreed by
hereof set forth all the promises, agreements,
premises, and that there are no promises, agre
set forth. It is further understood and agreed
tion to this lease shall be binding upon Lesso

29. Heirs and Assignees

All rights and liabilities herein given to,
and respective heirs, executors, administrators
be bound jointly and severally by the terms,
each and every person or party mentioned as
required or permitted by the terms of this le
by or to all thereof. No rights, however, sha
approved by Lessor in writing as aforesaid.

30. Approval of Owner Required

This lease shall not become effective un
Lessee shall be refunded to Lessee, but Lessor
having this lease considered approved. But in
pay the rentals and other sums due hereunder
all the terms, covenants and provisions hereof.
principal, to all intents and purposes as if th
cause Lessee to be ejected by an amicable acti
remedies, waivers and releases hereinabove se

31. Security Deposit

Lessee does herewith deposit with Lessor t
to be held as security for the full and faithful
to the demised premises. Said security deposi
Act of Assembly approved December 29, 1972
against Lessee arising from defaults under thi
Lessee at the expiration of the terms of this lease or any renewals or extensions thereof as provided for in the said Act of Assembly. It is understood that no part of any security deposit or Escrow Fund is to be considered as the last rental due under the terms of the lease.

32. Validity of Provisions

This lease shall be governed by the Laws of Pennsylvania. If any provision of this lease shall be declared invalid by judicial determination, or by Act of Pennsylvania Assembly, or by act of any other legislative body with authority to affect this lease, only such provision so declared invalid shall be thus affected, and all other provisions not inconsistent therewith or directly dependent thereon shall remain in full force and effect.

33. Headings No Part of Lease

Any headings preceding the text of the several paragraphs and sub-paragraphs hereof are inserted solely for convenience of reference and shall not constitute a part of this lease, nor shall they affect its meaning, construction or effect.

What if Aunt Minnie wants to stay with you for a month? You could be asked to move out! If it's not clearly stated in your lease how long a period must elapse before a long-term guest is considered a resident, you are subject to the whims of your landlord on this matter.

It's most important to have a clause in your lease which makes it the landlord's responsibility to see that prior tenants are out of the apartment at the time your lease begins. Otherwise it may be your responsibility to evict them! This depends on the area of the country in which you reside. But there are many places where you could arrive on moving day to find the "former tenants" still firmly ensconced in your apartment.

The number of landlords who pay for heat is on the decline. If apartments have individual heaters, furnaces, or heating units, the tenants are usually responsible for providing their own heat. But when several apartments are heated by one furnace, the landlord generally pays. If this is the case, there are two things to look for in the lease. The first is a fuel escalation clause, which gives the landlord the right to raise the rent to compensate for increases in the cost of heating fuels. A tenant on a strict budget can be in trouble when the rent increases unexpectedly. If this clause is in your lease and the landlord refuses to remove it, try to convince him to insert a percentage. The clause should at least state that the rent may not be increased more than, say, 6 percent per year (a commonly used figure) because of rising fuel costs.

Secondly, be aware that many landlords who pay for the heat also control it. This means you're likely to be cold. Look for a clause that says you will control the heat in your own apartment. Don't take a verbal agreement. The landlord may say, "It's not in the lease, but the thermostat is in your apartment, and you can keep it at the temperature you choose." Get it in writing! You could move in and find that the landlord has locked up the control on that thermostat. Or the property may be sold before your lease expires, and the new owner may not observe unwritten rules.

What rights do you have to the areas surrounding your apartment? You're not necessarily entitled to use the yard, for instance, unless it says so in your lease. You may not be allowed to put up a television antenna or have an air conditioner or a window box that juts out from the building.

The animal issue should be clarified at the time you sign a lease. If you are forbidden to have a pet, don't plan to bring one in after you've taken up residence. A clause precluding pets in an apartment is not considered unreasonable. It is also one clause that is usually easy to interpret because the landlord wants it to be clear. The only recourse you have in the pet issue comes if despite the no-pet clause in your lease you've housed a pet in your apartment over a long period of time during which the owner has been aware of the animal's presence in the apartment and has voiced no complaint. If the animal hasn't damaged the property, and the landlord suddenly decides to evict you because the pet is in the apartment, you may have a case. Because the landlord has accepted the animal, the court could find that he has waived his rights to enforce the no-pet restriction.

You may have a no-pet clause in your lease and a softhearted landlord, who, after getting to know you as a good tenant, will decide you can have a pet after all. That's nice, but get it in writing. After you've brought home the St. Bernard, the landlord may have second thoughts. With no witnesses to his approval and nothing in writing, it's your word against his. You and Fido could be looking for a new place to live.

Speaking of eviction, once the landlord has obtained a dispossess notice for any lease violation he cannot accept rent from you for the period after you were to have left his premises. If he does accept rent for that period, he nullifies the eviction. The landlord can, however, at a future date start the process over again by sending you another eviction notice based on the same violation.

There have been many efforts made to turn the lease into a fair and equitable agreement for both landlord and tenant. But many leases are still one-sided documents stacked in the landlord's favor. Progress is being made, however, and the day should come when a tenant can expect to sign a reasonable lease. Most landlords don't want to persecute their tenants. The majority do try to be fair. But the ones who don't can make life unbearable for the people who rent from them.

Undesirable Clauses

Any clause in any lease is superseded by the laws in the area to which the lease pertains. For instance, if you've signed a lease that entitles the landlord to keep your security deposit if he sees fit, but the law in your state says he must return it unless he can show just cause to keep it, he must return it unless he can show such cause. You can't be held to anything that's illegal.

Clause

In case of non-payment of said rent when due, or in case the leased premises shall be deserted or vacated, or if the Tenant shall break or evade any of the covenants or restrictions set forth in this lease, the Owner may forfeit and annul the unexpired portion of this lease, or any renewal thereof, and enter upon and repossess the said premises without process of law and without any notice whatsoever and/or may also relet the said premises as agent of Tenant for any unexpired portion of the term and receive the rent therefor.

COMMENT

This is a bad clause. It means that if you are even a little late in a rent payment, the landlord may repossess the apartment without notifying you of his intention to do so. You may come home from work and find that the locks have been changed and you're homeless.

Clause

The Tenant agrees that the public halls, passageways, stairways, and landings will be kept clean. . . .

COMMENT

A clause of this type permits the landlord to leave the maintenance of the common areas up to the Tenant. The hall outside your apartment might be cleaned only when you clean it. The stairs might stay littered unless you remove the trash.

Clause

The Tenant agrees that nothing shall be placed on the outside of the building, or on the windows, window sills, or projections and no signs or advertising notices of any kind shall be placed on any part of the building or on the doors of any apartment.

COMMENT

This means no air conditioners, so that in a third-floor apartment during a hot summer you will just have to suffer. It means no window boxes, and there go the flowers you'd planned. It means no signs, but this isn't so bad unless you were planning to have a small business in your home.

Clause

The Tenant agrees that the Owner reserves the right to rescind any of these rules, and to make such other reasonable rules and regulations as may from time to time be needed. When new rules and regulations are so made, and notice thereof given to the Tenant, they shall have the same force and effect as if originally made a part of this Lease.

COMMENT

Watch out for this one! It allows your landlord to set up a whole new set of rules for you mid-lease. You may not like or be able to live with his rewritten regulations.

Clause

If the Tenant shall continue in the occupation of the said leased premises after the expiration of the term hereby created with the consent of the Owner, it shall be deemed a renewal of this Lease, and of all the covenants, terms and conditions herein contained for the term of another year and so on until the lease is terminated by either party hereto giving 60 days notice prior to the expiration of any term of the Lease.

COMMENT

This puts you on a merry-go-round that you can only get off at one time each year. If you want to move in January and the lease renewal period isn't up until July, you're stuck with rent for your apartment until July. The best type of lease allows you to vacate the premises with a notice of 30 or 60 days at any time after the term of the first lease has expired. In other words, if your lease is for one year, you may vacate the premises without penalty after that year has passed providing you give the specified notice in writing to your landlord.

Clause

Tenant shall have complied with all the terms, covenants and conditions of this Lease, in which event the deposit so paid hereunder shall be returned to Tenant. Otherwise, said sum deposited hereunder or any part thereof may be retained by

Owner at its option, as liquidated damages, or may be applied by Owner against any actual loss, damage or injury chargeable to Tenant. Owner's determination of the amount, if any, to be returned to Tenant shall be final. It is understood that the said deposit is not to be considered as the last rental due under this Lease.

COMMENT

When you sign a lease with this clause, you are in effect giving the landlord the right to keep your entire security deposit for even a minor repair job. You can't even protect yourself by considering the security deposit to be the last month's rent payment in the event your landlord is the type who does withhold security deposits.

Clause

Tenant relieves Owner from all liability from any kind of injury which may result from any cause whatsoever on the leased premises or the building of which the leased premises is a part, including common walkways, driveways, and parking areas.

COMMENT

There is no need for the landlord to repair hazardous conditions when he has this clause in a lease. If you fall on a loose stair, trip on his worn carpet, or slip on an icy walk, it's your responsibility.

The Security Deposit

In the past, the security deposit game has been one of the biggest con rackets ever worked. In some places it still is, but in general things are looking up for the renter.

The security deposit is usually equal to one or two months' rent, and it's given to the landlord for *his* security—so he can feel secure that if you damage the apartment he will have your money with which to make repairs. This is fair as far as it goes. After all, there are people who move into an apartment and have wild parties, mark up the walls, let their animals soil the carpet and their kids break the plumbing, and an owner should be entitled to compensation for this type of thing. But where is the tenant's security? Can he feel secure that he will get the money back if there is no damage? The security deposit was never intended to be a way for the landlord to make additional money at the expense of his tenant. But this is what happens frequently. And until recently tenants everywhere have been helpless in their efforts to stop it.

If you have reason to believe your landlord is going to keep your deposit, you can try using it as the last month's or two months' rent unless it specifies otherwise in your lease, and provided you've kept the property in good repair.

In many areas, the law now stipulates that the landlord must keep all security deposits in interest-bearing accounts and return the deposits to tenants, along with at least a specified percentage of the interest money he has received, within a stated amount of time after the premises have been vacated. And there are states where the landlord is forced to pay the tenant as much as three times the amount of the security deposit if he fails to return the deposit within the period of time the law gives him to do so.

In other locations, any damages that an owner claims you have done must be itemized in writing and presented to you within a reasonable and stipulated amount of time in order for him to deduct these damages from your security deposit. Failure on his part to do this means that he forfeits the right to keep any part of the security deposit toward those repairs. Check with your local housing authority on what's legal in your area.

Things are getting better for the tenant as far as the security deposit is concerned. The landlord is now generally allowed to keep *part* of the security deposit—only enough to compensate him for damages that are not considered normal wear and tear. He may no longer, for instance, keep a $300 deposit because he has found a hole in the carpet made by your children that is going to cost him twenty-five dollars to repair. He may, however, keep the twenty-five dollars.

The owner shouldn't keep money for the holes you had to make in order to hang the curtains or drapes (unless they destroyed the walls). He should expect that the paint will have become older and show signs of wear; that the carpet may need cleaning; that a burner may have worn out on the stove. These things are considered normal wear and tear for which, almost everywhere, the tenant is not held responsible.

Where the security deposit is held in an interest-bearing escrow account, you will receive the deposit back with no hassle, but in some states, you have to sue if the landlord refuses to refund it. Where this may be the case, try discussing the security deposit issue with the landlord before you sign his lease. Ask what he considers a fair period of time for the return of your money after you vacate the apartment. If you can agree on this and on what constitutes normal wear and tear, see if he will include this information in your lease. A landlord who intends to play fair should have no objection, and it gives you a bit more legal clout should you need it.

LISTING PREVIOUS DAMAGES

When I move into an apartment, I always make a written list of any damages I find no matter how small they seem. Sometimes a lease restricts the tenant from putting up things like towel racks which screw into walls or doors. If this is the case, and there is a towel rack that has been installed by a prior tenant, I note it on my list. Small cuts on a kitchen counter also go on the list, as do any cigarette burns on carpeting, and similar damages. This isn't a list of things I expect the landlord to repair, it just lets him know that I'm aware these items were damaged when I took tenancy, and that I'm not going to take responsibility for them when I leave. I make this list in duplicate, giving one copy to the landlord and keeping one for my own records. This is not a legal document nor is it a part of the lease. It's just a way of avoiding honest mistakes and misunderstandings between tenant and landlord.

Rights and Responsibilities

LEGAL DISCRIMINATION

What if a landlord refuses to rent to you? Are you entitled to legal redress because of discrimination? Surprisingly, you may not be. There's such a thing as legal discrimination. In most places, a landlord can refuse to rent to you because he doesn't think you'll make a good tenant for his property on the basis of your profession (like a rock musician) or because he doesn't rent to people with children (some complexes are for adults only) or because there are going to be too many people occupying the premises (say it has one bedroom and you're a family of five). He can also refuse to rent to you because your salary isn't high enough for him to feel confident that you can manage to pay the rent. In fact, he can refuse to rent to you for almost any reason except race or religion.

In a landmark case in New York, a single, black, woman attorney was turned down by the owner of an apartment building. She took the case to court—and lost. The landlord claimed he didn't turn her down because she was a woman, because she was black, or because she was single. He turned her down because she was a lawyer. He claimed that he thought having a lawyer for a tenant would be a source of constant trouble. This man owned a number of apartment buildings. Many of his apartments were tenanted by women, many by blacks, many by singles—but none was tenanted by a lawyer. So the court concluded that his bias was on the basis of profession. This is a legal form of discrimination, at least in New York. My advice would be if a landlord doesn't want you as a tenant, you're better off with another landlord unless you have a point to prove.

THE PREVIOUS TENANTS

When you've signed the lease and have paid your security deposit and your first month's rent, you can expect to occupy the premises on the date specified in the lease. The landlord will have the apartment empty and waiting. Right? You would think so, but unless it's specified in your lease as the landlord's responsibility (as I suggested earlier), it's up to you to get rid of any previous tenants who may have lingered past their welcome and the terms of their lease. In most areas the landlord can collect rent from you even though you have been unable to occupy his apartment. He may not, however, collect rent from both parties for the same apartment. In effect you have possession so it's up to you to evict the loitering party.

You must go through the same legal eviction proceedings that you would if you owned the property. This means using the legal channels required in your area to evict an unwanted tenant. In the state of New York, for instance, you would have to institute eviction proceedings through a court. To have any hope of winning, you will have to hire a lawyer. You must prove to the court that your right to the property is stronger than that of the party who is residing in it. If you win the case and secure a warrant of eviction, you must then see that it is enforced by an officer of the law if the tenant is still reluctant to leave. Since the wheels of the legal system grind slowly, you're apt to find many months have elapsed between the time you were to occupy the premises and the time you actually get to move in.

This is another sensitive spot in the field of landlord/tenant rights that's being modified slowly. It has changed in some places, and it will be corrected in others in the future. But, as of now, get in writing that the premises will be delivered to you free of other tenants or squatters on the date specified in the lease. Then failure on the landlord's part to do this will mean that the lease is null and void, and all money will be returned to you immediately.

LIABILITY FOR ACCIDENTS

Suppose you rent an apartment that has an upstairs and a downstairs, and you discover that one of the stairtreads is loose. One day you have a guest who trips over that stair, falls and is taken to the hospital severely injured. You may assume that the landlord is liable for the medical bills and other expenses incurred by the fall. After all, the accident happened on his property, and you're only a tenant. Your assumption is probably wrong! Unless it so states in your lease or you have some other agreement with the landlord that he's responsible for repairs, you, as a tenant, will be held liable for the injuries of anyone who is hurt in your apartment. (See Chapter 9 for information on tenants' insurance.) As a tenant, you have control of the premises and are responsible for the welfare of those within. Even if you can prove that the landlord has agreed to accept responsibility for keeping the apartment in good repair, you then must prove that he was aware of the particular existing hazard. For this reason, it's best to notify him of any dangerous condition in writing (as well as verbally) and send it by certified mail, keeping a copy of the communication for your records.

An exception would be provided by a statute in your area stating that the landlord is culpable for injuries suffered on his premises. You also have a case if the landlord agreed to repair that stair and neglected to do so, or if he repaired it but did a slipshod job. But if he has agreed to make certain repairs and not others, he's not considered accountable for injuries occurring because of structural defects he hasn't specifically agreed to fix.

MORE ABOUT REPAIRS

If the elevator doesn't work, if there's no lighting in the hallways, or if the lobby is piled with junk which creates a fire hazard, you almost always have the right to make the landlord clear up the situation. But repairs within your own apartment are quite another matter, even in areas where the tenant is partially protected by an "implied warranty of habitability" (discussed later). All defects that need to be remedied don't qualify as health hazards or as conditions that make a place uninhabitable or dangerous.

Gray areas include things like paint and wallpaper, or kitchen flooring that's badly worn. In many complexes, the management accepts all responsibility and may request that you not try to paint, paper, resurface the floors, or fix any appliances yourself. The owner prefers to hire professionals and protect himself from amateur do-it-yourselfers.

But too often, unless otherwise stated, you must repair any appliance that breaks, or pay to have it fixed. If the landlord's refrigerator in your apartment goes on the blink, you have to get it fixed; if the dishwasher gives up, it's up to you to see that it's running again; if the place needs paint, you not only buy the paint, you apply it.

When you have signed a lease that says you will make certain alterations to the premises, such as painting, you had better do them. If you fail to, the landlord can sue you, or he may be able to keep your security deposit as payment for work promised but not done.

If your apartment is in disrepair and repeated efforts to enlist the help of your landlord in fixing it have failed, you have several options. You can try getting the necessary work done on your own and deducting the cost from the next rent payment. This is strictly legal in some places and illegal in others. Check! Be sure to keep all receipts and don't commission your brother-in-law to do the tasks for more than the going rate.

If the repairs your apartment needs seem to constitute a health hazard, call your local board of health and ask if the landlord is in violation of the local housing code. He may be forced to make the repairs without another word from you. If this doesn't work, you can take the landlord to small claims court and sue him either to make repairs or to reimburse you for work you have been forced to do on your own. Or you can go to the courts for a "constructive eviction." This means that you're being evicted not by the landlord but by the conditions of his property. You will not be required to honor the lease. The landlord will be ordered to reimburse you for your security deposit, and in some cases he may even have to pay you a portion of the rent you've already paid to live in his apartment while it was in effect not liveable.

IMPLIED WARRANTY OF HABITABILITY

According to Common Law, which we inherited from England, a property is leased "as is." This archaic law permits an apartment owner to rent a place to you that is virtually uninhabitable—something you may not find out until you actually move into it. Then, unless your area has a superseding law, you are a victim!

The efforts of many individuals and organizations to improve the lot of the tenant have resulted in limited changes in these ancient English common laws. Now, in some locales, a landlord cannot rent an apartment without guaranteeing that the place is liveable, which means there can be no defects that create a health hazard. This long-needed statute is called an "implied warranty of habitability." And it is overdue on a national basis as protection for all the renters in the country.

Where this statute exists, a landlord is held criminally liable for failure to provide sanitary conditions such as adequate heat and water. The "implied warranty of habitability" is in effect whether or not these repairs are specified in the lease. So if you're in an apartment where there's inadequate heat, for instance, and there are no provisions in your lease for the maintenance of the heater by the owner, you can still force him to fix that heater.

To many of us, the word "warranty" connotes something that expires after a certain, stipulated length of time, but an "implied warranty of habitability" is ongoing. It starts on the day you move in, and it stops only when your tenancy ends. This warranty is usually as weak or strong as the housing code in the area in question; and a violation of the housing code is generally a violation of the "implied warranty of habitability."

Some of the states that extend the protection of this warranty at present are: Alaska, Arizona, California, Colorado, Connecticut,

Delaware, Florida, Hawaii, Illinois, Iowa, Kansas, Kentucky, Louisiana, Maine, Maryland, Massachusetts, Missouri, Nebraska, New Hampshire, New Jersey, New York, Ohio, Oregon, Virginia, Washington, and Wisconsin. Perhaps other states will follow their lead soon.

Rent Payments

If the landlord doesn't provide a service he has promised in the lease, can you as a tenant lawfully withhold rent payments? In some places the tenant may deduct a portion of the rent. In others the rent must be paid into an escrow account which is not to be turned over to the landlord until the services agreed upon have been performed or the dispute is settled in court. Still other localities make no allowances for this type of injustice and force the tenant to pay the rent regardless of the circumstances. Your local housing authority can tell you what the law is in your area.

Within recent years, the "rent strike" has become a common occurrence. Dissatisfied tenants have common complaints about services not performed, inadequate heat, or some other responsibility of the landlord that they feel is not being met.

Acting as a body, they withhold rental payments, thus forcing the landlord to either sue them for payment or evict them. When he acts, they countersue, claiming noncompliance on the landlord's part with the terms of the lease. In some states rent strikes have proven to be effective tools, while in others they are not yet recognized as legal.

Must you pay rent if your apartment has been destroyed by fire, flood or any other disaster? Yes, usually you must—unless it says otherwise in your lease or you are protected by "implied warranty of habitability." You should get something in writing from your landlord stating that if the premises become uninhabitable due to a cause not of your making, payment of the rent will cease, and the lease will be void. If you have tenants' insurance, check your policy to see if it covers this.

EARLY RENT PAYMENTS

Paying rent more than a month in advance is a risky business at best. I have a friend who had a windfall and decided to pay his rent for the following year all at one time to get it out of the way and because he planned to be traveling extensively. This would have been a poor idea if only for the interest he was losing. But it became much more serious. After six months had passed, the property changed hands and the original owner vanished, and with him six months' rent from my friend. The new landlord wasn't impressed by my friend's protestations and demanded the money. The dispute went to court, and the landlord won. My sad but wiser friend ended up paying double rent for those six months. His only recourse would have been to sue his former landlord, but he couldn't find him.

A landlord doesn't have to abscond with your money in order for you to lose it through prepayment. He may declare bankruptcy. Your apartment could be destroyed by fire or some other disaster, thus making it unliveable. You can and should sue a landlord for return of any advance payments, but even though you're likely to win, you're unlikely to collect. You can't get money from someone who doesn't have it to give to you.

LATE RENT PAYMENTS

What if you don't have the money to pay the rent on the date it's due? Can the landlord appear on your doorstep on the second of the month if you fail to make the rent payment on the first when it's due, and, like the villain in an old movie, order you to vacate the premises forthwith? No, he can't. At least he can't legally. In most places there is a grace period allowed before the landlord can take legal action. But if you're too late with your payments, he can start eviction proceedings.

Let's say you fail to make payment on the first, and the landlord starts to evict you. You then come up with the money, at some date beyond any existing grace period. If the landlord accepts payment, the eviction proceedings are dropped automatically. To follow through on an eviction, the landlord must cease taking rent for the period of time after the eviction notice says you are to vacate. In other words, he can't evict you for nonpayment if he in fact has been paid. But if you again fail to make your payment on time in a subsequent month, the owner can start eviction proceedings against you all over again.

Often, the tenant is required to pay court costs incurred by the landlord in his efforts to evict the tenant, even if the action is ultimately resolved by the payment of rent.

Tenant Organizations

As apartment living has increased in popularity, many inequities against the tenant have surfaced, and tenants across the nation have formed tenant groups based on the premise that there's strength in numbers. Many of these groups have won victories in proceedings that a single tenant would never have dared to start and certainly would have had slim chance of winning alone. In a good, well-run complex there's no need for a tenant group. But when, for instance, the grounds are ill-kept, the halls are not cleaned, promised repairs are not made or are made on a haphazard, when-I-get-to-it basis, you need an organization.

To start one, talk to the people you know best in the complex or building. Ask if they're in agreement with your gripes and if they're willing to rally other tenants to the cause. If you don't know anyone very well, start recruiting those people in the complex who seem like leaders. Perhaps there's a lawyer among the tenants. If so, he or she would be a good person with whom to start. Remember to include women as well as men. In fact, make the group as heterogeneous as possible so there is a chance any tenant can identify with someone in your core group.

When you have a nucleus of four or more, prepare a list of general grievances. At this stage you don't need to be too specific. Take the list around to other apartments. Do this in pairs. If your complex is a large one where tenants aren't likely to recognize each other, try to have each pair consist of a man and a woman. This will make it easier to get doors opened. Some of your fellow tenants may be shy about allowing two strange men to enter their apartments.

After identifying yourselves and stating your purpose, find out if people are satisfied with the way things are run, or if they think that improvements should be made. Advise everyone you contact that there will be a meeting and that they, and all their complaints, will be welcome. Show them your list of grievances and ask if they agree. Most will have complaints and be eager to voice them. But don't be surprised or put out if someone is unwilling to participate. It's best if those who aren't with you at least remain neutral.

If you live in an area where people are security conscious, you may need to make your first contact through a written notice. *Do not* use the mailboxes to deliver these. This isn't legal use of a mailbox, and you could be fined by the Postal Service. If notices can't be slipped under doors or doormats, mail them. Include in the notice the reasons for organizing and the time and place of the first meeting. People who won't let you in their apartments if they don't know you, will generally read their mail.

Your first goal in getting together is to develop a list of specific annoyances that all of you feel are important enough to warrant action. The size of your organization, and of your complex or building, will dictate just how many committees you need and what their functions will be. In a fair-sized group you should have a committee to handle the money; one to take care of any printed matter you'll be circulating; and a committee to take your grievances to the landlord or whomever he appoints to represent him. These committees should be carefully selected, but the first meeting probably isn't the time to do this because you won't be acquainted well enough with each other and with each other's talents. Schedule a second meeting for this purpose.

As with any organization, you'll need to collect dues because you're going to need money to get the ball rolling and to keep it in motion. You'll need funds for the printed material that you'll be circulating; for the postage, if you opt for mailing; and for a lawyer to keep you from ending up on the wrong side of the law. The work of the tenants, of course, will all be done on a volunteer basis. In most instances, a few tenants will do the bulk of the work while the others will cast their votes, voice their complaints, pay their dues, and reap the benefits.

You're going to find that many tenants are reluctant to join the organization until it's in full swing. But once they see that they aren't going to get into serious trouble by becoming members, they'll be enthusiastic.

After your second meeting, the one at which you'll find out who is going to serve on what committee, set up a meeting with the landlord. Your landlord may be elusive. Questions to the management about who owns the apartment or complex can bring evasive answers. Don't give up. Call or write the County Assessor's Office, Legal Descriptions Department, and ask them who's paying the taxes on your complex. This must be a matter of public record, and the information can't be withheld from you. If the taxes are paid in the name of a corporation and you don't know who to contact, call or write the secretary of state in your state and request the names of the officers of that corporation. They'll provide this information for you.

When you locate the landlord, don't approach him like a tornado about to vent its full force. Simply ask him to meet with the three or four member committee which has been selected to speak for the group. Meet him either on neutral ground or in one of the member's apartments. Never congregate in his office because this gives him a psychological advantage. He will be "host" and, as such, able to set the tone of the meeting. You want to be in control. Be sure that the full committee attends this crucial first session between you and the landlord. It's your show of strength.

This committee should present the landlord with a written list of grievances agreed upon by the majority of the tenant organization. If the landlord says, "I'll go along with your first and third request, but I'm not going to fix the walks, or provide storm windows," your committee members must then go back to the entire organization and present the compromise. Unless previously agreed, they can't allow any alterations in the demands without the whole group's approval.

If the landlord agrees to everything, that's wonderful. But find out when he intends to make these improvements. If you think the time schedule is reasonable, give him a chance. If there are no signs that the landlord is going to keep his commitments, go back and ask for his intentions in writing. Always be polite, but let him know you mean business. Never make threats or say anything that you can't back up with legal action should it become necessary.

But what if your landlord is not responsive to your committee? He might refuse to meet with you; or he might meet with you but won't agree to anything. Now your lawyer goes into action. *Do not* take any steps without consulting him. If your complaints are mostly about repairs, find out if it's legal to have them made, and the bills sent to the landlord or the amount subtracted from rental payments. Whatever your complaints, take only the steps which are legal in the area in which you live.

The right to peaceably assemble gives you the right to picket. So you can, if you wish to, picket the landlord. But first find out whether a permit is needed. Picket in an orderly, nonthreatening fashion. Never let any of the picketers representing your organization get out of hand or try to prevent anyone from entering or leaving the landlord's office. Do notify the local newspapers of your problems and of the hours that you intend to be picketing. Give them a complete list of your grievances (the same one you gave the landlord). The knowledge you're going to do this is often enough to make an uncooperative landlord take a reasonable approach. Anyone who intends to stay in the business of renting apartments doesn't need bad publicity.

Arbitration or Lawsuit

Arbitration is a useful tool for settling landlord-tenant disputes. It differs from a lawsuit in that both tenant (or tenants) and landlord must agree they can't solve the problems themselves, neither wants to resort to a court hearing, and all involved are in favor of arbitration. This decision should be put in writing and signed by all involved parties. Then it's time to contact the American Arbitration Association or its affiliate, the National Center for Dispute Settlement. Generally, there isn't a long waiting period before you get action. These groups are nonprofit, so the charges to both landlord and tenant won't be exorbitant. The bill will be divided equally between both parties in most cases. When arbitration has been completed, the losing party may be required to reimburse the winner, but this is rare and only occurs in a very one-sided case.

Arbitration is legal, and it is binding. Neither you nor the landlord have any right of appeal, but this isn't really a drawback. The arbitrators are skilled, fair, and impartial. They can see both sides of the issue, something you and the other tenants may not be able to do even though you think you can. These cases have a way of getting muddied with emotion and personal assessments after they've been going on for awhile. It's possible the landlord has a few points in his favor which you fail to recognize, just as he's failed to recognize his obligations to you, his tenants.

Lawsuits can be expensive. They usually bring out the worst in people. And often everyone is a loser of sorts. But your tenant organization can, as a last resort, sue the landlord. If the conditions you're complaining about can be shown to constitute a health hazard, you have an excellent chance of winning.

The landlord may start eviction proceedings against members of your organization. But if you stick together as a group and stand your ground, he is almost certainly going to drop his action. He can't afford to evict all the tenants that are members of a strong tenant organization. That would leave him with too many empty apartments. He knows it will be easier for you as tenants to find new lodgings than it will be for him to find new tenants.

The majority of landlords will be cooperative with a tenant organization once they know the group means business. It's only in a few extreme cases that the matter must go beyond the first few negotiations.

An Intruding Landlord

Some landlords just can't let go of their property. Before you move in, they hover over your apartment as if it were an egg about to hatch. And after you've taken up residence, they still seem to be on the doorstep or, worse yet, inside at alarmingly regular intervals. Must you put up with this? In many states there's a "quiet enjoyment of the premises" clause in all leases, which is generally interpreted to mean that for a landlord to enter your apartment uninvited, he must have a very good reason to do so. A growing number of states have renter's privacy laws which have even stricter terms for protecting the tenant's rights of privacy. If you have this problem, find out what your rights are.

But just as the landlord can't be unreasonable in his visitations, you shouldn't be unreasonable about letting him in if he does have a valid reason for being there. The owner, or a spokesman for the owner, usually has the right to enter the premises for the following reasons: 1) to make necessary repairs or to alter the apartment for your betterment; 2) to show your apartment to a prospective tenant once you've decided to move and have given notice that you will be vacating the premises; 3) to show his property to prospective buyers if he has decided to sell; 4) to make periodic inspections to make sure the apartment isn't being abused. But he isn't allowed to overuse these privileges of entry. In other words, if you feel you're being harrassed, you may well have a right to do something about it.

In all but a few jurisdictions, the law now reads that the landlord must give the tenant at least 24 hours notice before he enters an apartment for any reason that doesn't qualify as an emergency. When the pipe in your bathroom is leaking all over the apartment underneath you—that's an emergency. If the landlord thought he'd stop by and weather-strip the door—that's not an emergency. You aren't required to let him make these appointments for unreasonable hours or when his visit is going to seriously disrupt your way of living. For instance, if he works until 12:30 at night and wants to stop by to fix something on his way home from work, you probably aren't going to have to let him do it.

Your landlord can't make it a habit to enter your apartment frequently even for repairs. For example, he may be showing up every week—one week he replaces a washer in the kitchen sink, then stays to talk for a couple of hours; the next week he comes back to fix a light fixture, and the next for something else. You have a right to feel he's harassing you. (Actually he may just like your company.) It's hard to ask him to leave you alone if he happens to be a friendly fellow. But if you don't want him around, the sooner you let him know it the easier the problem will be to solve.

If nothing else works, you can sue the landlord for damages and invasion of privacy, or you may be able to get a court order saying he may not enter the premises except at intervals that the court will stipulate and which it will deem reasonable. When you win this type of case your landlord is stuck holding the tab for your attorney's bill and the court costs. So if you think you're on firm ground, you have little to lose by taking the legal route when the owner has turned a deaf ear to your pleas for privacy.

Moving On

It's necessary to adhere to the terms of your lease in giving notice that you intend to vacate the apartment when that lease expires. Most tenants prefer a lease that allows you to vacate after the term of the first lease is up with a notice of thirty to sixty days. You find these in complexes that have no trouble renting when a unit is vacant. But most leases say that if you have not given notice within sixty days before the expiration of the lease, it will automatically be renewed. So if you have a lease of this type that expires in July, you can't give notice in June. You will be held responsible for that next full term just as though you had signed a new lease.

SUBLETTING

If you find yourself with another year of a lease that you don't want and you have a sublet clause, you can, of course, solve your problem by subletting your apartment. But remember, you'll be liable for its condition so be selective whom you sublet to. You also will be the one who collects the rent and pays the landlord. If the party to whom you have sublet fails to make the rent payment, you must do so. The person who is subletting from you is, however, required to observe all of the clauses in your lease. If the lease says, "no pets" he can't have pets, "no late parties" he can't have late parties.

When your lease says you may not sublet, or when there is no sublet clause and the issue isn't addressed, if you go ahead and sublet anyway, a landlord (in most areas) can't accept any further rent from you if he wishes to evict you or the people in your apartment. Once he takes the money, providing he is aware that you've sublet, the law usually waives his right to hold you in violation of the lease.

If you're not allowed to sublet, but your lease doesn't say how many people are allowed to live in your apartment, what happens if you decide to take a roomer who will share expenses? Taking in roomers isn't the same as subletting. The person whose name is on the lease is still in possession of the premises and is simply allowing the roomer to use part of those premises for a fee. This is allowable as long as your roomers don't create a nuisance or in any way violate the terms of the lease. This has been put to the legal test many times, and, in most of them, the landlord has lost. If the property were sublet, the original signer of the lease would be waiving all jurisdiction over the apartment. In this case he is still the tenant and is living up to the terms of the lease.

BREAKING THE LEASE EARLY

Suppose you answer an advertisement for a beautiful apartment in a garden-type setting in the quiet of the country and move in, only to discover that there is a noisy factory just over the hill where you couldn't see it; that the garden isn't going to be planted for another two years; that the maintenance is nonexistent and that none of the things that were described so beautifully in the ad are actually there. Must you live there for the term of your lease? In many states, you do have the right to break your lease if an apartment was advertised falsely. If this happens to you in a complex, your best bet is to form a tenant association and approach the problem with the force of numbers. But when it occurs in a small apartment building, you still have a good chance of winning the right to vacate the premises without penalty.

The apartment which seemed right for you when you looked at it and signed the lease may not seem at all right a few months later. Maybe your dream house has come up for sale just after you've signed a lease; perhaps you've found that the apartment you've chosen just isn't big enough for your needs now that the baby has arrived; maybe you're getting married and your spouse also has a lease on an apartment. There are many reasons for breaking a lease other than dissatisfaction with the premises.

You may find that you're locked into that lease and will have to pay a penalty (if not the balance of the lease) in order to break it. But you also may have a landlord who's willing to release you from it if you request that he do so. If the apartment is a good one, he shouldn't have any trouble renting it to someone else. It's best to get this agreement in writing if your landlord says he has no objection to an early termination of the lease agreement. However, a verbal agreement and his acceptance of the keys to the property are enough to make it legal. You may offer to pay for the ad to rent the property. This small act will sometimes placate a landlord.

The landlord may withhold your security deposit to cover his expenses while he's finding a new tenant. He will, after all, probably have to advertise, and to paint earlier than he had planned, as well as generally clean up the apartment. You would have trouble fighting this in court as technically you owe him the full balance of the rent due on the lease even though you've moved out. If he lets you out of the lease and keeps your security deposit, you should consider yourself lucky. In some complexes, you'll be released from your obligation on the lease if you pay until the apartment has been rented again. If the complex is a desirable one, the time should be minimal. In this way, the landlord can allow you to break your lease without penalizing himself.

Taxes and Tax Deductions

Until recently, all real estate tax breaks went to homeowners. Those of us who rented paid and paid and paid, but we got no breaks. Gradually this is changing. In many states, apartment dwellers are now entitled to deduct a certain amount of their rent payments from their taxable income. This new trend still has a long way to go before it's of any major benefit to most of us, but a start has been made.

Many states allow senior citizens who rent to deduct a portion of the rent paid from their state income taxes. Wisconsin, which was the first state to allow renters any tax break, is also one of the states which doesn't impose an age restriction. Arizona, California, Colorado, Connecticut, Illinois, Indiana, Iowa, Maine, Michigan, Minnesota, Missouri, Nevada, New Mexico, New York, North Dakota, Oregon, Pennsylvania, Vermont, and West Virginia are among the other states which now offer some sort of tax break to those who rent.

In most states which recognize that renters already pay real estate taxes through their rent, there are certain restrictions. First, if you're on welfare, you don't get a tax break. Second, you need rent receipts to file with your income tax to prove that not only have you agreed to pay the stipulated amount of rent, you actually have been paying it. Third, the apartment for which you're deducting must be your home. If it's an apartment you only use on occasion, or if you use it as an office instead of living in it, you cannot take the deduction.

It's likely to be some time before there are tax breaks in effect in all the states, and even longer before apartment dwellers can have a break on the federal level. But when this does happen, it will be a giant step toward recognizing the apartment dweller as a first-class citizen.

Nor will it hurt the landlord's pocketbook. The portion of rent he applies toward taxes isn't taxable income to begin with. So he'll come out about the same as he does now, and we as renters will come out ahead.

Chapter 3

Dressing Up Your Apartment

Furnishing and decorating an apartment should be fun, but sometimes the project gets overwhelming, and, too often, the results are disappointing.

One way to avoid disappointment is to set reasonable goals before you start and keep them in mind. Your apartment should reflect you, your lifestyle, and your personality. It doesn't have to look just like a magazine cover. For instance, have you ever seen a photo in a decorating magazine of a room with electrical cords that showed? No matter how many electrical appliances are shown, none ever seems to be plugged into anything. In contrast, the cords in your room are going to show to some extent no matter what you do!

Know Your Needs

There are several questions you should ask yourself before you begin decorating. The answers will help you to achieve an apartment with which you'll be happy.

1. First, how much can you afford to spend? Is it a "sky's-the-limit" project, or are you pinching pennies? Whatever your pocketbook permits, with a little work and a lot of imagination, you can have an apartment of which you can be proud.

2. Must your apartment be child or pet-proof, or is it to be tenanted by adults only? Is your family the white sofa, eggshell rug variety. Or are you more apt to have a good-looking apartment longer if you stick to earth colors such as brown and dark green.

3. Are you party people who need space for entertainment, or do you need only books and records for companionship?

4. What is the natural traffic pattern? Can you decorate the way you wish to without blocking this movement, or must you change your plans?

5. Is your taste traditional, modern, eclectic? Are you formal or informal?

6. What colors do you want to live with? Are they practical? Will your lease let you use them on the walls?

7. Do you already have all the furniture that you plan to use? Are you going to completely refurnish? Or are you planning on adding just a few pieces?

8. Will you use the services of a decorator or a designer? There is a difference. You'll usually find decorators at large furniture stores or in the furniture departments of department stores. Their job is to decorate your home with their employer's merchandise. Some of these people are extremely good at their profession and can give you valuable tips on how to make your apartment more attractive. A designer is one who works for or owns a decorating or interior design firm. Designers shop all the stores and outlets, as well as other sources (some known only to them), for just the right touches to turn your home into that something special you want. A good designer will work with *you*; get to know *you*; and take the lead from *you* so that the end result will be something you can take personal pride in and will not be just an extension of the designer's tastes and preferences. But most designers are expensive. Unless you're awfully rich, or have no confidence in your own taste, you should be able to handle the decorating yourself.

Imagination is the key word, whether you're decorating on a shoestring or have unlimited resources. Good taste isn't for sale, and expensive poor taste abounds in the apartments of those who lack imagination. Your imagination may be titillated by perusing home fashion magazines, even though you're not going to duplicate their ideas. Study rooms you like, and ask yourself what appeals to you about them. Is it the colors, the furnishings, the accessories, or the fabrics?

Start with Color

Color will play a big part in your decorating plans. Decide which of the three basic color schemes you're going to use in a room before you determine anything else.

An *analogous* color scheme uses colors which are adjacent to each other on the color wheel. For instance, you might use red, red-orange, and orange, or you could move up a color and select orange, yellow-orange, and yellow. The middle color is the unifier. This type of color scheme might incorporate four colors such as blue, blue-green, green, and green-yellow. But four colors are trickier to use than three.

Monochromatic color schemes are variations on one color. Medium blue, light blue, and dark blue form an example of a monochromatic scheme. This kind of color scheme can make a mish mash of various styles and types of furniture seem to go together when they actually aren't all that harmonious. If you opt for a monochromatic color scheme, your room will be enlivened with the inclusion of a small dash of another color. For instance, a beige to brown theme sparked up with a touch of orange can make the difference between dull and dazzling.

A *complementary* color scheme is your other choice. It uses two colors which appear opposite each other on the color wheel, such as pale green and pink (these are light values of red and green). A complementary color scheme using the colors at full strength can be dramatic or, in a small room, can be overpowering.

Select colors and color schemes that you'll find easy to live with. A handsome effect can be achieved by using royal purple and gold (a complementary color scheme) but you may find that after the first month or so you've grown tired of it. Subdued shades, while not as dramatic, sometimes retain their appeal for longer periods of time. Also bear in mind, when selecting wall color for an apartment, that you're probably going to have to paint over it with a pastel, if not white, before you vacate the premises and your security deposit is returned to you. Most (but not all) leases state that you can't paint walls with a dark color, or that if you do, you must cover them with a pastel. And by "cover" they mean cover so that the dark color won't burn through in time.

You can add neutral colors to your color scheme, such as white, black, or beige, without interfering with the basic colors you've chosen. When you've selected the colors for your walls and floor covering, it's time to pick colors for drapes and furniture. When purchasing big pieces of furniture, choose fairly neutral shades. These furnishings usually represent major investments, and you'll want them to fit in with any decor you have in your next apartment. Even if you decide to stay in the apartment you're in, you'll want to redecorate someday. A bright, floral sofa, or a multi-colored stripe, or even a solid bright red can severely limit you when you want to change a color scheme or give your room a different atmosphere.

Draperies are another story. You needn't spend the world for them, and they probably won't fit the windows in another apartment anyway. This is a good place for color expression and the daring use of patterns.

When you're working on the color dilemma, you should be aware that the tiny paint chips, or swatches of wallpaper or fabric will appear lighter than they will when they are actually on a wall, used in a curtain, or on an upholstered piece. The more of a color you use, the darker it will look. Some colors, such as yellow, are particularly deceiving. What looks in a paint chip like such a pale yellow it's almost white can simply scream "yellow" at you when it's applied to a wall. Always select something that looks lighter than what you think you want.

The natural light source should be taken into consideration, too, when you're deciding what colors to use in a room. Warm colors such as red, orange, and yellow may be too much for an already sun-drenched room, while blues, greens and orchids can make a sunless room seem even colder and less cheerful.

Plain or Patterns

Are you going to go for patterns in your apartment or plain colors? Patterns are usually more interesting (for all but those expensive pieces) unless you have many pictures and artifacts from which you don't want to divert attention. The faint-hearted stick to just one pattern per room. This is the safest way, and it can be effective when the pattern is carried from drapes to pillows to a bedspread. But there's nothing wrong with mixing two patterns if you know what you're doing. You can take the sure route on this and purchase fabrics already paired by a decorator and sold as mates. Most of these were designed to go together before they were manufactured. You may prefer to mix your own, thus coming up with an original match instead of one that's going to be found in many apartments.

Be sure the colors in any patterns you select match your preselected color scheme and that the colors in both patterns go together. Don't decide on two large or two small patterns unless they're completely different. Generally, one pattern should be dominant. A large plaid could be used with a large floral, however, and a small floral with a small geometric, and so forth. Some decorators use two florals together, one small and one large. If you do this, be sure there is a *great* variance in the size of the two patterns. One should be much larger than the other one. Three or more patterns also can be mixed successfully, but I think anyone who isn't a decorator or doesn't have a definite flair in that direction is courting failure to attempt it.

If you have Oriental rugs or any other patterned rugs on your floors, they count as a pattern and must be dealt with accordingly. If you're introducing other patterns into a room where you have a patterned rug, follow the large–small rule.

A small room won't take a large pattern well, especially on the walls. And if you use a large pattern on drapes or a piece of furniture, that's where all eyes will go in that room. An area covered by a pattern will dominate. In small rooms it's best to stick to small patterns or solid colors.

If your living room is large, and you don't have much to put into it, make every piece count. Pattern will help with this. The larger the fabric pattern, the larger the furniture will appear to be. Use slipcovers rather than upholstery. This makes the decor much easier to change in the future.

Before you invest in fabric for drapes, for furniture, for a tablecloth, or for anything else that constitutes a fairly large investment, purchase a yard of the material so you can see how it looks in your apartment with your things. Drape the fabric over something in the room in which you're planning to use it, and leave it there for a few days to see if you're going to enjoy living with it. Never make your selection from a tiny swatch in a book if there's another way of doing it.

Don't overlook sheets as possible decorating material. There are some gorgeous sheets on the market now, and they aren't expensive compared to the material in most fabric shops, especially if you buy them during white sales. Sheets are now doubling as wall coverings, drapes and curtains, slipcovers, tablecloths, cushion and pillow

When you're mixing patterns, don't disregard the rug. The Oriental adds an intricate pattern to this room. *Courtesy of the Kirsch Company.*

covers; almost anything you care to cover with fabric can be taken care of with a sheet. And they're luxuriously wide to work with—you don't have to make so many seams.

Floors, Windows, and Walls

There are three main elements in every room: the floors, the windows, and the walls. These are the places to start using your imagination and applying your decorating knowledge.

FROM RAGS TO RUGS

Rugs can consume a good portion of your furniture budget if you allow them to. Good quality broadloom is expensive, and Orientals can cost a king's ransom. But there are less expensive ways to cover your floor stylishly and with an individual flair.

Are you, or is anyone in your family, handy with a crochet hook? (Crocheting is simple to learn, and it doesn't take long since the yarn works up much more swiftly than it does with knitting.) With a bulky yarn, a crochet hook, and very little know-how, you can add a dash of color to your apartment with crocheted rugs. Simple instructions can be found in most yarn stores. And the salespeople in these shops are normally able and willing to help you if you're a novice or if you run into any problems with your project.

Your talents might not lie in the direction of crocheting. Perhaps painting is more in your line. An apartment with dull, old, wooden floors that need refinishing can be brought to life by painting a rug right onto the floor. A good deck paint works best. First, paint the rug area of the floor with your base color. Let it dry thoroughly. Then stencil the rug design you want to use onto the floor, filling in the design with the colors of deck paint you've chosen for the pattern. Paint the area around the "rug" a neutral color. (Be sure to get your landlord's approval before starting this.)

In Colonial times rug designs were painted onto pieces of canvas that were cut into whatever shape and size was needed. Today, inventive people have improved on this old practice. An interesting do-it-yourself rug can be made from a piece of painter's canvas that has been primed and cut to the desired size. Select a fabric with a design you'd like for a rug. Cut it so that it's at least three inches larger than the canvas on all sides. Place the canvas, gesso-side-up,

A crocheted rug is inexpensive and easy to make. This one can be completed in a short time. *Courtesy of Fieldcrest.*

on an old sheet or a large piece of plastic. Coat the canvas with paste (wallpaper paste works well). Then place the fabric, design-side up, on top of the canvas. Smooth it so it will be even. The same amount of fabric should be left on all sides. Push thumbtacks through both the canvas and the material at the corners. Allow the paste to dry thoroughly. When it's dry, remove the thumbtacks, turn the rug over, and paste down excess material around the edges. When this has dried, coat the fabric side of the rug with polyurethane. Allow this coat to dry twenty-four to forty-eight hours before applying a second coat. I have a small rug that I made this way. It's a conversation piece, and I get satisfaction out of knowing that it's my original, a one-of-a-kind creation.

A poor person's rug, maybe, but this rug, painted right on the floor, is a creative answer to floor decoration, and one in which even a wealthy person might take pride. *Courtesy of the Kirsch Company.*

Another unusual and inexpensive rug can be put together with sample pieces of carpeting. These sample rugs are on sale from time to time in just about any store that carries carpeting. You can purchase a good quality piece for an extremely low price. Select enough of these samples to make a rug of the size you need and in the colors you've elected to use. One store may not have enough of these remnants to suit your needs; you may have to go to two or three before you're satisfied. Try to get pieces that are all the same size. I've seen this type of rug made effectively from odd-sized pieces, but for a first-time rugmaker, they present problems.

Arrange the remnants on the floor in the manner you think looks best. When you're satisfied that you've achieved the most eye-pleasing pattern, sew the pieces together on the wrong side with a strong thread and a heavy needle. You can use large stitches. A pad under this rug will enhance its looks, but you can use it without one. Sample rugs are almost always bound, and can be used singly anywhere you need a small scatter rug.

Beach towels are made to suit every taste and mood. And they too can be used as area rugs. Select a plush one. With a towel rug, you will need a pad to keep it from wrinkling when it's walked on. You may have to glue the edges of the towel to the padding to avoid any tripping accidents.

Straw mats have become fashionable in the last few years. Their popularity has been a boon to those who are decorating on a budget. These inexpensive mats can solve your rug problems. But they do have drawbacks you should be aware of before you invest in them. It's essential to have a sturdy pad under a straw rug otherwise the fiber will cut right through the padding and ruin the floor. These mats aren't too comfortable for bare feet either. If you take your shoes off at home, straw rugs probably aren't for you. Finally they tend to ripple when it's damp, so they must be pulled taut and stapled to the pad. Still, after taking into account all the negatives, straw or sisal rugs are a lot of rug for the money. And they will go with almost any decor.

WINDOW DRESSING

The windows in your apartment and the way you dress them can make the difference between success and failure in your decorating efforts. There are many types and sizes of windows, and with each comes a different problem or set of problems—too much light, not enough light, poor view, off-size, strange shape—the list goes on and on. But there isn't any window that can't be made to enhance the room it's in with a little know-how.

Tiny windows usually are installed to allow more wall space for furniture or because the view is offensive. But the small window itself is often unattractive. The problem can be solved in several ways. First, you can hang your drapes way out to either side of the window, bringing them in only to the edge of the glass, thus giving the illusion that the window is much larger than it actually is. If the window is too high, try hanging a café rod just at the window's bottom edge. Then put a drape or opaque curtain on this rod. Select one that goes to the floor, or adds whatever amount of length you want. The upper half, or the part of the arrangement that's really a window, can be covered with a traditional curtain or a café curtain. Something sheer to let in light is best. If the window is both high and narrow, combine these two treatments.

A window that looks out over the dump can be depressing. Semi-sheer curtains will help this situation by blurring the scenery while still allowing light to filter through. If this doesn't block the view enough, try covering the window with rice paper. It won't allow as much light in as semi-sheers, but it will screen the offending sight and let in some natural light.

Glass shelves installed across a small window with an ugly view and filled with plants will take the curse off of a bad view. But be sure you select the right plants for the amount of light that strikes the window.

Casement windows can defy attempts to make them beautiful. But they still can be dressed up. Old casement windows are even more of a challenge than the newer ones as they were almost always made to open in. Most drapery devices won't work unless the windows are always left shut. If you have this type of casement window, your best bet is the type of curtain that's shirred and stationary, attaching to the window frame itself, both top and bottom. You can also have a draw drape, providing the space on either side of the casement window is sufficient so the window won't tangle in the drape when it's open. When these windows swing out you can use almost any treatment, except the one that attaches to the part of the frame that houses the glass.

Some older apartments have lovely arched windows. These are beautiful to look at and devilish to curtain. It's next to criminal to cover up the arch, an architectural asset seldom found in modern buildings. But you can drape just the bottom part of this type of window. Hang your rods just below the arch. Since these arched windows are usually large and the arch high up, you will probably find that this provides you with adequate privacy. If you don't feel comfortable having that exposed expanse of glass, try using a semisheer curtain (it will have to be custom made) that gathers on a rod shaped to the contour of the window. If you resort to using a full drape, which when closed covers the whole window, at least hang it so that the entire shape of the window is visible when the drape is open.

A bay or bow window is another architectural asset. Don't upstage it with the window dressing you select. Allow the window to be the star of the room. Avoid splashy patterns or startling colors. Use a quiet drape or curtain that will blend into the background.

Older apartments sometimes have a series of windows with window frames or a sliver of wall space showing in between. These can be treated together as one whole window, or, if you prefer, you can put a piece of fabric between the windows, covering the frame or wall. If you consider it to be one window and use one pair of drapes, you will be happier with the appearance if you have stationary sheers underneath to cover the entire expanse of all the windows and fortify the unified look for which you're striving.

A big room with a picture window is a perfect place for a large, bold, colorful print. If the room is large but the window isn't, you can hang a mural on a blank wall (there are some rather handsome murals made of wallpaper that can be hung in panels) and hang a drape on the entire wall over the mural as though the mural were a window. This is dramatic either open or closed, and gives you the opportunity to change the ambience of your room just by opening the drapes. Woven wood shades can be hung over an entire wall, too, for an individual look that you can take with you when you leave the apartment.

The magnificent chandelier and the window dressings make this ordinary apartment seem elegant. *Courtesy of the Kirsch Company.*

For an elegant, formal room use a swag, or cornice, or some other top treatment on your windows. Most of these are custom made, but you'll find a few are carried by large department stores and mail order houses. They are made to match their manufacturer's drapes. If you purchase drapes from one of these places, check to see that all the material comes from the same dye lot. The companies mass produce and different lots often end up intermingled. If you first hang your drapes at night or in dim light, you may not notice that one pair doesn't quite match another pair or that a valance is just a shade off.

Fabrics

Drapery fabric can be as confusing as patterns and colors. You should keep several things in mind when purchasing drapes or material from which to make them. Do you want a washable, shrinkproof fabric? How important is it that the fabric from which your drapes are made is fire resistant if not fireproof? Are the colors going to fade? Will the sun rot the material? Is mildew a problem in your area? What will happen to the fabric when it folds and rubs against itself (which is inevitable for a window covering)?

Know your fabrics and choose them according to your particular needs. The following information will help you.

Cotton has come back into favor as an all-purpose material. This easy to launder, long-wearing material holds its shape well. It doesn't show wear from the abrasive affects of being rubbed together. However, cotton fades quite rapidly in a strong sun; and it is flammable.

Acetate holds its shape well through either washing or dry cleaning (some kinds need one, some the other), and it stands sunlight a great deal better than cotton does. It is also more resistant to fire. But it doesn't wear as well as cotton.

Nylon and *polyester* have similar properties. Both hold up well as drapery materials and don't wilt or mildew under damp conditions. These fabrics are washable. Nylon fades considerably faster than polyester. Both tend to melt rather than burn under a direct flame or intense heat.

Rayon is durable and holds its shape well when it's dry cleaned. It doesn't fade except under extremely bright and sunny conditions. But it's not a good choice for the careless smoker as it's a rapid burner.

Acrylics darken rather than fade in the direct sunlight. But these fabrics will pass almost any other test. They're durable, they don't wear out from rubbing and folding, humidity doesn't seem to hurt them, and they're fire resistant. Some acrylics wash well, while others do better when they're dry cleaned.

Fiber glass is a less popular fabric for drapes and curtains than it was a few years back. I don't recommend it for an apartment with children or pets. It's very abrasive, not only destroying itself but rubbing little glass particles into the skin of anyone who handles it. Although fiber glass is washable, coming out looking like new, the washing machine is left with tiny, usually invisible shards of glass that will cling to other washables for many loads afterwards.

Even though you've carefully selected the fabric for your drapes and curtains, it won't hurt to further protect the material with liners. They will add to the price a little, but you're protecting an investment. The use of sheers or semi-sheers under your drapes will act as a sunscreen in protecting your drapes, too.

Rods

Drapery and curtain rods are as important as what you hang from them. They come in many styles and colors, and using those that complement the furnishings in your room can make quite a difference. If your drapes are nothing special, they can become special with the selection of just the right rod. For instance, if your room has a Spanish motif, carry it through to the drapery rods. Your ordinary drapes will suddenly look Spanish. Chrome furniture can be accentuated with the use of silver curtain rods. This small item seems like a minor detail, but it's the minor details that make a well-appointed room. But cheap rods do look cheap. This is an area where it usually shows if you spend a little more (and it *is* only a little more) and get the best.

Draperies and curtains aren't really essentials. Ready-made window shades (the room-darkening variety, please) afford you the privacy of draw drapes at a small fraction of their cost. But they don't do much for the looks of a room unless you dress them up. You can let your inventiveness have full reign on this one. Colorful stenciling works well, or, if you have artistic talents, you can paint an original scene on the shades. A ruffle glued or stapled to the bottom slat dresses up a shade, especially in a feminine room. You can wallpaper the inside of the shade, too. Shades are available in a variety of colors or even in stripes or plaids.

Shutters fit in with almost any decor and give an apartment a decorator look. But they're expensive, and chances are they won't fit in the next place you live.

FOUR WALLS

Since walls compose the largest single area in any room, their decoration is important. There are some basic rules for coping with problem walls or room shapes. Tall ceilings in a relatively small room can give you the feeling of sitting in an elevator shaft. But you can decorate the walls to compensate for the ceiling's height. Stripes applied horizontally are one of the most effective ways of giving the illusion that a wall is longer than it actually is. On the other hand, if the ceilings are unusually low, as sometimes happens in apartments with drop ceilings, a striped paper that runs vertically will tend to push up the ceiling visually. This same principle applies when a room is long and narrow. Stripes running vertically on long walls will appear to shorten them, while horizontal stripes on short walls will stretch them out.

Small rooms always look smaller when they're painted or papered in dark colors or large patterns. Save these measures for big, airy rooms if you're lucky enough to have them in your apartment. An exception to this is that small, lackluster place such as the end of a hall, or a nook you don't know what to do with. It doesn't really matter if these areas look smaller, so a touch of vibrant color, or the use of a dramatic pattern are acceptable ways to bring these trouble spots to life.

Reflections work magic. Mirror one wall of a small room and, presto, it doubles in size. The adhesive-backed mirror squares aren't difficult to apply. Start at the ceiling when you do this so that any wall space that's too small to take an entire mirror square will be at floor level where it won't be noticed or will be masked by furniture.

Metallic wall coverings also add spaciousness to tiny areas. But walls with imperfections aren't good subjects for this metallic paper, which seems to point up the flaws in whatever is under it.

Although it's no longer the "in" thing it was twenty years ago, there's nothing wrong with papering just one wall of a room. The investment in paper is diminished considerably and the results look dashing, especially if the paper you use has a matching fabric with which you can make a bedspread, drapes, or a slipcover.

Sometimes old plaster walls are just too bumpy and pitted to respond to anything but extreme measures. Every flaw shows up on a wall of this sort when you paint it. It seems that the fresh coat of paint is wasted. And paper may just look lumpy. Injured walls take a lot of sanding and filling to make them look well again once they're painted or papered with anything but a paper carefully chosen to mask the imperfections. What is needed is wallpaper with a small overall pattern and a matte finish. It's surprising how it will camouflage the problem spots.

Don't be afraid to attempt hanging wallpaper. Until I tried it, I thought hanging paper was best left to the professionals. But I found that it's not only simple, it's fun! I find the paper that requires wallpaper paste is actually easier to put up than the paper that you just wet on the back and then stick up. Wallpaper paste is gooey enough to allow you to move a piece of paper around after you put it on the wall. Prepasted paper grabs more firmly and is less adjustable. But paste is messier, no question about it!

For those of you who don't want to go to the trouble and expense of paper and don't want to settle for the plainness of paint, there are other solutions. One is called Rollerwall. It's a roller on which a design has been imprinted. The design transfers to the wall when you saturate the roller in paint and then apply it to the wall. This gives the look of wallpaper for the price of paint. You do have to purchase the special design roller (available in about 100 different patterns) and a paint tank to help you apply the design. But a middle-sized room takes only about a quart of paint and can easily be completed in one or two hours (including coffee breaks).

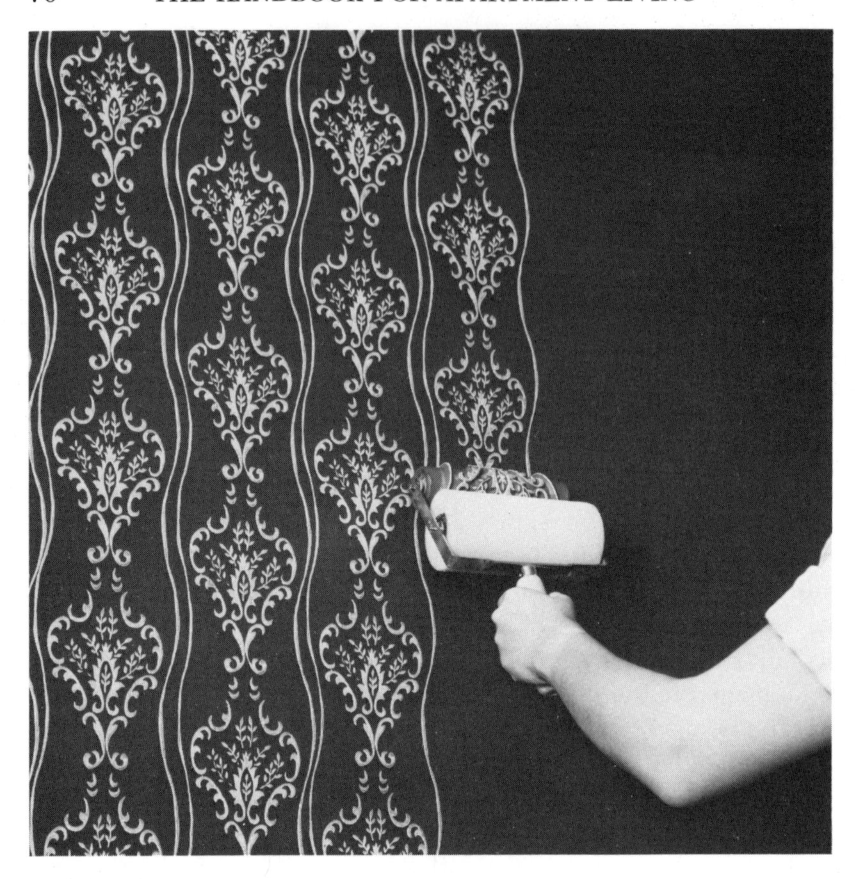

You can roll a pattern right onto your apartment walls at a fraction of the cost of wallpaper with the use of a roller, a little paint, and some elbow grease. *Courtesy of Rollerwall, Inc.*

The Rollerwall idea originated in Europe and has just recently begun to catch on over here. It can be used on fabrics as well, so you can have matching draperies made out of sheets or another inexpensive material that will give your room a coordinated look. Since you can roll these designs over any color, this is a good place to start with your basic color scheme.

Stenciling on walls or woodwork is another way to give your apartment a custom look at an economical price. I've seen stenciling used effectively as a border around a ceiling of a living room, on kitchen cabinets, around mirrors, and in a mural-like arrangement over a sofa. One color or a rainbow of colors can be used with equal success. Cut stencils from heavy, nonporous paper. The design is your own original creation.

Another inexpensive way to spruce up a room is to add a molding. You can make an ordinary room look classy with this simple touch. A fancy wooden molding can be painted one of the colors in your color scheme and nailed at the top of the wall right against the ceiling.

Use your imagination to create a design out of adhesive-backed paper and apply it to a wall area. This should only take about thirty minutes to do, and you can use a plain color, a metallic-type paper, or one of the many available patterns—whatever fits in best with your decorating theme. Or you might outline a window with a strip of wallpaper or adhesive-backed paper.

A wall that's badly scarred, and needs more TLC than you're prepared to invest in it, can be covered with a shirred fabric, such as a sheet, hung from a rod at ceiling level. It's possible, and in many rooms looks first rate, to cover all the walls in this manner. And it gives the room a cozy feeling. For a luxurious look, cut your material

Ingenuity, creativity, and a bit of adhesive-backed paper are the main ingredients for making a bedroom wall that would delight any child. *Courtesy of Comark Plastics.*

two to three times as wide as the area you're going to cover. Otherwise the shirring might look skimpy. Café rods hung an inch or so beneath the ceiling and the same distance off the floor will hold the fabric taut. You will, of course, have to do a narrower rendition of the same thing over doors, and over and under windows. If you just want a gathered effect on the walls, you can eliminate the bottom rods. But the shirred walls really are lovelier.

The walls can be brushed or vacuumed when they get dusty, and the material should come down for laundering every so often. When removing the panels be sure to mark each one so you can return it to the wall where it belongs.

Affordable, Portable Furniture

The growing trend toward mobility in our society has created a challenge for the designers of furniture. The big, sturdy pieces of yesteryear have fallen into disfavor. People rapidly lose their enthusiasm for these heavy pieces of furniture after they've moved them once or twice or paid a mover (most of them charge by weight) to move them from place to place.

While it seems that most of what's in the stores today is lighter furniture, the real boon for apartment dwellers is the knock-down, easy-to-assemble furniture that makes moving, if not a joy, at least tolerable.

One manufacturer makes an entire bedroom set which, when packaged, fits into a Volkswagen. That's progress! K.D. (as knock-down furniture is affectionately referred to) has not been known for its quality in the past. But it's coming out of the closet and some truly fine pieces are made now in K.D. The furniture is designed with the average, all-thumbs apartment person in mind. You don't need sophisticated equipment or a degree in engineering to put it together. You may need a screwdriver and sometimes a hammer for all but the newest pieces. The instructions are explicit, and all the necessary holes are already drilled. K.D. is going one step further and some of the latest pieces are being made to fit together with pegs, or with an interlocking tongue and groove construction. These don't even require a screwdriver or hammer for assembly.

The neat thing about this furniture is the price. It is fabulously inexpensive, costing far less than its already-assembled counterparts. And it comes in just about any style or period you're liable to want. A major reason for the low price tag is the ease with which K.D. is shipped. Everything can be packed flat, taking up about half the room needed for preassembled furniture. The shipping price is therefore substantially less. K.D. doesn't take up much storage room either, so a retailer isn't using so much expensive space to keep the items in stock.

There are stores opening up which cater only to the K.D. buyer. They are an apartment dweller's dream. In some stores, all the K.D. furniture in stock is coded to denote ease of assembly. Although no piece is unduly hard to put together, some do require a bit more time and effort than others. The coding is valuable information for those of us who definitely don't make it in the do-it-yourself category.

Furniture Refinishing

It's rather difficult to strip furniture in an apartment. If you're determined to do so, you can cover your floor with plastic, open all the windows, turn on the fans, and go to it. But there are any number of furniture strippers in business in most areas, who are able to dip even large pieces in a solution strong enough to remove all of the old finish. The cost is reasonable, but you probably will have to sand the piece down fairly well and, in most cases, reglue the joints before you paint or refinish it.

The best furniture strippers use a solution that doesn't contain lye. Ask about this before you leave your furniture to be worked on. I find that hard woods, such as cherry, lend themselves to this dip-and-strip process better than the softer woods, such as pine, which seem to lose their resins in the stripping process.

It is a good idea to consult one of the many helpful books on furniture refinishing. Doing a good job is not so hard as you may think. And the reward is great when that old, painted dresser you bought for a few dollars turns into an elegant piece that's perfect for your bedroom.

The Wonderful World of Second-Hand

Second-hand is more exciting, individual, and, unless you're in the market for genuine antiques, less expensive than new. And you can usually get much better quality for your money. There are many places to start the hunt for second-hand treasures to furnish your apartment. You don't have to deal with Sotheby Parke Bernet to achieve a perfectly sensational second-hand look. You can do a lot with what you find picking through someone else's abandoned goods.

GARAGE OR HOUSE SALES

These sales provide a never-ending source of wonders with which you can furnish an apartment. If you're a discriminating buyer you may get a spectacular buy. In an effort to rid their houses and apartments of discarded items, people often overlook an article's true value. What is junk to them may not be junk to those in the know. This is why it pays to get to a sale of this type just as soon as it's scheduled to begin. These sales are favorite hunting grounds for antique dealers and those collectors who bank on owners not knowing what they're selling. Garage sales are usually advertised in the newspapers, and a few of the items for sale will be listed. Select a sale that has articles in which you're interested and be among the first in line. If it's furniture for which you're hunting, have a vehicle large enough to transport your purchases.

Something that you like but think is overpriced, either for your pocketbook or for what you think is its intrinsic value, could still be yours. Don't be too timid to make a lower offer. If the person who's having the sale won't accept it, ask if you may leave your phone number so you can be called if the article in question isn't sold during the sale. A garage or house sale rarely clears out all the merchandise that's up for sale. A price that seems too small to the seller on the first day of a sale, may seem great on the day the sale ends.

If you come upon an inviting object that's unpriced, ask what the owner wants for it. Never make an offer until you've been told an asking price. Then you can offer lower if you think it's too high. If you make a blind offer, it may be much more than the person expected to get for it, or you could be so low you'll offend the owner and ruin your bargaining chances.

AUCTIONS

There are good auctions and bad auctions. If you're thinking of spending an appreciable amount of money, get there in time to

This lovely room holds many treasures that were found in the wonderful world of second-hand. *Courtesy of Bill Hedrich, Hedrich-Blessing.*

Don't overlook garage sales, auctions, and flea markets. They offer bargain treasures for the discriminating buyer.

inspect the merchandise before the sale. It may look different from the back of an auction house than it does up close. You could miss a good buy or get a raw deal if you don't take a close, thorough look.

Don't resist bidding on a good, solid piece of furniture just because you don't like the finish or paint. It can be stripped down and refinished or painted a color you like. The lines (are they pleasing to you?) and the condition (is it sturdy?) are the important considerations, along with the price, of course.

If you're antique hunting at an auction be cautious. Many auctions are salted with reproductions. Unless an auctioneer says he knows something is an antique he isn't violating any law or code by letting you think it is. "I think this is an example of an 18th century sideboard . . ." is different from certifying its authenticity. The jargon is misleading and often intentionally so.

If you see something you want for your apartment at an auction, decide what that piece is worth to you, and don't bid any higher.

Bidding is contagious! It's tempting to add just another dollar or so to what someone else has bid and then, if they raise your bid, to add another dollar. Before you know it, you may own something for which you've paid way more than you intended. Some unscrupulous auctioneers even have people in the audience who bid things up for them. If the person who's working for the auctioneer gets "stuck" with an item, it can always go in next week's auction sale. Of course, there are many honest auctioneers who would never do this.

Second-hand television sets can be had for a few dollars at most auctions. Some of them are worth much more, and some of them are worthless. Never bid on a television that the auctioneer doesn't guarantee as being in good working condition. "It only needs a minor repair" should be a warning sign. It may, in fact, need a new picture tube and not be worth fixing. Forget it!

Any kind of appliance is suspect at an auction unless it's a home auction where the people who owned the merchandise are deceased or for some reason are breaking up housekeeping. In this case, the appliances have likely been in use and are okay, although on occasion things are brought in from outside to be sold at sales of this nature. Years ago, I bought a washer and dryer at a fantastically reasonable price at an auction. I couldn't believe it! The auctioneer told me the washer was "on a dare," something I later learned meant "you're taking a chance." He said the dryer worked. Since we needed these things badly, I was delighted with my purchases—until I tried to use them. The washer didn't work, and I found it couldn't be repaired. The dryer had a malfunctioning heating unit which was so hot it melted my clothes. That was an expensive lesson, and I since have been extremely cautious when I purchase appliances at auctions.

Upholstered pieces are quite another thing. They usually cost very little at auctions. Sometimes the fabric is worn, but if the springs and frame are good, you can slipcover the furniture and have a solid, attractive piece for just a few dollars. I've purchased overstuffed chairs for as little as ten dollars at these sales.

Old, unattractive pictures are sometimes auctioned in lots just to get rid of them all at once. For a dollar or two you may get five or six of these. Look over the frames before the sale begins. Just one good frame makes it well worth the investment. I have two huge, beautiful mirrors in my apartment whose frames were originally on unappealing pictures. My husband painted them gold, antiqued them, and we purchased mirrors to go in them. They cost only a few dollars total, and I've seen mirrors the same size in department stores for twenty times what we paid. They weren't as good looking either.

FLEA MARKETS

Flea markets and church bazaars are a source of wonderful apartment furnishings. You're likely to find some surprising bargains, depending on the expertise of the person running a booth. The list of things to look for at a flea market is almost endless. Old sheet music often sells for pennies a sheet, and it can be framed and hung on your apartment walls. Old prints or old postcards also make unusual wall displays, or they can be used to decorate the top of a glass-topped table. Look for interesting bottles and outdated items that can be converted to lamps. Bird cages, painted brightly, are great planters. An old sewing machine table can be made into a handy end table by adding a new top to the iron legs. Musical instruments make interesting wall arrangements for the apartment of a music lover. Odd cans or jars can be used as cannisters, or a cradle as a magazine rack.

It was at a flea market that my husband and I found a 1930s phonograph cabinet for ten dollars, which didn't even need refinishing. That cabinet now houses our stereo turntable and radio, and it blends in beautifully with our apartment's decor. I'm as pleased with it as I would be with a thousand-dollar cabinet.

USED FURNITURE STORES

Unlike the flea market and the garage sale, the second-hand dealer almost always knows how to price the merchandise. He's aware of the true value of the furniture and knick-knacks he has in the shop. Even so, occasionally you will find something that has slipped by him and is priced lower than it really should be. Nobody knows the true value of everything.

Look around the back rooms in these establishments. Sometimes you'll find a piece of furniture the proprietor has had for a long time and is anxious to get rid of. He may let you have it cheap just to regain his initial investment.

Goodwill and Salvation Army outlets are second-hand stores where the money that's made goes to the charity the store represents. Much of this merchandise comes from the homes of the well-to-do. These places are fertile hunting grounds for the person who's furnishing an apartment on a shoestring but who wants it to be chic.

RULES FOR SECOND-HAND SHOPPING

No devotee of second-hand items ever attends any type of sale without three things in hand. One is a flashlight to aid in close inspection of merchandise. The second is a magnet to tell brass from iron and other metals. Brass won't attract a magnet. Iron (which is far less desirable and which can be purchased for considerably less money) does. A magnifying glass is the other piece of standard equipment. It's used in spotting signed pieces, inspecting jewelry for flaws, or looking for sterling or gold markings. Anything that's signed is automatically worth more money (if the signature is authentic).

One hard and fast rule I now stick to in shopping in the wonderful world of second-hand is never to buy anything I don't like, even if it's a bargain. Maybe you can turn around and sell it for its actual worth, but you're more likely to get stuck with it. I don't purchase anything I'm not going to be comfortable living with.

If you're tempted by an antique at any of these sales, proceed with caution unless you like the piece so much that it doesn't matter to you if it's old or not. There are a great many reproductions out there masquerading as the real thing. A reputable dealer won't try to sell anything as authentic unless it is, but all dealers aren't reputable and often an individual who's selling a piece at a house sale doesn't know whether it's old or not. In the 1920s the market became glutted with new pieces being touted as antiques. In order to make these look like authentic early 19th century, the manufacturers used wood with knotholes when, in fact, an authentic early 19th century piece is unlikely to have these knotholes. So if you're about to buy a 19th-century piece of furniture, look for this clue. It could help you avoid buying a fraud.

Whatever is presently in vogue will have a higher price than other old items, and the value isn't always inherent in the piece. I don't advise buying with the fads. Anything well-built will serve you well even if it isn't considered stylish at the moment you purchase it. And since these fads come and go, you may find in the future that your purchase has become worth many times what you spent for it—due to demand. The only way to buy a faddish item is to anticipate the fad and buy early. If you don't want to spend the money for a brass bed (a voguish item), consider the less expensive iron ones. They can be painted to be truly exquisite. But be sure anything that you purchase has all of its parts. The knob off a bedpost is difficult to replace, and its absence detracts greatly from both appearance and value.

From Room to Room

Here are a few suggestions for ways to deal with the various rooms in an apartment.

THE KITCHEN

If you have the room for a kitchen table but either can't afford one or don't want to use up the room, you can install an eat-on counter. The most space-saving way to do this is by attaching a piece of planking, Formica, or pressboard onto the wall with hinges. This can be kept out of the way when it's not in use, and it will provide extra space when you're preparing for a crowd and need to spread out.

Food is the theme of every kitchen. Capitalize on this by using potatoes, onions, and fruit as decorations. Hang these in baskets, or put them in a bowl on the kitchen table.

If your kitchen and dining room are one big room, or if your living room and dining room run together and you'd like each to be set apart, build a simple, wooden platform for the dining area of the room. Redwood is a pleasing choice for this (although plywood will work, too). Most lumberyards will cut the wood to your specifications. You need only build the deck up about an inch or two from the floor to get the desired effect. Stain it, or wax it, and you don't even need to use a rug. This will give you a separate and quite rustic dining area.

If you don't have kitchen cabinets, or the cabinets you do have don't have doors, your dishes and other utensiles are going to collect grease. And you'll have to keep everything super neat all the time. One great cover-up is to install window shades over the open cabinets, or to put up shelves and cover them with window shades. You can decorate the shades, or purchase them in bright colors to match the rest of your kitchen. Either install runners on the edges of the cabinets on which the shades will run, or have a hook for each shade to latch onto at the bottom of each cabinet when closed.

Scatter rugs with non-skid backings will add a splash of color to your kitchen, and they'll be comforting to your feet when you stand for any length of time preparing a meal, doing dishes, and the host of other chores that always seem to need doing in that room. Add a few to strategic spots in your kitchen.

Kitchen curtains take more wear and tear and get dirtier quicker than curtains in any other room. Select the curtains for your kitchen with an eye to washability. If your windows are anywhere near your stove, be sure the curtains don't hang where they could be in danger from a flaming pot or pan. To be extra careful, look for a flameproof fabric.

Coffee cans covered with wallpaper that matches your kitchen walls make attractive canisters. You could also paint the cans or cover them with a washable fabric that can be slipped off for easy laundering.

THE BATHROOM

When you're decorating your bathroom keep safety uppermost in your mind. Put colorful, nonslip strips in the bathtub or shower. Don't use scatter rugs that will skid when placed on a tile floor. Use rugs with a good, rubber backing.

If the fixtures are old and tired-looking, divert the eye from them by using strong colors on the walls and hanging up bright-colored towels. A busy pattern on the walls will also make the old tub and sink fade into the background.

Curtains for this room should be mildew resistant and of the type that won't droop when the humidity elevates.

THE LIVING ROOM

This is the room in your apartment that you'll probably be using the most, and the one you want to look just right for company. When

This modern seating arrangement offers the opportunity for cozy chats, and it's also comfortable for sleeping. *Courtesy of H.U.D.D.L.E.*

you plan your living room think first in terms of conversation. If you've only two chairs, don't place them at opposite ends of the room so their occupants will have to shout in order to converse. Two sofas (if you have them) placed opposite each other with a coffee table in between makes for a workable living room that's cozy for conversation. There's a seating arrangement called Huddlecouch on the market which is a large, three or four-sided sofa that can also be used as a bed. Any number of people can sit on it for easy intimate conversations. This should have great appeal to the young and garrulous.

An easy-on-the-pocketbook way of having adequate seating is to invest in stacking pillows. Not only do they provide portable seats, they can be stacked when not in use so they won't take up much floor space in a small apartment living room. The original stacking pillows come in a pile of various-colored, vinyl-covered pillows. But you can also use large decorator pillows for this purpose, selecting a harmonious group that fits in well with your other furnishings.

Wicker furniture is easy on the budget. Old wicker is harder to find, and it's more expensive—but it is handsome. Either old or new can be used as is or spray painted. The addition of covered pillows on the seats and backs makes this furniture infinitely more comfortable. Versatile wicker will match either a traditional or modern decor depending on the finishing treatment you elect to give it.

Most people want sofas in their living rooms, and new sofas are costly. But a substitute sofa can be made with a mattress and box spring. You may have extra ones around. These can be any size, but twin works best. Your substitute sofa can be covered in a variety of ways. Quilted mattress covers (the type that the mattress slips into) can be dyed to fit your decor. You need one for the mattress and one for the box spring. Or, you might try covering both pieces with a colorful quilt, stapling it to the corners of the box spring. The box

Old wicker furniture can be painted to look better than new. With the addition of colorful cushions, it gives a festive touch to a living room. *Courtesy of the Kirsch Company.*

spring with the mattress on top of it can be placed directly on the floor, or it can be placed on bricks (painted or plain) or cinder blocks. You may even want to build a small platform. A selection of coordinated throw pillows against the wall adds the finishing touch.

The old rocking chair still has a prominent place in many homes. They are cheap, tasteful, and come in all sizes and styles from old-fashioned to ultra-modern. Most of them are comfortable, which is something you don't always find in inexpensive seating.

Don't overlook slipcovers in your efforts to make your living room livable. There are many angles from which to attack the problem of slipcovering your living room pieces. You can purchase ready-made, and hope for a good fit. You can have them custom made. This is not as costly as you might think, especially if you purchase your material at a fabric outlet. You can make your own if you're handy at that sort of thing. Or, you can cover the furniture with sheets, blankets, bedspreads or anything else that's large enough, taking a tuck here and a pleat there and holding the whole thing together with ribbons and bows. (Both *Family Circle Magazine* and *Woman's Day* carried instructions for doing this in their October 1979 issues.) This idea is for the novice decorator, not for the experienced seamstress, although the results look amazingly polished.

When you're shopping for a new piece of upholstered furniture for your apartment, do so with care. Push up and down on a chair or sofa to find out if the springs creak. See if the frame gets wobbly or seems stable if you sit down hard on it or even bounce a bit. If you're going to buy really good furniture, be certain the quality warrants the price tag. The rear legs and back frame should all be one piece. A frame that's made of wood (and most of them are) should be reinforced with supports on the corners.

Fine furniture with coil spring construction should come with eight-way ties on the coils. And no matter how much of a bargain a piece is, don't buy it unless it has at least four-way ties on the coil springs. This has a huge bearing on how long that piece is going to stay intact. There should be webbing on the bottom of any upholstered piece, and the webs should be so close together you can't easily push your fist between the bands. Find out, too, how many layers of padding have been installed over the frame. One layer is generally not enough. Two or three will insure you of longer lasting comfort.

You need more than seating for your living room. You need tables, for instance. Cocktail and end tables needn't be store-bought. Even an old wooden crate sanded down and refinished makes an interesting table in a rustic room. Large spools, like the ones the electric companies use for wire, can also be sanded and refinished for use as tables.

Plastic parson's tables can be found in most thrift stores. While they are not extremely chic, they are cheap and the lines are clean. You can dress them up to suit your living room. I wallpapered one parson's table to match the paper on one wall. It helped tie the whole room together. If you attempt this, use a washable, fabric-backed wallpaper. Adhesive-backed paper will work well this way, too. I covered another parson's table with a flowered sheet. First, I cut the sheet in pieces to fit. Then, I pasted them on with wallpaper paste, lacquering over when the paste was dry. This looked fine, but it was much more work than using the wallpaper.

Many people make the mistake of moving a huge piece of furniture to a fairly small apartment and then trying to conceal it in the living room, pushing it into corner. If you have a piano or other large item with which you're loathe to part, don't try to hide it—you won't succeed. Make it the focal point of your room. An upright piano doesn't pose the problem that a grand does because it's not as large, but it's not as elegant either. A grand piano doesn't have sounding space if it's placed against a wall. An upright, however, generally should go against a wall, but do consider the balance and feel of the room. If the piano is battered, try painting it to match something else in the room. Any piano should be treated gently, never left in strong sun or near a radiator. Put the piano in the place it will perform best, and then plan your seating arrangement around it.

THE DINING AREA

For an informal, inexpensive dining arrangement, let your stack pillows double as dining cushions around a plywood rectangle supported by bricks or cinderblocks. Cover the table top with a festive fabric. Or you can cut the legs of an old card table to the appropriate height for the stacking cushions, and fold it away when it's not in use. But sitting around Japanese style on stacking cushions isn't for all of us. A piece of pressboard or plywood can be set on two sawhorses for a higher table. A cloth to the floor will conceal the unsightly legs.

Chairs need not be mates to work well for you in your dining room. An odd set of chairs can be unified by painting them all the same color, or you can have a confetti look by painting them different colors in the same value. If you purposely select chairs that don't match, make sure they are truly different from each other, not near matches. You want the difference to look intentional.

Give your dining room a dado effect by putting a molding around the room at chair height (the height of the top of the back of the chair) to separate the bottom and the top sections of the walls. You can then paint or paper the two sections differently.

When you're selecting colors and fabrics for your dining area, bear in mind that most people prefer a serene setting in which to eat. Save the really garish decorations for another room in your apartment.

THE BEDROOM

The bedroom isn't the first consideration for most people when they decorate their apartments. It usually can be closed off when company arrives. But it is a room in which you're going to spend a great deal of time. If at all possible, use one end of the bedroom for a sitting room. This makes the apartment seem less confining and allows more privacy when there is more than one tenant. If one spouse or roommate wants to watch television while another wants to quietly read, this extra "sitting room" offers a simple solution. Just a comfortable chair or two and a table for a lamp can provide that spot for privacy.

The bedroom is one place in which you should definitely keep privacy in mind while you're decorating. The drapes or shades should be opaque. Not only does this protect you from the eyes of a peeping Tom, it keeps out the sun should you care to sleep late.

Headboards are unnecessary purchases. If a pile of throw pillows at the head of the bed doesn't satisfy you, build your own headboard out of plywood. Have the lumberyard cut a piece that's the width of your bed and the height you want. The top of the piece (the part that's going to show) can be either cut square or in a half circle. Use a good grade of plywood if you want a finish that shows the grain of the wood. If you are going to paint the headboard, you can use a lesser grade. A spread or quilt to the floor will hide the bed frame, or you can build a three-sided, box-like arrangement around it, made of plywood to match the headboard.

Bedside tables needn't be costly, either. There are quite adequate ones made of cardboard which when covered with a floor length cloth look lovely. Or you can make one from plywood or pressboard and cover it in the same way. This looks especially stylish if you coordinate the cloth with your drapes or bedspread.

Artistic Touches

Pictures and wall ornaments are among the touches that make your apartment uniquely yours. You don't need an original Dali or Renoir to have an impressive wall display. You can spend as little or as much as your circumstances allow and still have something of which you'll be proud. Reproductions of classic pictures can be found in many gift shops and through mail order firms. Some of these come matted and ready for framing. Many of the shops keep these pictures in bins and boxes where customers can go through them at their leisure without a salesperson in constant attendance.

Small, empty spots on the walls can be filled with greeting card or calendar art, mounted and framed. Posters have been in vogue for some time now. They depict everything from favorite rock stars to peaceful bucolic scenes, and they're available in gift shops, record shops, and department stores. Some of the more arty ones are rather expensive. If you like the scenic type, you can obtain them, gratis, from some foreign embassies. I sent for some from the Swiss Embassy and received a tasteful selection of ten posters of various sizes. But two other embassies failed to respond to my requests. For the travel minded, these posters are a happy answer to what to hang on the walls, and you can't beat the price.

Family pictures, especially older ones, make interesting wall arrangements. They can become conversation pieces too, when you explain that Aunt Tillie, in the lace dress, was married to Uncle Lester, in the high-button shoes. If you come from a family of champions, frame the diplomas, awards, and citations and use them to spruce up a dull wall.

Don't limit yourself when you're decorating walls. Think of all the possibilities. Mirrors make dramatic wall hangings, and seem to enlarge a room. A wall of mirrors in various sizes and in different frames is eye-catching. I had an arrangement like this over a sofa in a rather narrow living room, which eliminated the feeling that the walls were closing in.

A very plain, large mirror can be made to look custom done by mounting it on a rug that's several feet larger than the mirror. Mount the rug on a sturdy piece of plywood or pressboard first. You can use an old rug for this if you're trying to give it an antique appearance, or you can use one of the rug remnants mentioned earlier.

Anything graphic can be made into a wall hanging. A colorful beach towel or an elegant piece of material stretched over a frame or a canvas stretcher, or a handsome, fragile Oriental rug look lovely hanging on a wall. Coins, shells, or beads can be worked into a charming wall display. Try mounting some of these items on velvet, then framing them. Or cover plywood with felt of a color that fits in with your room's colors, and mount these articles on the felt.

When you frame your treasures, do it with frames that don't command more attention than the item itself. Simple frames can be created out of pieces of molding, and five and dime stores have a variety of inexpensive frames.

Hanging pictures so they look appealing and don't fall down is more of an art than selecting what you're going to hang. Light pictures or objects don't pose quite the problem of heavy ones which need to be secured to something firm. Use a stud finder to locate the studs inside the walls. You don't want to puncture a pipe or put a nail into a wire. If the stud finder you're using is an electronic one, so much the better. It will light up and stay lit if you're tracking anything metal. When you locate the stud, the light blinks on and off as you go over the surface.

Groups of pictures are generally more interesting than single pictures, but they are harder to hang and arrange. Before you hang a wall grouping, place a large piece of brown paper on your floor and put the pictures on it. Move them around until you've found just the proper place for each one. Then outline each picture on the paper, and mark the spot where the hooks will go. Now put the paper on the wall and mark each spot that requires a picture hook. I prefer to use an eye on each side of the picture frame, which fits over its own hook on the wall. This really secures the picture. Those hung with a

An old light fixture picked up at an auction or in a second-hand store adds drama to a dining area. *Courtesy of the Kirsch Company.*

wire are forever getting crooked. Just the slam of a door or a breeze will move them.

All pieces of sculpture don't need to be set on a table or bookcase. They can be displayed on individual shelves hung on a wall. Many interesting art objects are being offered now in limited editions and for fairly reasonable prices.

Baskets come in all shapes and sizes and many of them don't cost much. A group of baskets hanging on a kitchen wall creates that individual look for which we're all striving.

Old light fixtures are interesting replacements for the standard ones found in the dining areas of most apartments. You don't have to purchase an expensive one to add interest to your room. Again, expense usually depends on what's in vogue. Until Tiffany lamps came back into style a few years ago, dealers couldn't give them away. Now they bring thousands of dollars. The light fixture you buy today for a few dollars may be in favor a few years from now.

LIGHT UP YOUR LIFE

Lighting sets the mood in any apartment. It can work with or against the decor you've so carefully selected. A living room should be well lit. The minimum number of lamps suggested by lighting experts for an average size living room is five. Two of these should have three-way bulbs for versatility in lighting.

Your bathroom and your kitchen also should be strongly lit rooms.

High wattage bulbs give more light per watt than do low watt bulbs. For instance, one 100 watt incandescent bulb will provide you with as much light as six incandescent twenty-five watt bulbs. And fluorescent bulbs give off five to six times as much light as incandescents do for the same amount of electricity.

The mood you're setting with lighting should also be a prime consideration, and fluorescent lights come in a variety of mood setting hues. A plain, natural white light bulb is the right choice if you're in doubt. It won't distort most colors. But the warm white light will remove some of the coldness from a room that's decorated in blues or greens. There's a yellowish white bulb that changes the blues in a room, so you might want to avoid it if you've decorated in this color. Daylight fluorescent is to be avoided at all costs. It gives people a pale, ghost-like appearance that puts a damper on any gathering (unless it's a seance or a Halloween party). Soft white has a kiss of pink that muddies a room decorated in yellows, but it does marvelous things for complexions, giving them a warm, glowing look. Deluxe warm white is another flatterer for skin tones as it adds a touch of red. It also serves to deepen color tones. Cool white is clinical looking and best left to offices and industry for whom it was designed in the first place. But deluxe cool white is a cool white with a hint of red; it presents color in an almost true value, sometimes attractively graying those things nearest it.

A DOZEN DIME STORE DECORATIONS

The name five and dime lingers on, but its meaning is just a memory in our society of escalating prices. Still you can find some buys for your apartment in these stores. Here are a few ideas to which you'll undoubtly be able to add:

1. Construction paper can be put to many uses. Cut it up for placemats to decorate your table. You may even cut the silhouette of a piece of fruit or a flower from a second piece of paper that's a complementary color, and glue it on the mat. These are for one time use only unless you spray them with an acrylic finish, in which case they can brighten up your dining room or kitchen for many meals.
2. Poster paints are inexpensive, easy to use, and you can paint an original mural on your wall with them if you're artistic. If you're not, try projecting a colored slide on the wall and filling it in with poster paints.
3. Plastic, porcelain, or metal clothes hooks which screw into the wall can be used to make a decorative kitchen display of your pots and pans, or potholders. Screw them into a one inch by four inch strip of wood painted to match your kitchen and nailed to your kitchen wall.
4. Fish bowls don't have to house fish to look pretty. Partially filled with colored sand into which a candle has been inserted, they make a lovely and safe candle holder. All the items to make this are available in most five and dime stores.
5. Picture frames of all types can be bought at the five and dime. Adjustable plastic frames are great for hanging record albums featuring your favorite musicians.
6. For decorating the children's room, head for the toy department. A set of paper dolls can be used as wall decorations. You can find something that will please the fancy of any child. Cut out the paper dolls and attach them to the walls with double-sided masking tape.
7. Liven up a dull kitchen by bordering cabinets with ribbon or designs cut from gift wrap. A bit of glue (also available in the five and dime) serves as the adhesive for this.
8. An inexpensive bulletin board can be made by covering a piece of pressboard with burlap or any other fabric which catches

your eye in the fabric department and will blend with your furnishings.

9. Don't forget adhesive-backed decorative paper, a boon to the apartment dweller who is striving to have an attractive home without making a huge cash outlay.

10. Decorate with ornamental switchplates to be found in different colors and patterns to please any taste. This little touch adds a custom look to any apartment.

11. The housewares department will yield colorful, inexpensive towels suitable for making curtains for either a bathroom or kitchen. The cost is not the only attribute of curtains made from these towels. They wash wonderfully well and aren't damaged by high humidity, both pluses for curtains that are going to grace either of these rooms.

12. Brightly colored doorknobs are another easy-on-the-money decorating touch that makes a room look as if it were expensively appointed even if it isn't.

With swelling expenses which make incomes appear to shrink, most of us have more ingenuity than cash to use in decorating our apartments. It's easier to stretch our minds than our wallets, and often the results are more rewarding, and certainly more individual.

Chapter 4

Apartment Greenery

After being out of vogue for a long time, house plants came back in a big way a few years ago. Everyone was purchasing them—small plants, medium-sized plants, large plants, flowering plants, foliage plants, and even fruit trees to grow indoors. People felt that they had been missing the fun of having live plants around their homes, and they hastened to rectify this.

Plastic flowers were to be found in some of the best trash cans. The "in" people were opting for the real thing. Many long-time plant lovers as well as small time entrepreneurs thought they'd strike it rich opening shops that catered to this obsession. But in those days, new plant owners often did not know how to give a plant the care it needed to flourish. As a result, many followed their plastic counterparts into the trash cans.

Although the plant craze still goes on, it has been altered. Most of the vendors who knew nothing about plants but sought only to make their fortunes have gone out of business. Buyers have become wiser and considerably more selective, choosing only those plants they can care for and which suit their lifestyles and tastes in decorating. Sadly, some people have simply given up growing plants in their homes. Many apartment dwellers, plagued by what they think are insurmountable problems of space and lighting, are in this group. But there's no need to forego the pleasures of plants just because you live in an apartment. You, too, can have a green thumb, albeit a selective one.

Let There Be Light

Lighting is probably the first consideration in choosing house plants. The apartment dweller often runs into problems because so many apartments have only one exposure and offer little light. But there are plants which will grow well with a bare minimum of light, thrive on a northern exposure, or flourish under grow lights. In fact, most foliage plants don't thrive in direct sun. Plants, like people, can get sunburned.

Many apartment dwellers don't take full advantage of the natural light they have available. No matter how good that light is, it's useless if you have all the shades drawn. While you may covet privacy, and understandably so, you can pull up the shades and open the curtains just before you retire at night so your plants will get the benefit of those wonderful early morning rays.

The color of your wall affects the available light. A pastel room will offer more light for your plants than will a dark green or dark brown room. The ever-popular flat white finish that you find in most apartment complexes today is just about the best when it comes to reflecting light. Believe it or not, the white finish gives between 100 to 150 foot-candles more light than dark green or dark brown would give in the same room, everything else being equal.

Dust and grease can build up on the surfaces of leaves and prevent them from getting the full benefits of light rays. Keep your plants clean, especially if you have a light problem.

The regular incandescent lights you use to work or read by may be sufficient to keep your plants healthy if you place them judiciously and have the right type of plants. These incandescent light bulbs give off far-red as well as red rays, which are especially advantageous for flowering plants. A bit of sun during the day will provide the blue rays and you may have it made in the shade, so to speak.

Place your floral plants near floor lamps, desk lamps, under reading lamps, wherever they look attractive and are close to the light source. But be cautious—incandescent bulbs get hot. If you can feel the heat of the lamp on the leaves of the plant, your plant is too close.

While incandescent lighting should help your flowering plants, most foliage plants call for blue rays. That's where fluorescent lighting comes in. Just because the plant needs blue rays doesn't mean you have to buy the harsh blue fluorescent light bulbs. The white ones will work as well and the light from them is infinitely softer and more flattering.

Fluorescent lights don't give off anywhere near the amount of heat that incandescents do, so you can have your plants quite near to a source of fluorescent light without fear of burning them. In fact, you can have them as close as one inch from the light. But most plants prefer to be six to nine inches away. If the fluorescent light source is too far off, say more than 18 inches from your plants, chances are that any benefits will be minimal.

A few years ago, artificial grow lights became widely available. And although those early lights were helpful, they lacked some of

Some plants flourish under incandescent lights, but if you can feel heat on the leaves, the plants are too close to the lights.

the rays vital to a number of types of plants. This problem has been corrected and the later models are great. They almost succeed in duplicating the rays of sunlight that are necessary to promote maximum plant growth. When you're shopping for these lights, which are made by several companies, look for the ones with blue, far-red, and ultra-violet rays. Used correctly, these lights may make your ordinary plants into show pieces.

You can make the natural light in your apartment do double duty. Line the windowsills where your plants are growing with foil. Or for more plant space, attach a topless, three-sided box to the windowsill with the open side toward the window. Then line the back, sides, and bottom of the box with foil. The foil reflects and intensifies the sun, making the most of every ray. (But make sure the box doesn't get too hot.) Since the foil reflects light onto the backs of the plants, you don't have the problem of plants leaning toward their light source. If your plants are small and not too heavy, you can use a cardboard box. But you may prefer to make a more permanent wooden container, painting the outside, wallpapering it, or covering it with adhesive-backed paper so that it will fit into the decor of your apartment.

When to Water

Different plants require different amounts of water just as they require different degrees of light. Some plants need to be soaked well but not too often, while others need frequent light waterings. For specifics, check any of the good books on indoor plants now available, or consult your nursery or florist.

Large plants tend to need watering more frequently than smaller ones. If your plants are in ceramic or plastic pots, you need not water so often since these pots are nonporous and hold moisture longer than clay pots do.

During hot weather, especially if it's dry heat, plants may need more water than they do ordinarily. A plant you'd usually water once a week could need watering three times that often.

Do not use tap water. More often than not, the chemicals are more than the plant can cope with. Distilled water is the best bet. And use it at room temperature. Cold water shocks plants.

The most common crime committed against houseplants is overwatering, providing too much at one time or watering too often. Many zealous plant lovers apply an excess of tender loving care, diligently watering their already saturated plants daily. About 80 percent of all houseplants die in their first year. A great many of these deaths can be attributed to drowning.

There are ways to tell if your plants are getting too much water. Look at the lower leaves. Are they becoming bedraggled and droopy? If so, you have a slight case of overwatering. If all the leaves, or at least a good many of them, are beginning to look lifeless or show signs of turning yellow or brown, you are dealing with a more advanced stage of overwatering. When roots are saturated, they usually surface, and you'll see them near the top of the pot. Roots also may turn yellow or brown from too much water, and your plant's in real trouble when the roots start to soften. That's a sign they're also starting to rot. A little neglect may solve these problems.

Some other cautions: A plant sitting in the brightest spot in your apartment should not be watered when the sun is shining on it. The roots will rise to the moisture and may get burned. Likewise wet leaves are liable to sunburn and, with some plants, invite disease and insects. Finally, make sure your pots drain properly. A plant should never have to stand in water.

Humidity is, of course, moisture. The more humid the atmosphere the less likely a plant is to dry out and the less often it will need watering. However, the air in many apartments during much of the year tends to be quite dry, and few apartments offer an ideal degree of humidity for either plants or people. There are ways, short of buying a humidifier, to help remedy this problem for your plants anyway. A large metal, water-tight pan with shallow sides can work wonders. Decorate it, fill it with pebbles, and add water to the top of the pebbles. Rest your pots of plants on top of this, and the water will add moisture to the air surrounding the plants without their actually sitting in water. For larger plants, a handsome outer container fitted with a rack (the type used for cooling cakes can often be used) will accomplish the same thing. Fill the container with water up to the bottom of the rack. Place your pot on top, and your plant will get humidity without its root system becoming waterlogged.

An arrangement of plants which includes a few vases or contain-

Because of their high humidity, bathrooms offer the perfect environment for plants that love moisture and don't require much sunlight. *Courtesy of Fieldcrest.*

ers of water is an attractive way of providing necessary humidity. Misting is another way of solving the low humidity problem. Plants with thin leaves benefit the most from misting. But know your plants. Never mist a plant that has a fuzzy or hairy leaf. You're almost certain to end up with a sick plant. Instead of the leaves absorbing the moisture, the small follicles hold it on the surface, creating an unhealthy condition. Bugs love this environment, too.

To provide proper humidity for plants, rest them on pebbles placed in a large, watertight pan with water added just to the tops of the pebbles.

The Infirmary

One top priority in protecting plants is to quarantine any new ones that you bring into your apartment. The gorgeous purple passion plant that you proudly bring home from the local supermarket may be harboring mealy bugs, and if it's placed with your older plants they are apt to end up having mealy bugs, too. Keep new plants by themselves until you have had a chance to observe them for at least two weeks, and you're convinced that they're fine, healthy specimens. By this time any eggs or diseases should have surfaced.

Plant diseases can come from bacteria, a fungus, or a virus which has attached itself to the plant. These unhealthy organisms usually are in the soil in which the plant was started—a good argument for using sterilized or synthetic soil. You can sterilize soil from the garden, if you wish, by placing it in a shallow pan in a 500° oven for about four hours. Personally, I don't think it's worth it. It smells awful while it's cooking; you don't always get it completely sterilized; you can buy sterilized soil at a garden center or a five and dime store, and it's not expensive. This soil comes with a variety of ingredients in varying proportions. You can purchase the one that's just right for your plants' needs. Be sure, though, that it's marked "sterilized."

I don't know anyone who has ever had any luck saving a diseased plant. The best thing to do is burn it. If that's not possible, throw it out. Just cross your fingers that none of your other plants has contracted the disease. Don't be tempted to cut one little shoot from the sick plant so you can start another one. And don't use any seeds that may have come from the plant. If a plant is diseased, so are its cuttings and seeds. If it was a favorite plant, buy another just like it.

Bugs are a different matter. If you see them soon enough, chances are you can save your plant. But the minute you notice anything you suspect might be a bug, isolate the plant. That way you can avoid starting an epidemic. It's preferable to use an organic or nonchemical pesticide on your houseplants. Be careful, especially if you do use one with a chemical base, to do so in a well-ventilated part of your apartment. Weather permitting, the patio would be a good choice. Take care if you have animals or children that you keep a plant which you've sprayed with a chemical far from their reach. Even then you may have to contend with falling leaves.

Where do bugs come from? Sometimes it seems they just drop from the ceiling! Actually, the eggs have probably been there waiting to hatch, or if your plants have summered on the patio or in an outside windowbox, the bugs have likely been brought in from outdoors.

Identifying bugs as bugs isn't always as easy as it would seem. They may be so small they're almost invisible, or they may look like something else and show up only through the damage they've done. There are four types of insects that are most likely to appear on your houseplants. It's a good idea to know what to look for so that you can deter their efforts before they make real inroads. You don't want to make the mistake of thinking the plant is diseased and throwing it out, when it only has a slight case of bugs.

Aphids. These common pests are usually of a greenish-white color. But there are some that are black. Since they develop in clusters, they're reasonably easy to see. The best treatment I've found for ridding a plant of aphids is a simple one. In a deep pot, mix a solution of mild soap (use real soap, not detergent) and warm

Common houseplant pests, from left to right: aphid, mite, mealybug.

water. Cover the soil in the pot with a cloth or a piece of foil, anything that will prevent the dirt from falling out during the next step. Now turn the plant upside down, keeping the soil in place, and dip the leaves into the soapy solution, swishing them around gently. Then dip them into plain warm water to rinse them. If the leaves are hairy or fuzzy, dry them thoroughly. Repeat this process every week for four or five weeks. Each bath will get rid of the bugs but not the eggs. Misting plants with non-fuzzy leaves every few days between baths will help chase away the aphids.

Mealybugs. These little pests can fool you. They like to begin their dirty work on the undersides of leaves and in dark places rather than out where you can spot them easily. At first glance, they really don't resemble bugs but look more like spun sugar or white cotton candy. Attack them with cotton swabs dipped in rubbing alcohol, touching the plant softly so that you don't bruise the leaves. Scoop the bugs off with the cotton swab. When you can no longer see any sign of them, rinse the leaves off with lukewarm, distilled water and dry gently.

Red Spider Mites. This is a misleading name. Red spider mites come in an assortment of colors. Although many are truly red, some are yellow, green, white, or a burnt-orange in color. But whatever their color, they are nasty little things that attach themselves to the undersides of the leaves and literally suck the life out of a plant through its veins. A plant infested by red spider mites appears to have little fine webs under its leaves. In an advanced stage, the plant will lose much of its color. A large, strong plant may be helped by putting it in the bathtub upside down and attacking the mites with a strong warm spray from the faucet. A more delicate plant is not likely to survive this drastic treatment and should be treated with the warm soapy water method used on aphids.

Scale. Ferns and fruit trees are favorites of this crawly nuisance. If your indoor garden includes such plants, be on the alert. Another hard-to-see bug, the scale becomes easier to spot as it matures. It has a hard brown shell and burrows into the stems of the plant. They are persistent and clinging little devils. They will hang on during even a vigorous washing or spraying. To destroy them you literally have to pick off each individual one with a wet rag.

If a plant isn't looking well, it doesn't necessarily mean that it's diseased or has bugs. Any plant left too close to a cold window, for instance, may develop limp, pale leaves. The answer is simple. Move the plant to a more temperate place in your apartment.

Plants with thin, delicate leaves will suffer if you leave them close to a heat source. Yellow edges on their leaves is a sign they're drying out from the unwelcome heat. Again, just move the plants.

Displaying Your Plants

"I'd love to have plants, but I don't have room for them in my small apartment." I've heard that statement from apartment dwellers who haven't considered the variety of ways plants can be displayed without plunking them down on a surface needed for something else. Imagination is the key to placing plants so that they give maximum eye appeal and take up a minimum of precious space.

If you're fortunate enough to have a fireplace, it's a marvelous place to show off plants during the seasons you're not using it. In front of, on top of, or right in the fireplace—the bounty of greenery adds life to any room.

Bay windows yearn for plants to dress them up. If you don't want to use the sill in your bay window for plants, hang them all around

When heating season is over, a fireplace is a dramatic setting for your shade-loving plants.

it. There are magnificent hanging pots to be found and some unusual hangers. Another space-saving way to display plants, and one that is usually beneficial to light-loving plants, is putting them on glass shelving in your windows. They not only look festive inside, they dress up your windows from outside as well.

While the conventional place for window boxes is outside, there is no reason they can't be indoors. In fact, you can make a convertible window box and have plants that add color to the outside in the summer, then move the box inside when the weather dictates.

Given the right lighting situation, you can build your plants right into your furniture. I once had an old china cupboard I didn't use and couldn't figure out what to do with. But it did seem a shame to discard it. After much contemplation, I removed the door, installed fluorescent lights under each shelf and inside the top and filled the

This indoor window box will brighten an apartment all year long. *Courtesy of Comark Plastics.*

shelves with plants. I've received more compliments on that than on any other piece of furniture. A version of the same idea is a plant shelf under a glass-topped coffee or end table. So stretch your mind. Look around your apartment for furniture you might convert. Something lackluster can be brought to life with a fresh coat of paint and a few plants.

There are ways to hang plants in an apartment other than using the conventional hooks. A friend of mine took an old wagon wheel, painted it light green to match her decor, and hung it from the ceiling in front of the picture window she was fortunate enough to have in her apartment. Then she hung a variety of beautiful plants from the spokes. She had added that something to her apartment that only plants can give, and she had not sacrificed any table or floor space to do it. An old, or even a new, wooden ladder (not the stepladder type, but the kind you lean against something) can do the same job.

There's an interesting product for hanging plants that looks like a drapery rod. It comes in four-foot lengths with hooks, and it attaches to the ceiling. The hooks are on pulleys, so you can hang plants at whatever heights you choose. You can pull them up or down until you hit upon the arrangement that you and the plants like best. If a plant isn't doing well in one position, move it until it is getting more or less sun, whichever it seems to need. These rods can be hung individually at every window, or they can make an impressive display when hung the length of a wall.

Be sure that whatever you use to hang your plants from is securely fastened to a wooden beam or something solid in the ceiling before you hang the plants. The hanger may seem strong enough to support the plants' weight when you put them up, but then when you water, it might come down. It's amazing how much weight is added when you water just one plant to say nothing of a group of plants.

Large, tree-like plants make an attractive and moveable room divider, setting the dining room off from the living room, or providing a private corner (so hard to find in many apartments) for reading or sewing. It's convenient if these large plants are kept in containers on wheels. When you want to change the room or water the plants, you can just roll them away.

Plants for the Lazy Apartment Gardener

Here are brief descriptions of a few plants that have flourished in my apartments. I can't guarantee they'll grow well for you. But they have for me, and I'm not known for my green thumb.

African Violets. African violets (which incidentally aren't violets at all) may not always be easy to grow, but they are beautiful. If you have the right place for them, they're worth the effort, adding cheerfulness to the average apartment. They're prolific bloomers, offering an almost constant profusion of flowers if the conditions warrant it.

Light is probably the most important factor in growing African Violets. They simply won't bloom without it. But light doesn't mean strong sun. Start them with grow lights. When they appear to be thriving, place them in bright, indirect sunlight.

These delicate lovelies can't stand to have their roots in water so be certain that the pots you use provide excellent drainage. They don't like drafts, sudden changes or extremes in temperature. Actually, they're happiest when kept in a place where the temperature never varies from between 65° to 75°F.

I use half sand and half vermiculite to grow my African violets, and I water them with tepid water when the top soil feels dry to the touch.

Airplane Plant or *Spider Plant.* These look marvelous hanging at windows. Easy to grow, the Spider plant has trailing, spiky leaves and long stems that end in baby plants complete with roots. The babies can be cut off and planted in standard potting soil to start other Spider plants. They are almost indestructible, and need water about once a week (unless the surface gets really dried out). You only need to buy one because they keep having babies which supply you with all the new plants you can use. I only feed my Spider plants twice during each growing season.

Aralia, also called the *Balfour Aralia.* This tree-like plant has shiny, wide, dark green leaves. A few placed in a row can be successfully used as a low room divider. They need a bright room if they're to do their best, but the lighting can be artificial. They thrive in standard, all-purpose potting soil and need to be kept fairly moist. Mist on a regular basis—about once a week—and feed two or three times a year, preferably during the spring and summer months.

Aspidistra. The plant Gracie Fields made famous is great for all situations. It lives through temperatures ranging from 45° to 90°F. It doesn't need frequent watering. In fact, over-watering is one of the few ways you can do it in. You can stick it out-of-the-way in a dark nook, or you can put it in the direct sun; and its many short, dark green, spiky leaves will still flourish. It can be easily divided to make a new plant by cutting a piece of plant, along with some root, from an existing aspidistra. Follow these simple directions and you may end up with "the biggest aspidistra in the world."

Begonias. An extensive family of handsome plants answers to the name begonia. Tuberous begonias are a popular choice for patios. Since their blooms are beneath their leaves, they look prettiest in hanging baskets. Their large blossoms floating in a shallow dish with a few leaves make an exotic centerpiece for a dining room table. The rhizomatous and fibrous rooted begonias are better suited for indoor display than the tuberous variety. All three varieties of begonias come in myriad types, shapes, and colors. None are partial to direct sunlight. Summer sun simply wilts them.

They like to be evenly damp—too much moisture makes them soggy, too little makes them droopy. They are easily harmed by strong fertilizer. I use only a mild liquid fertilizer added to the water every three or four weeks and only when the plants are blooming.

Bromeliads. Another family with many members, bromeliads have striking foliage which resembles the top of a pineapple in shape. (In fact, the pineapple is a member in good standing of the bromeliad family.) Bromeliads feature one, usually magnificent bloom which protrudes from the middle of the leaf formation. These blossoms are durable and add charm and color to a room for up to three months at a time. The plants like light, but not direct sun. They can go without water for weeks without any long-lasting ill effects, and they don't require feeding. I consider bromeliads a must for the lazy plant grower who likes maximum benefits with minimum effort.

Cacti. Literally thousands of types exist. And horticulturists continue to experiment, achieving interesting results by grafting cacti. These plants, which originated in the desert, need strong, direct sunlight. As long as you have that to offer them, they need little else. If you water them every other week during growing season,

Cacti add a spot of green to an apartment, and they thrive on neglect. The pots and tray are covered with Contact paper. *Courtesy of Comark Plastics.*

they are content with water every six weeks or so in the winter months. Plant them in light soil with good drainage. They simply can't survive if their roots are standing in water.

Coleus. Although the occasional flowers produced by coleus are less than spectacular, the infinite array of colorful foliage offered by this family more than compensates. Sunlight enhances their colors, but coleus will grow in shade. They do need frequent watering—

every day isn't too much for the average coleus. They cheer up an apartment in the winter and make interesting patio plants during the summer.

Corn Plant. These good-sized plants are so named because their leaf formation slightly resembles a very elegant corn stalk. The long, wide green leaves have an attractive yellow stripe down the middle. If that stripe disappears, it doesn't mean the plant is dying, but that it isn't getting enough light. The plant will still grow, although not as fast, but the leaves will remain a solid green.

Corn plants like soil that's barely moist and they need exceptionally good drainage. The leaves should be wiped off occasionally with a cloth dampened in warm water. But this plant doesn't require a great deal of tender loving care. I've gone away for weeks at a time and left my corn plant without care, finding it healthy, if a bit thirsty, when I returned.

False Aralia. You would think, looking at its delicate leaves and stalks, that this pretty plant needs a lot of coddling. Not true—a false aralia can reach a height of five feet with little tending, provided it isn't pot bound. It doesn't require much light. In fact, direct sunlight can kill it. It likes a good thorough soaking every week to ten days, but you can allow it to dry out a bit in between. I feed my false aralia about every three weeks during the growing season.

Fittonia or *Nerve Plant.* The striking thing about this vine-like plant is its colorful veins, red or white depending on the variety you choose. (It does have some white blossoms from time to time, but they're small and spindly.) Fittonia likes shady spots. If the only windows you have in your apartment face north, try growing one. It should do well for you. It likes moisture, so keep the soil damp. Put it in a humid setting if possible.

Geranium. While geraniums may be common, they're also beautiful. And they come in a large variety of shapes and colors. You can have an apartment full of white, pink, red, or coral flowers—all from the geranium family. There are also varieties of geraniums with scented foliage that will add the fragrance of nutmeg, peppermint, or lemon to your apartment. They don't require feeding, but they do need lots of sun and lots of water. Unfortunately, this lively plant is not for you if you have only a northern exposure.

Jade Plant. The popular jade plant has been known to turn into a tree six feet tall. The mature jade is a handsome addition to any room setting. When small, the plants make lovely centerpieces. Since they are succulents, jade plants don't tolerate much water. A thorough soaking when the plant appears dried out seems to do it. They do like light, but not direct sun. Unless you want a giant plant, don't feed it often if at all. Jade plants will stay a nice coffee-table size for years if they're a bit potbound and kept slightly undernourished.

Mimosa. These little plants, commonly called shame plants, are easy to grow, and they're a conversation piece because the leaves curl around any object that touches them. While they don't have a long life span, they're so simple to grow from seed (seeds germinate in about a week) and they put forth such attractive pink or lavender flowers, they're certainly worth the small effort needed to restart them periodically.

Mimosa plants shun sunlight and prefer indirect lighting. Artificial light is just fine for this shy plant. However, they are fussy about water. A mimosa needs even moisture at all times, not too much and not too little.

Palms. My favorite plant is my palm tree, which was just two short shoots about five years ago and now stands four feet tall and spreads out majestically. It gives the apartment just enough flavor of the tropics to get me through the northern winters.

Palms come in many varieties, all of which prefer a filtered, natural light. They can be moved out to the patio in summer if they're not subjected to hot glaring sunshine, which will wilt them fast. Palms love a good soaking about once every five days. Never let them dry out. If you want them to grow fast, feed them about every two months, year round. But if you're satisfied with the size of your palm, don't feed it at all.

Peperomia. This is a popular succulent plant which lends itself nicely to neglect. Peperomias come in both tall and trailing varieties. Some have smooth leaves, some are deeply ridged; some are an even shade of green, some variegated. A northern window suits them fine, and they don't need much water. I water mine when I happen to think of it, which isn't very often, and it's thriving. Peperomias should be fed with a mild liquid fertilizer about three times a year during the growing season. If your plant gets leggy, trim it to shape. You can put the cuttings in water, and they'll root to start new plants.

Piggyback Plant. This plant acquired its name because of the strange way in which the leaves grow, one on top of the other, almost in layers. These hairy leaves resemble grape leaves in shape. Unfortunately, the plant is temperamental and will wilt if you don't keep it evenly watered. Although piggybacks flower occasionally, the plant is enjoyable even without blooms.

This plant needs bright light but not direct sun. A northern window will suffice. It's a good idea to fertilize your plant about six times a year with a mild fertilizer.

Portuacaria. Although this plant comes from South Africa, it has an Oriental look and blends well with an Oriental decor. Its succulent leaves resemble those of the jade tree but are not as large. The one thing this plant needs is good light. But the good news is that it only needs water when it has completely dried out. Portuacaria can be trimmed into interesting and different shapes.

Prayer Plant. This plant doesn't need direct sunlight. It will thrive on artificial lighting or just a bit of filtered sun. The leaves, which fold into a praying pose each night, are wide and colorful, offering a blend of all shades of green with bright red veins on some varieties.

Mist your prayer plant daily. It needs a humid atmosphere. During winter, you can let the soil dry out a little, but the rest of the year, it should be kept really damp all the time. This plant requires little fertilizing and can, in fact, get by with none.

Purple Passion Plant. This exquisite plant, which looks wonderful in a hanging pot, owes its name to the tiny purplish hairs that cover its many small, pointed green leaves. Since it needs direct sun, hanging it in a southern window is ideal. Unfortunately, it has a tendency to attract mealybugs. Don't overwater your passion plants; they can't take soggy soil.

Snake Plant. Sansevieria is the proper name for this plant, but its nicknames, including mother-in-law's tongue, are much more descriptive. It won them through its ability to survive almost any kind of treatment, and because the leaves are long and sharply pointed. I find it an ideal plant to brighten a dull entry hall and just right for that small table on which nothing else seems to grow. About the only way to kill one of these plants is to pamper it. Dark corners won't do it, bright light makes it flourish; dusty leaves are okay; infrequent watering doesn't faze it. But try watering it daily, and it probably won't survive!

Swedish Ivy. This is a great hanging plant that doesn't like strong sun but needs light. Each plant has hundreds of small bright green leaves. The plants need to be kept quite moist or they will droop perceptibly. But if you thoroughly water a drooping Swedish ivy, it will revive within an hour. You can actually see it come back to life. Since it sheds leaves regularly, if you're a fastidious housekeeper, you may not be happy with a Swedish ivy.

Weeping Fig. Bright, indirect light is the choice of the weeping fig, but it will survive in dim light. It has small, shiny dark green leaves and grows into an attractive little tree, even though its drooping leaves give it rather a woebegone look. Grown in sandy soil, and kept evenly moist, this tree does well in most apartments.

Zebra Plant. With its striped foliage and bright yellow bloom, this plant is gorgeous. Each plant has only a single bloom, but it's a spectacular one. When the plant isn't flowering, the foliage itself is well worth the effort required to keep a zebra plant happy. It should be kept in a bright but not sunny location. Water only when the top soil feels dry to the touch. After it has bloomed the zebra plant tends to get leggy, and you may want to take a cutting from it and start again.

When You Have to Move

The temporary feeling some people have about their apartments makes them hesitant to invest in plants they don't know how to move. Here are some hints for making moving day easier.

If you're about to move into a new apartment and you already have plants, there are several precautions you should take so they will continue to grow and be healthy in their new environment. Plants find moving a stressful situation, and they need proper care if they are to survive. Whatever you do, don't repot either just before or just after moving. If possible allow two or three months on either side. Repotting is, in itself, a traumatic experience for a plant, and combining it with moving is subjecting your plants to two traumas at once.

If your move is to be a lengthy one and the temperature will be either extremely hot or cold, you would probably be wise to find new homes for your plants. They might never recover from those harsh conditions.

Here's what to do to protect your plants. Trim off all new growth before you pack them. This means all flowers and buds as well as the tender, new leaves which will sap the energy of the plants. It's going to take all their energy to make the transition. Next, unless chilly winter winds are blowing, water your plants well. (In the winter, let them get fairly dry before the move. This will lessen the chance of having the roots freeze.) Wrap your small plants in newspaper, making sure that the leaves are all pointing upward. Place the wrapped pots in large cardboard cartons—the divided ones that you can pick up at liquor stores are ideal for this. If you can't get any cartons, use brown bags for your newspaper-wrapped plants.

For large plants and trees, the easiest and most efficient thing to use when packing is brown paper or large paper bags. Wrap large plants so that the leaves are pointed upward and fitted rather snugly against the trunk or main stem of the plant. But don't push the leaves so tight that they break off.

Although many people advocate packing plants in plastic bags, I haven't had much success with this method. The plastic seems to hold heat or cold. Since it's not porous, the plants can't breathe and tend to wilt.

The last thing on, and the first thing off, the moving truck should be your plants. If you're doing the moving yourself, see that the taller plants are placed so that they won't fall over. If you have professional movers, don't assume that they'll place your plants correctly in the truck—check to see that they do.

When you have unpacked your plants at your new apartment, put them in a dark corner and let them rest for a few days, gradually bringing them back into the light. Plants should be watered as soon as they arrive in the apartment, but delay fertilizing them for approximately eight weeks.

A Miniature Vegetable Garden

When I took the big step of moving from a house into an apartment, I cast a long, regretful, backward look at my vegetable garden. I was certain that I was forever to be denied the pleasure of tasting tomatoes right off the vine and the satisfaction that comes from watching vegetables grow to their succulent best, then preparing them at the peak of their flavor.

It was a pleasant surprise to find this part of my life need not be lost because I was to be an apartment dweller. I've had some bountiful crops from my apartment vegetable gardens. All it takes is adapting to a slightly different way of gardening. If you have a patio, can get a window box, have access to a doorstep or a flat rooftop, you're in business as a vegetable gardener! Even if you only have a windowsill, you can grow a few small things to liven up your menus. You need containers, soil, and either seeds or seedlings to begin this project. And right in your apartment there are probably enough potential containers to make it unnecessary to spend any money in this department.

PLANTERS

I've used a variety of household objects as planters. A large wooden box is ideal, of course. Paint it to complement your furniture, line it with plastic, and add a good layer of gravel to allow for drainage.

If you do not have a large wooden box you want to sacrifice, wastebaskets or any kind of large plastic container will do. But allow your plants room to grow. Vegetables such as peppers, eggplant, tomatoes, and cucumbers need at least two quarts of soil per plant to have room to stretch their roots. Bushel baskets treated like the wooden box are useful too. You can leave them *au naturel* if you have a rustic setting, or you can paint them for a more formal decor. Large coffee cans or old pails are also acceptable. You can dress them up with contact paper. And, if you're just not one for makeshift measures, garden centers carry pots that will make any apartment garden a showplace.

Drill holes in the bottoms of your containers unless you're going to put in a good thick layer of stones, cinders, gravel, or pieces of broken crockery. (You get the best drainage using both holes and stones.) Make the holes about ½ to ¼ inch in diameter, and place them on the sides of the container, about an inch from the bottom. Four or five per container should guarantee the roots won't rot from standing in water. To prevent the holes from getting clogged with dirt, carefully pack the spaces around them with stones or pieces of broken crockery. Do this whether or not you're lining the bottom with a drainage material.

GROWING FROM SEED

When selecting seed, choose the smaller varieties, not necessarily miniatures although most of them are quite adequate. You'll want insect and disease resistant seeds, of course, and be sure to check the dates on the packages before you buy them. Outdated seeds are no bargain. Although some will probably germinate and grow, most are likely to be duds.

My favorite method of starting vegetables from seed employs peat pellets, available from any garden supply house. Put some pellets in a shallow pan, a tray, or a cardboard milk container cut down to about an inch or two high, allowing room for expansion. Add water until the pellets have swollen to three or four times their original size. With the end of a pencil or your finger, make an indentation about a quarter of an inch deep in the top of each pellet. Put in two seeds, cover well with peat, and water thoroughly. If you want to hasten growth, place the container in a large, clear, plastic bag. How long you have to wait for seedlings to appear depends on what you've planted. Some vegetables take much longer than others to push through the soil. When they do start to peep through, take the containers out of the plastic bag and place them where they'll get some filtered sun but not so much they'll wilt. When a seedling grows two leaves, it's ready to be transplanted. Most often, both the seeds you've planted in a pellet won't produce. But if they do both put out shoots, uproot and discard the smaller before the root structures can become entwined.

VEGETABLE CHART

Vegetable	*Inches Between Plants*	*Date to Put Outside*	*Light*	*Harvest Time*
Beets	2 to 3	2 to 4 weeks before frost-free date	full to partial	1 to 2 in. around
Cabbage	12 to 18	4 weeks before frost-free date	full to partial	when firm
Carrots	2 to 3	3 weeks before frost-free date	full to partial	½ to 1 in. around
Cucumbers	18	2 weeks after frost-free date	full	6 to 8 in. long
Eggplant	36	1 week after frost-free date	full	when firm
Lettuce	4 to 5	5 weeks before frost-free date	full to partial	when leaves are useable size
Peppers	16	2 weeks after frost-free date	full	2 to 3 in. around
Radishes	½	3 weeks before frost-free date	partial	about ¾ in. around
Summer Squash	1 plant per 5 gal. container	1 week after frost-free date	full	varies according to type
Tomatoes	1 plant per 2 gal. container	1 week after frost-free date	full	when almost red

I advise using synthetic soil to avoid disease and bugs. The combination that has been most successful for me consists of horticultural vermiculite, peat moss, and fertilizer. You can purchase this mixed, or you can mix your own. I use 1 bushel of vermiculite, 1 bushel of peat moss, 1 cup ground limestone, ½ cup of 20 percent superphosphate, and 1 cup of 5-10-5 fertilizer. I add water as I'm mixing. It keeps down dust and makes it easier to blend the components together.

Once your vegetables are transplanted in their new containers, keep them inside at least two weeks to toughen. Some plants should be placed outside before the local frost-free date, others not until well after it. The seed package should give you that information. For the frost-free date in your area, contact your local Cooperative Extension Agent.

Arranging your vegetables outside so each will receive the best exposure and also look attractive is an art. Most vegetables need sun, but in varying degrees. Leafy vegetables, for instance, will thrive with a bit of shade now and then, while root vegetables need more sun. And the vegetables that bear fruit, such as cucumbers, peppers, and tomatoes need a great deal of full sunshine to produce the firmest, most delectable vegetables. If you have a shady spot where you want to tuck some vegetables, try growing garden cress. It really takes to the shade.

FERTILIZING

To fertilize or not to fertilize, when to fertilize, and what to use for fertilizer on a patio vegetable garden can be perplexing questions. If you fertilize too often, at the wrong time, or with a fertilizer that's too strong you'll damage the crop. If you don't fertilize at all, you probably won't get maximum growth, and your vegetables won't attain their succulent potential. The best solution I've found is to use 1 level teaspoon of liquid 5-10-5 fertilizer for approximately 1 square foot of soil and apply first when your plants have two leaves. Reapply about every three weeks thereafter. You can add the fertilizer to the water you use to water your plants or apply it to the soil just before you treat your plants to a deep watering that will carry the nutrients through to the root structure. Some people prefer using a milder solution and applying it every week. Experiment and see what works best for your plants. Some experts say that fruiting plants (those with vegetables growing on a vine or plant above the ground, like tomatoes and cucumbers) should be given a fertilizer with a high phosphorus content.

There is a small, compact composting machine available for the apartment plant enthusiast. For this you definitely need a concrete surface, such as a patio or balcony, on which to put it. It takes eggshells, assorted food scraps, and whatever grass clippings and dry leaves you can forage from the groundskeeper if you live in a complex. Throw them all in the composter and in two to three weeks you'll have a good, rich compost that will make your plants flourish.

Herbs—Dual-Purpose Plants

One of the loveliest indoor gardens you can grow is a kitchen window herb garden. These plants add that much needed touch of life to a kitchen and a gourmet touch to your cooking. Snip off what you need; they'll soon replenish themselves. I hang my herbs from the kitchen ceiling in small pots in front of the window.

Herbs don't seem to contract the diseases nor be prey to the insects that plague many other plants. They will survive even when there's an epidemic among your other plants. When you're caring for herbs, remember they are going to be used in food. This means no poisons of any sort should be sprayed on them. If you do have a rare case of insect infestation, use only natural, organic pesticides.

Herbs are eager to grow and need little coaxing. You can start them either from seeds or cuttings, or you can purchase plants from garden supply stores. I plant herbs in standard potting soil, mixing in about one tablespoon of sand for each small pot just to lighten the soil a little.

Keep your kitchen herb garden simple. Chives, sweet marjoram, dill, mint, basil, and parsley all have small root systems, making them good candidates for an indoor herb garden.

Chives are delicate onion-flavored spears which do best in a pot with good drainage. And they like to bask in the sunlight. Provide these two things and in return they'll produce luxurious growth all year long.

Sweet marjoram is a beautiful little plant, and it's easy to grow. You can use cuttings in lamb stew, sprinkle on a vegetable dish, flavor a chicken casserole, or even mash some into softened butter to make a tasty herb spread for hot bread.

Dill is one of my favorite herbs. It flavors my egg dishes, stews, and some breads. It's so easy to snip the flavorful shoots and add them to whatever is cooking. It's delicious added with sour cream to baked potatoes.

Mint grows in several varieties, peppermint and spearmint being the most popular. Keep the soil moist around your mint plant. It droops badly when it gets too dry. And keep mint out of direct sunlight. You can add its leaves to teas, jellies, desserts, vegetables, and sauces. It also gives a fresh fragrance to your kitchen.

Basil is another herb that has versatility. It's almost a must in any tomato dish, stews, salad dressings, and with veal, lamb, or pork. And I guarantee you that the fresh basil from your kitchen will be superior to any you've ever had dried. When flowers appear on your basil plants, pinch off the heads or the leaves won't grow to their fullest.

Parsley has long been used as just a garnish to be thrown away. What a waste! Parsley has so much going for it. It's delicious, and it's good for you since it provides vitamins A and C, as well as calcium, niacin, and riboflavin. Parsley's medicinal uses date back to ancient times, and it's said that many Romans wore crowns woven from sprigs of parsley when they attended banquets because it was thought that parsley absorbed the fumes of alcohol, thus removing its powers to make them intoxicated. And, of course, many a garlic eater has saved a night's romance by chewing on a sprig of parsley.

Toxic Houseplants

Unfortunately, some plants are poisonous when ingested. Before you add a new spot of green to your apartment garden, you should be aware of its potential danger, especially if you have pets or children around. The American Medical Association claims that plants are the third most common reported cause of poisoning in the country each year. Among the top offenders are bulbs and berries. Unless you're certain otherwise, assume that any bulbs or berries are not to be eaten.

It's a good idea to keep a written list of the botanical and common names of all your plants. And tuck a bottle of ipecac (to induce vomiting) in the back of your medicine cabinet. If a pet or child does swallow a leaf and you're concerned about the consequences, call your local poison control center. They can tell you exactly which plants are dangerous. This is where a written list comes in. Instead of just being that mottled green plant with spiky leaves that grows in the corner of your living room, you will have a name to give the person at the poison control center.

The following is a brief list of some of the most common poisonous apartment and patio plants.

Azalea. All parts of this lovely, harmless-looking plant are poisonous when ingested. The symptoms to look for are watering eyes, excessive salivation, a discharge from the nose, complete loss of appetite, nausea and vomiting, pain in the stomach, and, in severe cases, paralysis of arms and legs along with convulsions.

Dieffenbachia. The toxic substance in this common plant is calcium oxalate crystals and it is contained in all parts of the plant. Swelling of the tongue and throat, along with severe irritation of the mucous membranes are the symptoms to look for if you think someone has partaken of your dieffenbachia plant.

English Ivy. All parts of the innocuous-looking English ivy are permeated with a toxic substance which has the impressive name of hederagenin of steroidal saponin. Excessive thirst, nausea, vomiting, and diarrhea accompanied by severe abdominal cramps are the symptoms it produces.

Hyacinth. This flowering plant contains toxins in the bulbs, leaves, and flowers but is only really dangerous if eaten in fairly large quantities. Nausea, vomiting, abdominal pain, and diarrhea may result.

Lantana. Several members of this plant family, including hens-and-chicks, bunchberry, and the plant simply known as lantana, contain a poison called Lantadene A which causes vomiting, diarrhea, visual problems, and a lethargic feeling. While all parts of the plant contain the toxin, the berries are especially poisonous.

Narcissus. This family, which includes the narcissus, daffodil, and jonquil, has an unknown toxic substance present in the bulbs. The flowers, stems, and leaves are apparently harmless. Abdominal distress followed by nausea, vomiting, and diarrhea are the signs to look for.

Philodendron. This ever-popular houseplant contains calcium oxalate crystals (as does dieffenbachia). Symptoms are swelling of the tongue and throat and severe irritation of the mucous membranes.

Chapter 5

Apartment Pets

An apartment just doesn't seem like a home without a pet, at least to some of us. Many landlords do allow pets, even dogs and cats. But there are usually some restrictions, and not all pets are suited to apartment life. Unlike their country cousins, apartment pets can't roam. Dogs must be leashed, cats restrained, even birds shouldn't sing too loudly. Pets create problems for the apartment dweller. But they can be solved; and if you're an animal lover, it's definitely worth the extra effort.

One of the common problems for apartment pets is obesity. With their relatively inactive lives, they're prone to the same middle-aged spread that humans are. An obvious remedy is diet. Find out how many calories your animal should have daily, and stick to it in his diet. Apartment pets often overeat out of boredom. Give your pet things to chew on other than food, such as a toy suitable for the type of animal you own. Overweight animals are no healthier than overweight people. They, too, have heart problems and respiratory troubles. Love your pet enough to feed him right.

Dogs

Most people prefer to own a dog. If your lease doesn't preclude it, there's no reason you can't successfully keep one in your apartment. But you will find he or she requires more care than other animals. So before you acquire a canine, ask yourself the following questions.

1. Am I willing and able to devote the amount of time necessary to insure that the dog will be healthy and happy?

2. Is the apartment large enough so the animal won't be miserably cramped?

3. How much money do I want to spend on a dog, including the purchase price and the cost of maintaining the animal? (This includes equipment, food, vet's bills, and boarding in case of travel.)
4. Do I have the patience to walk the dog as often as is necessary to see that it gets proper exercise?
5. Am I willing to take the time to train a dog so he is housebroken, doesn't bark, and won't jump on people?

Of all the apartment pets you might choose, a dog will be the most demanding!

EXERCISE

All dogs need some exercise. How much depends mainly on the size and the breed you select. Regular walking is essential—thirty minutes a day for smaller breeds and up to two hours for those that are larger and more muscular. If you love the outdoors and enjoy a walk in the park, you won't mind this. But if you only desire fireside and slippers when chilly weather comes, you may do better with another type of pet. Dogs need exercise not only in the balmy spring but in the cold of winter too. And even that apartment dog who doesn't require much exercise or can stretch his muscles scampering about indoors must be taken out three or four times a day to relieve himself.

If you're not big on walking, but you still want a dog, you can hire someone to do the walking for you. Some larger cities have dog-walking services. These walkers usually take several dogs at one time, so it will also give your pooch the chance to fraternize with those of his own kind. Doormen in apartment buildings or complexes can often be persuaded to take on dog-walking duties to make a little extra pocket money (sometimes a lot of extra pocket money).

You'll need a collar and leash on which to walk your dog. Be sure the collar is a good fit. If your dog is a puppy, you'll have to check the collar often and purchase new ones as the old ones become too tight. Select a collar that's not so tight that it will choke the dog and not so loose that the dog can slip out of it. The width of a collar is important, too. One that's too narrow can cut into the animal's neck. One that's too wide can keep the dog from moving his head about freely. Choke collars are for big, powerful dogs, the kind that aren't recommended for apartment living, so you shouldn't have to concern yourself about the pros and cons of the choke collar. If your dog is of a really small variety, you may prefer to use a harness. They're useful on a dog that's picked up frequently.

Leashes come in different sizes and varying lengths. Long ones are usually best for small dogs, giving them a sense of freedom, but a large dog has to be kept on a short lead.

PAMPERING YOUR POOCH

Apartment pets are pampered more than other animals, and a whole industry has sprung up around this pampering. There are gourmet treats for pets, salons to beautify them, galoshes for their little feet, sweaters and overcoats to protect them from inclement weather, and umbrellas to shelter them in the rain. There are even rubber hydrants for male dogs.

The doting dog owner is tempted to treat his pooch to all these splendors. There is no need to in most instances.

Your dog will do well on a good brand of dog food. Most dogs should be fed both dry and moist food. Gourmet feasts are unnecessary.

If you have a poodle or other dog that needs clipping, you may want to have it done professionally rather than attempt it yourself.

Unless a dog's feet are injured, there's no need to put galoshes on them. They only will make it difficult for the animal to walk and probably humiliate him. (Dogs do get embarrassed.)

Overcoats and sweaters are another matter. While most dogs don't need them and are better off without them, an apartment dog of a small, delicate breed may well need protection of this sort in cold or rainy weather.

A dog coat or sweater should be functional, not just cute. In order to protect the animal, it should cover the stomach and chest areas. If it's to be worn in rain or snow, it should be water repellent as well as warm. You'll be happier with it if it's washable. Dogs' apparel gets filthy on a rainy day. Umbrellas a dog can do without!

Male dogs seem to like the rubber hydrants. If there's a special yard for walking pets in your apartment complex or in a nearby park, you may find a hydrant already installed in it.

Unless you want to get you and your pet into trouble with the authorities, you should carry a scooper to clean up after your animal. In many cities, there's a stiff fine for neglecting to do this. Many complexes will evict your dog and maybe even you and your family if you're a chronic offender in this delicate matter. Other tenants become irate when the common areas of a complex are strewn with dog droppings.

Aside from exercise, your dog is going to require feeding once a day at a regular time. If you opt for a puppy, you'll have to feed him four times a day, to begin with, working down to once a day.

A dog should have a bed of his own, something he knows is his territory.

Bathing dogs is overdone by excessively conscientious dog owners. Most apartment dogs never get dirty enough to warrant washing them—ever. But if your dog does roll in the mud, or in some way gets filthier than you can stand, bathe him in the sink or tub using a shampoo specifically formulated for dogs and being cautious not to get it in his eyes. A few drops of vegetable oil, applied around the eye area, will help to protect them.

Bathing is seldom needed for an apartment pooch, but if you feel it necessary, use a mild pet shampoo, taking care not to get it near your dog's sensitive eyes.

Unless your dog likes a bath (which is rare, indeed), bathing him will be a two-person operation. First the dog should be leashed. One person is needed to hold the leash and reassure the dog, while the other person rolls up his sleeves and gets down to the nitty gritty. When the dog is suitably bathed, rinse off all the shampoo, thoroughly. A residue is liable to give him dry, scaly skin. Towel dry the animal and put him in a warm place to regain his composure. I don't think a dog should be washed in winter, but if he is, do keep him in for twenty-four hours after the bath. If he's housebroken, this will upset him as he'll be forced to relieve himself in the apartment, but it's preferable to having a sick dog.

GET A DOG THAT REALLY SUITS YOU

Deciding on the breed of dog that's right for you, your apartment, and your family can be difficult. There are so many from which to choose. But as an apartment dweller, unless you're in an unusual situation, you can pretty much eliminate the larger breeds. Many apartment houses and complexes permit maximum shoulder height of fifteen inches, which will automatically limit the size dog you may select.

One of the comforts of having a small dog is that they tend to live longer than the larger breeds. With all the love and attention lavished on a pet, we want to enjoy it for as many years as possible. Some of the smaller breeds have been known to live for more than twenty years with proper care. Even if the apartment in which you're living permits large dogs, you'll be better off with a smaller one. Should you move, you will be more likely to find another apartment that will accept your Chihuahua than you will be to find one that will welcome your Great Dane. Pet ownership is a responsibility, requiring a commitment for the lifetime of the animal.

Another plus to owning a small dog is that it won't eat you out of your apartment. A large dog consumes a large amount of food. A small dog consumes a small amount.

Do you want a long-haired or short-haired dog? If you're a meticulous housekeeper, you'll be more content with a short-haired dog who doesn't shed much. Short-haired breeds don't require the amount of grooming necessary for the long-haired dogs, either. If hair bothers you, short or long, you might want to consider a small poodle. They don't shed at all! Poodles and schnauzers have hair that's different from that of other breeds. Some people who are allergic to dog hair, and can't be confined in an area with a dog, can own a poodle or schnauzer happily, suffering no ill effects. The hair and dander on these animals is similar to that of humans.

Generally speaking, the smaller breeds need less exercise. But if you're looking for a dog to take you for a walk in the park, a toy dog won't suit your purposes.

Barking is another consideration. Some breeds tend to yip shrilly. Small dogs seem more prone to this than larger ones.

In your search for the perfect pooch, don't overlook mongrels and crossbreds. They can be obtained for far less money and often make loyal friends. True, they don't have the snob appeal of a purebred, but if you're only looking for a warm, loyal, furry companion, this could be the answer. However, beware of getting a snuggly puppy of unknown origin who might grow up to be a giant. This is less apt to happen if you select a crossbred. Some crossbreds are registered with dog breeding associations since they are a cross between two recognized purebreds. Crossbreeding often results in a new breed of dog that has the attributes of both the dam and sire.

Mongrels, on the other hand, are sometimes the result of a chance meeting in a back alley. And the resulting size of the offspring is questionable. Some people do know the parentage of the pups they're selling or giving away, and they can probably tell you how large the dog will be when it's full grown. When you get a mongrel, you may get a one-of-a-kind pet. This in itself has a certain snob appeal. Since these animals haven't been too finely bred, they usually are of good temperament. And they aren't heir to all of the congenital disorders suffered by the higher-class pedigreed dogs of more royal ancestry.

When you have decided what kind of dog you want, you must then decide where you're going to get it. Professional breeders are the best source of a pedigreed animal. They're well versed in the pitfalls of breeding, and you're more likely to get an animal with a good disposition and a healthy body from a professional breeder.

Homebred dogs are often a find, too. But you are running more of a risk buying from the homebreeder, who may breed two animals without knowing what weaknesses or strengths will be passed on to the pups. Home breeders are usually honest, sincere people and are most apt to be concerned with the type of home you have to offer to the pup. Professional breeders, however, are more likely to guarantee the pup against both physical disability and bad disposition. If the pup of your choice doesn't work out for you, the professional breeder will probably take him back and either replace him with another pup or refund your money.

It's difficult for the average animal lover to pass by a pet shop without wanting to visit the wiggly little creatures in the cages. But pet shops aren't the best places to purchase animals. Though some are painstakingly careful in their efforts to sell healthy animals, they're dealing with animals from many different sources. If one animal is infected, they're all likely to get infected. A dog who has been kept in a pet shop cage for too long is apt to be withdrawn and shy, not making a good pet. If you do purchase a pup in a pet shop, be certain that you get a written guarantee, and then, before you bring him home and get attached to him, take him to a good veterinarian to be thoroughly checked.

Animal shelters are another source. A visit to one of these places is not for the tenderhearted. Viewing the assortment of animals lined up in cages and knowing that if they don't get homes they'll be destroyed is heartbreaking for an animal lover. But you often can get a wonderful pet for just a few dollars. If you're not looking forward to the task of housebreaking (a hard chore for the apartment dweller) you might consider an older, already housebroken, dog from a shelter. Another advantage to selecting the grown dog over the pup is that you can see what the dog looks like as an adult. His size, character and disposition are set. (Pups rarely are hostile even if they're going to grow up to be nasty or aloof.) If you find a purebred (unlikely) or a mutt that's to your liking, question the shelter officials as to why this dog has been brought in and put up for adoption. Some of the animals have been abused and will require almost infinite patience before they'll learn to trust people again. If you don't have this to give, don't adopt such an animal. It's not fair to you or to the dog. Other dogs will be in a shelter because their former owners were forced, for one reason or another, to part with them.

Some breeds lend themselves to apartment living better than others. The following are some of the breeds that are most adaptable to apartment life.

American Cocker Spaniel. The cocker reigned as the most popular dog in this country for many years. It enjoyed the largest number of AKC registrations from the year 1936 until 1953. This floppy-eared canine was originally a hunting dog, but it has now been bred into a playful housepet. Because they have an unusually strong desire to please and are by nature dependent upon their masters, cocker spaniels are easily trained. They welcome the voice of authority. Their affection is unsurpassed by other breeds, and they're wonderful pets for children since they'll put up with being mauled and tugged. Cockers are slow to mature. They act like puppies long past their puppyhood, so be prepared for lots of tricks and games.

This isn't a good pet for the apartment person who's gone a good deal of the time. Cockers require more than the usual amount of attention or they won't be happy. And those floppy ears must be taken care of. They should be cleaned often and checked for signs of infection. An adult cocker will stand 14 to 15 inches shoulder height and should weigh 23 to 27 pounds. Unfortunately, cockers really tend to become fat. They love to overeat. The owner of a cocker must be vigilant on this score. They're bred in an assortment of colors.

Chihuahua. We have Mexico to thank for this little dog with the giant, bat-like ears. The Chihuahua is a favorite of apartment dwellers who want a tiny dog that can be carried around easily. Although short-haired Chihuahuas are more familiar to us, there are long-haired varieties, too. Chihuahuas fit best into an adult family because they are not terribly fond of children. At full growth, a Chihuahua is unlikely to weigh more than 6 pounds and will stand only 5 inches high. They're available in many colors.

Dachshund. This is one of the best dogs for apartment dwellers. Although they are inclined to be slightly independent, dachshunds are intelligent and make delightful pets. They'll go for long walks with you, making their short legs go a mile a minute to keep up, but they don't need nor crave this exercise and will be equally happy curled up at your feet at home.

Dachshunds are keen observers of the daily life of their families and are not averse to using any turn of events to their own advantage. A dachshund will size you up and quickly determine just what he can get away with. So be on guard against spoiling. For such little dogs, they are strong, and they'll use this strength if necessary to protect their owners against any threat, real or imagined.

There are two sizes of dachshunds: standard and miniature. They may have smooth hair, long hair, or wiry hair. An adult standard dachshund should have a shoulder height of 8 to 10 inches and weigh between 18 and 30 pounds. A miniature, when full grown, should have a shoulder height of 6 to 8 inches and weigh no more than 10 pounds. (Don't let a dachshund get overweight. It will make it difficult for him to get around.) A dachshund's coat can be red, black, tan, or chocolate and tan.

French Bulldog. This little dog looks like a small version of the English bulldog. They're unusually placid dogs, but they don't give or expect a large amount of affection. The French bulldog might be a good choice for you if you're out a great deal. These dogs normally have a pronounced wheezing sound to their breathing. They're a bit on the lazy side and neither enjoy nor need more than minimum exercise.

If there's anything a French bulldog dislikes more than a brisk walk, it's a small child. So unless you're an adult family, forget this breed as a possible pet. The French bulldog has a shoulder height of 11 inches and weighs about 27 pounds, and can be fawn, white, brindle and white, or brindle.

Lhasa Apso. Little and long-haired, the Lhasa apso came to this country all the way from Tibet. They were originally bred as watchdogs in Lhasa, the seat of the Dalai Lama. Lhasa apsos have appealing faces, and the pups have a "take me home" expression that's hard to resist. Their thick coats need a lot of care. In fact, their hair is so long and thick, legend has it, that in Tibet it used to be woven into yarn. While this breed seems to be increasing in popularity, they do tend to nip people, even their owners. However, they do make fine apartment dogs, requiring little exercise. An adult Lhasa apso should have a shoulder height of about 11 inches and weigh 14 to 16 pounds. Their fur can range in color from golden to black.

Maltese. This breed is the oldest European miniature. Its long, silky hair hangs to the floor, suggesting a white cape. Maltese have droopy ears and endearing large, round eyes. Unfortunately, the grooming duties that go along with one are no small matter. Be sure you want to undertake them before you decide to share your apartment with this intelligent, affectionate, mirthful little dog, who at full maturity will stand only 5 inches at shoulder height and weigh a mere 7 pounds or so. Maltese are white.

Pekingese. A tiny powerhouse, the Pekingese is by no means a lap dog. He is fierce, and can be nasty when spoiled. A native of China, this ancient breed was once the darling and exclusive possession of the Imperial family of China. He's playful, personable, and interesting. And he's so loyal to his owner that he'll fight even to death to protect him. His looks are probably responsible for the legend which proclaimed him a cross between the king of lions and a monkey. The Pekingese, if not overfed, will live longer than most other breeds. A gluttonous appetite spurred on by an oversolicitous owner has been the undoing of many a Pekingese. The Pekingese needs considerable grooming. It weighs about 12 to 14 pounds when full grown and has a shoulder height of around 9 inches. This dog is bred in many colors.

Poodle. Super-intelligent, extremely popular, a poodle—either miniature or toy size—can be a marvelous addition to any apartment family. Because they love to learn and enjoy pleasing their owners, they're one of the easiest breeds to train. Poodles are good watchdogs and are highly protective of their homes and those they love. Most poodles only bark when there is reason to do so. And, of course, the big bonus is that the poodle doesn't shed.

You will have to spend more time with this dog than you would with another breed. Poodles won't tolerate neglect. They enjoy pampering and will remain still for long periods of brushing and grooming. They are wonderfully happy, patient playmates and a wise choice for the apartment that houses children. Poodles are inclined to take a chill easily and appreciate the benefits of a coat or sweater for strolling in cold weather. Miniatures can range anywhere from 11 to 15 inches in shoulder height and weigh 13 to 18 pounds when full grown. The toys must be under 10 inches in height and weigh about 6 pounds. Poodles are bred in many colors.

Pug. This intelligent, short-haired, snub-nosed dog is one of the least nervous of the small dogs. But his wheezing can often be heard across the room. He doesn't need as much attention as some other breeds, although he's loyal to his owner and does respond to affection. His patient, quiet nature makes it possible to leave a pug alone while you work.

Tending to obesity, the pug does best on a simple diet with few treats. For a small dog, he does need quite a bit of exercise. With a shoulder height of about 11 inches and a weight of between 14 and 18 pounds at full growth, this dog fits well into the average apartment scene. Pugs are available in fawn, apricot, black, or silver.

Miniature Schnauzer. This popular dog is hardy, playful, and good with children. Although he is a good watchdog, he isn't a yipper if properly trained. A schnauzer doesn't need pampering since he has a rugged constitution. No need for overcoats for this one, but he does like exercise. His affection is unbounding, and he'll treat you to many hours of fun. The miniature schnauzer has a shoulder height of 11 to 14 inches at maturity and weighs between 13 and 17 pounds. Colors: salt and pepper, black, or black and silver.

Scottish Terrier. This short-legged bundle of mischief became popular in our country when Franklin Roosevelt was president, and the press delighted in the antics of Fala, Roosevelt's Scottie. These dogs have a regal air about them and are aloof with anyone they don't know well. Unless a Scottie is raised with children, he will have a contempt bordering on hostility toward them. And even if he was brought up in a family with youngsters, he won't be fond of any other children and probably won't tolerate being handled by them. But he'll be loyal and playful with all family members no matter what their ages. Scotties are indifferent toward exercise, and their take-it-or-leave-it attitude makes them good apartment pets.

You must use restraint when training a Scottish terrier—*never* strike him, or he will not forgive you. A firm word should be enough. Scotties want to please, and they respond well to praise or scoldings. Known as a dog with a sense of humor, the Scottish terrier will keep you amused with his antics as long as you'll be his audience. Standing about 11 inches at shoulder height at maturity and weighing between 11 and 21 pounds these dogs, whom most people think of as being black, are also bred in gray or wheat colors.

Sealyham. The Sealyham is a fine apartment dog because he needs little exercise and is not a barker. With their coarse, wiry hair, they slightly resemble Scottish terriers except for color. This breed is inclined to be strong-willed, and a rigid routine and a firm hand when it comes to training is absolutely necessary if a Sealyham is ever to learn who's boss. He thinks he is. But they won't knuckle under to unfair treatment, either. These loyal pets are fine watchdogs and great protectors. Sealyhams stand 11 to 12 inches at shoulder height and weigh about 22 to 25 pounds. Most Sealyhams are white, but some have brownish markings on their heads and ears.

Skye Terrier. It's difficult to tell what a Skye terrier is thinking because long hair covers his expressive eyes. This very old breed derives its name from its place of origin, Scotland's Isle of Skye. Although they have extremely long hair, they don't need as frequent combing as you might think, and they never need clipping. A fast daily brushing and a weekly combing will keep a Skye terrier well groomed. These are one-person dogs. They'll decide on whom to shower affection and they may be a bit snappy to others. A Skye terrier isn't a wise choice for a family pet but is an excellent dog for anyone living alone. They stand about 10 inches at shoulder height when full grown, and weigh between 23 and 31 pounds. Cream, to black colors are available.

Yorkshire Terrier. The long, silky hair on this tiny dog is parted from the tip of his nose to the tip of his tail, and it requires constant care. If you want a dog to dote on and spend time grooming, this is the one for you. To keep him in shape, you should spend at least an hour a day with him. The Yorkshire is affectionate and definitely a lap dog. He's intelligent, fun-loving, and a very lively addition to any apartment family. He should tip the scales at no more than 7 pounds and have a shoulder height of just over 6 inches when full grown. The Yorkshire terrier, which originated in England, is usually steel blue in color, although a few are tan.

TRAINING YOUR DOG

Whether you've obtained your dog from a professional breeder, a home breeder, a pet shop, or a shelter, if it's a pup, housebreaking will be in order. Unless you have ready access to the outdoors, you have to do this by paper training. Select a corner of your apartment, put down a thick layer of paper, and introduce your pup to the spot. Every time he makes a mistake, take him to that corner. Praise him when he uses it. Scold him when he doesn't. Some people put the papers right in front of the door so the pup will associate the act with the outside. Young pups have little control of their bladders and bowels, and they won't be fast learners. But a four-and-a-half to five-month-old pup should be trained in a matter of a few days. As the pup learns to use the papers, make the area that the papers cover smaller and smaller until it isn't there any more. Then you'll have to take the animal outside quickly when he approaches the spot where the papers were. Praise and tone of voice work better with most dogs than spanking. The latter is apt to make a dog skittish and hand shy.

If your pup isn't going to be allowed on the furniture, start right off scolding him when he jumps on it. Don't allow him up on things when he's a puppy and rescind the right when he's grown. Barking, which can be a major problem with an apartment dog, is another training area. You may want your dog to bark as a stranger approaches your door, but you don't want him to bark at every little noise. He will learn to discriminate between when he is supposed to bark and when he is not to if you praise him and scold appropriately. Let him know, by getting him acquainted with visitors, that it's all right for certain people to be there. Scold him if he continues to bark or is threatening to your friends.

A dog that barks when you've left your apartment can really drive the neighbors crazy, resulting in complaints to the management. If you know or suspect that your dog is doing this, leave and then come back. Wait outside your apartment door or down the hall until the dog starts barking, then go back and scold him. Let him know you're displeased. Then leave again and do the same thing. It may take a few days or even a week of this type of action, but it does work. Dogs want the approval of their owners. When he sees that you're truly angry, he'll mend his ways.

Elevators create a problem for the dog owner who lives in a high-rise apartment. Never enter an elevator with an unleashed dog. You may think he's cute and friendly, but someone else who doesn't like animals may be truly frightened if they're closed in an elevator with a dog. Even if your dog is obedience trained and you know he won't even give a sniff to the other person in the elevator, keep him leashed and close to you. If at all possible, don't take your dog onto an elevator unless it's empty or at least not crowded. If you're going to unleash your dog, don't do so until you're in an open area and then only if you know he'll obey your command to come when you call him.

Cats

The second most popular pet in this country is the cat. Cats are symbols of all sorts of things, lucky and unlucky. In England a black cat is considered a sign of good fortune, while in America the opposite is true.

Cats are ideal apartment pets since they're easily litter trained and you don't have to contend with the many daily excursions outdoors that a dog requires. Most cats can adjust nicely to an apartment, and never need to go outside except for an occasional visit to a vet. But don't try to make an apartment cat of one who has been used to having access to the outdoors. You'll probably be disappointed. Start with a kitten or with an older cat who has been kept indoors.

If your cat shows signs of boredom (often marked by attacks on its owner) the acquisition of another cat to keep him company will sometimes solve the problem. (If it doesn't, you've got double trouble.) Two male cats, however, don't generally take to one another, even if they're altered.

NEUTERING

There is no reason not to alter your apartment cat, unless you're showing it or planning to mate it. The average cat will be a much happier, more contented animal if he or she is neutered, and a male will be considerably more affectionate. Females should be neutered at about six months, males at seven. A male cat confined to an apartment will start spraying the furniture, walls, and maybe the people if not neutered by ten months. Once he has started to spray, having him altered may curb it, but it may not. I recommend having the cat altered when very young, both for his comfort and yours.

DECLAWING

Another operation you might want to consider for an apartment cat is declawing. While neutering is a simple and relatively painless operation for a cat, especially a male, declawing is extremely traumatic and painful. It's recommended only if the cat or kitten is destroying your furniture. This procedure is best done at about 12 to 16 weeks old. It's even more of a trauma for an older cat. In most cases, having just the front claws removed will take care of the problem.

Many cat lovers are violently opposed to this operation, and I agree that it shouldn't be done routinely. If you do have your cat declawed, you should be willing to make a commitment to take care of it for the rest of its life. It can no longer be an outside cat as you've removed its main line of defense against attackers. But once the painful paws have healed, a cat can live happily in an apartment setting without his front claws. It's possible he will forget he doesn't have them. I've seen clawless cats make raking motions across furniture just as if they were sharpening their claws.

SPOILING

Cats are loners and can be left for longer periods of time then dogs can. While quite independent, they do need care, some more than others. I had always been told and had believed that cats were absolutely no trouble--until we got a cat. He soon got the feel of the apartment and sized us up as pushovers. By the time he was four months old, he ruled us with an iron paw. He resented it when we left him alone and chewed up whatever was available for chewing. However, we were devoted to him and remained his faithful servants for his entire life. Cats can be sneaky and, unlike most dogs, will take advantage of every situation. The secret, which we learned too late, is don't spoil them.

SELECTING THE PURR-FECT PET

A kitten is easily come by, and, unless you go in for an exotic breed, much less expensive to buy than a dog. If you're going to get a pedigreed cat, obtain it from a professional breeder. But if you just want a playful kitten, try to find someone whose cat has had kittens. Home-raised kittens are apt to be healthier than pet shop cats or those available at shelters. Take the same precautions in selecting a cat that you would in choosing a dog.

A kitten displays signs at an early age that indicate the type of pet he's going to be. You should look for a kitten that seems neither extremely aggressive, nor unduly shy. A sudden motion or loud noise will cause any kitten to startle, but if he's psychologically sound, he should recover rapidly and be playing again in a matter of seconds. Kittens are innately curious creatures. Any tiny feline that doesn't show this trait should be avoided as a potential pet. If the kitten you've decided on won't relax when picked up and handled, he will probably be uneasy whenever he's held. Choose another one. A young kitten shouldn't be tense.

Kittens are ready to leave their mothers at about eight weeks of age. Don't take one any younger than that. If you take your kitten home in the morning rather than at night, he will have the entire day to wander around and get used to his new surroundings before nighttime. He will probably get any crying done during that first day and leave you to a peaceful night's sleep.

Another point to keep in mind when selecting your feline friend is that most, but not all, blue-eyed white cats are deaf. There's nothing wrong with having a deaf cat, especially in an apartment where he won't have to contend with the outside world, but it is something of which you should be aware.

KEEPING YOUR CAT HAPPY

A cat needs a bed, and will prefer something he can get into, rather than on top of. There are many styles of cat beds available in pet shops, but your cat will be happy if you just put a pillow in a box for him.

You'll also need a litter box. This isn't a beautiful addition to your apartment's decor, but it is a necessity. The latest design in litter boxes features a high, dome-like cover over the litter pan. An opening in one end of the cover allows the cat to enter and exit. The nice thing about this pan is that the cat doesn't get litter all over the place when he scratches around furiously, as he will every time he uses the litter box. A litter box needs to be cleaned often, and the litter should be changed every day or so. This is the most expensive aspect of keeping a cat in an apartment.

Cats are simple to housebreak. Usually all you have to do is show them where the litter is and from then on, they'll use it unless they're sick. Should your cat for some reason make a mistake, the odor is one of the most difficult to remove. Don't try conventional methods—you'll only worsen the situation. Your local pet shop should carry cleaners and odor killers for this particular occurrence.

Cats do need some exercise, and while a few (mostly Siamese) will allow you to walk them on a leash, this is too much for the average alley cat to put up with. Provide a play area for your cat and lots of toys. But do be careful about what you select. I've found that many of the toys made for cats aren't safe. They have small parts that can be swallowed easily.

Take the time to play with your cat. He will enjoy this, especially while he's a kitten, and he'll become a more affectionate, responsive cat. If you haven't had your cat declawed, try giving him a scratching post. They're available in pet shops, or you can make one from an old carpet remnant. A cat that's sluggish and not given to frivolity might be introduced to the wonders of catnip. This magical herb has turned many an old crotchety cat into a foolish kitten—at least for a little while.

Cats are by nature clean and will take care of themselves, bathing regularly. But if you have a long-haired or semi-long-haired cat, do brush him frequently. Otherwise he's going to swallow fur balls while he's grooming himself. This will make a cat vomit and won't help his digestion, either.

What you feed your cat is important. Milk, which most people associate with kittens, is one thing that most vets recommend a cat never have in his diet. It can produce worms and cause kidney trouble, especially in a male cat.

Cats don't attack their food with the enthusiasm displayed by most dogs, but they do like to eat if only in snacks now and then. Keep a supply of 100-percent nutritionally balanced, dry cat food always available to your cat. If you want to give him a treat, you might try one of the canned cat foods at night. But offer him one that doesn't have any bony pieces in it. These can cause problems for your cat just as they would for you. Most canned cat foods aren't 100-percent nutritionally balanced, so they should never be relied upon as the main ingredient in a cat's diet. Some veterinarians don't advise using them at all, claiming a cat doesn't need and can't adequately handle the amount of protein the food provides. Moist cat foods are also available. Most of them are 100-percent nutritionally balanced. They're more expensive than dry food and a bit cheaper than most of the higher-quality canned food.

Always have fresh water where your cat can reach it. He can exist for several days without food, but most cats won't live a day without water.

The old wives' tale that felines always land on their feet has led to the demise of many a cat. Never let your cat sit in the open window of your apartment or lean out over the edge of your patio. While cats do have fairly good balance, they can also lose that balance. You can install metal grillwork on a window to prevent your cat from falling out if you don't have a strong screen to protect him.

"No Dogs—No Cats!"

Many apartments don't allow either dogs or cats, but they will let you have other types of pets. If you want to stick to the fur bearing variety, here are some suggestions.

Rabbits. Rabbits are fine pets, especially for children. Domestic rabbits (the only ones you should have as apartment pets) are amazingly docile. Pet shops and breeders have a ready supply of these prolific little creatures. Contrary to common opinion, rabbits can, with some effort, be housebroken to a litter box filled with cat litter. But they must be watched when not in a cage since they love to nibble at furniture and even electric wires.

If you're going to keep a rabbit in your apartment, see that its nails are clipped on a regular basis. A big patio offers the opportunity to keep your pet bunny in a large pen outside. These great lovers of greens only need to be fed once a day. Don't feed them anything that has been grown above ground and sprayed with insecticide. Rabbits are fond of raw carrots, raw cabbage, raw parsnips, oats, clover, and rabbit pellets. They need fresh water, and since they're gluttonous must be discouraged from overeating. Don't get a boy bunny and a girl bunny and put them in a cage together unless you want little bunnies.

Gerbils. Although these animals are banned in some states, they're popular pets in others. One thing gerbils have going for them is that they don't smell. Another is that they're not noisy. These sociable little creatures should be purchased in pairs. They need mates, and they mate for life. A drawback is that they reproduce often.

Gerbils can be kept in a cage or in an aquarium tank, but they should have plenty of nesting material to snuggle into. They're easily tamed and not likely to bite. Gerbils enjoy eating mouse or hamster chow and should also be given seed to nibble on. This simple fare, plus an occasional helping of fruit or a green vegetable, and constant fresh water is all they ask of life. A well-cared-for gerbil should live for four to five years.

Hamsters. This pet suits the nocturnal apartment person. Hamsters sleep all day. They are much less friendly than gerbils and considerably noisier. They love to run on an exercise wheel, which should be provided for them, and night is their favorite time for this sport. Their tiny muscles need to be in motion. If you don't provide an exercise wheel, you will end up with a paralyzed hamster. Put two adult male hamsters together, and you're almost certainly going to have a fight. One hamster per cage is enough.

These animals are clean and odorless, but they do need roomy cages in which to roam, and a temperature between 65° and 75°F. to maintain good health. A diet of hamster food, apples, green leafy vegetables, crushed oats, and peanuts will keep your hamster happy enough to live to the ripe old age of three years.

Guinea Pigs. These animals are not from Guinea (they come from Peru) and they are no relation to the pig (they're rodents). In some places they are known as "cavies." Among the most docile of pets, they have no interest in play or affection. But they're popular children's pets since they're not apt to bite, either. They are odorless, but they gnaw constantly and can be destructive as well as annoying if they happen to be gnawing on something which you value. They'll gnaw their way out of a wooden cage. Guinea pigs, which can be kept singly, in pairs, or in groups (but no more than one male to a cage), make squeaking and whistling sounds when they're trying to communicate.

Since a guinea pig's system is not able to synthesize vitamin C, it must be provided in its diet. Try feeding them a good cavy chow (vitamin enriched), green vegetables, and a treat of fruit on occasion. They like to overeat and should be fed only about a half a cup of food per day. Keep fresh water always available to your guinea pig. He may live to be five years old.

Skunks. Don't back off. These nocturnal animals can be affectionate, rewarding pets. But obtain one from a pet shop; never try to capture a skunk (or any other wild animal) with the hope of domesticating it. Rabies are a very real threat from wild animals. The female skunk makes a far better, more affectionate pet than the male. If you're a night person, a skunk will be right there with you, bright-eyed and bushy-tailed. But he'll sleep during the day.

Some people, understandably, prefer to get their pet skunks descented, while there are other skunk lovers who believe this is unnecessary and that a skunk will not spray once it's been domesticated. If you prefer a descented skunk, have this operation performed at about six to eight weeks of age.

Skunks can be housebroken fairly easily to litter boxes. However, it's inadvisable to use cat litter, as a skunk will use it to burrow in. Fill the box with shredded paper instead. He'll burrow in this, too, but it won't make such a mess.

The bed you provide for your pet skunk should be covered—something into which he can really snuggle down. A beehive-shaped cat bed is ideal. Skunks thrive on canned cat food, supplemented with fresh fruits and vegetables. As with cats, always provide fresh drinking water.

Fish. If the flick of a fin will do it for you, try fish. No one will complain that they're either messy or noisy. Cold, freshwater fish are by far the easiest to raise. Goldfish have been known to live as long as twenty years. They aren't as finicky about water as their tropical sisters, who need just the right pH balance and exactly the proper water temperature, and are apt to flop over and die if the water is too hard. But many people have been successful in keeping lovely, tropical fish in their apartments.

When you select fish there are certain things for which to look. Both the body and the fins should look healthy and should not be covered with white blotches or other signs of erosion. The eyes shouldn't look too bright, but neither should they have a hollow appearance. Any fish with torn fins or missing scales should be passed over. With rare exceptions, a healthy fish will swim upright and smoothly through the water holding the dorsal fin high. Select fish that are compatible. Many species will kill each other given the chance.

You'll need equipment for your fish. Goldfish are easy. You can make do with a bowl, although it isn't ideal and should never house more than two fish. If the bowl has a broad rim, it should be kept full of water. If it's tall and narrow, it should be only half-filled. This is to keep the oxygen supply at optimum level. Lack of oxygen and dirty water are the two leading causes of death in goldfish.

Tropical fish require tanks. There are three types of fish tanks from which to choose, and there are drawbacks to all three.

Be sure your pets are compatible.

An *all-glass tank* is made by cementing together glass sheets. These tanks are inexpensive, they are strong, and there is nothing to corrode. The problem comes if the glass breaks or cracks. They should be kept on polystyrene sheets to lessen this possibility.

Angle iron tanks are put together with metal frames. The frames tend to rust, which causes leakage. There are sealants you can use on the joints if you notice the problem before too much damage has been done.

Plastic tanks are molded in one piece so there are no joints to crack. But the difficulty with these is removing the algae from the sides of the tanks. Unless this process is done with extreme caution, the plastic gets hopelessly scratched. Although there are special scrapers for this purpose, I don't think they're very efficient.

The water in your fish tank should be changed partially (about 10 percent) at least once a month. Impure water will make sick fish. Be sure the water you put into the tank does not contain chlorine or any other undesirable chemicals.

Fish should be fed three times a day and given no more than they can eat in five minutes. Fish pellets, flakes, crumbs, and powders are available from pet shops. Ask someone there to tell you which form is best for the type of fish you've purchased. Fish need a well-balanced diet of vitamins and minerals. See that this is present in whatever food you decide upon.

Birds. Parrots and myna birds don't lend themselves to apartment living. They can make more noise than a dog and a cat put together. (Since they cost up to thousands of dollars, this news isn't all bad.) Canaries and parakeets, however, do make nice apartment pets.

The *canary* is really a finch that comes from the Canary Islands. While the most prevalent color is yellow, they have been bred in a rainbow of colors including green, blue, and red. They'll treat you to many hours of song once they learn to sing. I've known people who have been disappointed when their birds never uttered a note. This may be because they had female canaries—only the males sing.

A bird cage with an enclosed bathing cage is appropriate for a canary as he needs to take a bath at least three times a week. Feed your canary rapeseed, canary seed, cuttlefish bone, and some form of grit such as sand. A bit of linseed oil may be needed in the diet from time to time. Don't ignore your canary or he will die of a broken heart. They need attention just as much as other pets.

Parakeets are a member of the parrot family. They've enjoyed their position of family pet for quite a few years. Blue and green parakeets are the most popular but they are available in other bright hues, as well. These little birds should be raised very much as you would raise a canary. They do love to escape from their owners, so if you take your parakeet out of the cage be sure that all exits are blocked. Feed a parakeet seed, cuttlefish bone and grit.

Other pets are adaptable to apartment living, also. If none of the ones mentioned in this chapter is to your liking, look around in pet shops, and talk to animal breeders. There is an animal for almost any lifestyle.

Chapter 6

Creating Storage Space

A person new to apartment living can be dismayed by the lack of usable space in the average apartment. "Where am I going to put this?" becomes the cry of the inexperienced as they move into their new homes. Indeed, space is usually limited in apartments. There are never enough places for storage, clothes closets, room for an office area, for that extra bed—even the kitchen cabinets won't hold everything!

The solution is to utilize every inch of room that you have to its fullest. Select furniture that is dual purpose. Then use the space over, under, and beside it. Section off closets and storage areas. And rid yourself of things you really don't want or need, which are just lying around in places needed for other items. The apartment dweller needs to be super-organized. Storage must be thought out so it will work with you and your way of life instead of against you.

Dead Storage

Your apartment building or complex may provide you with an area for dead storage. If so, look it over carefully before you decide what to put into it. If the space provided is a wire coop in a basement, check it on a rainy day to see if it's dry. Even if there's no sign of water, still select carefully what you'll store there—wiring, after all, is susceptible to wire cutters.

Most basements are damp and musty even when they don't actually take in water. If your storage area isn't made of wire but has regular wooden, plaster, or fiberboard walls, build shelves on which to store your possessions. You can store more and it will be easier to reach. Vinyl-covered wire shelves are easy to install, and they have the marvelous advantage of allowing the air to circulate underneath your stored items. This can lessen if not eliminate the threat of mildew—the curse of storing anything in a damp place. Take the time to label all boxes as to contents, and put the ones you'll need most frequently toward the front.

Basement storage isn't always what you'll find in an apartment. In the complex where we live now, there's a medium-sized storage closet off of the patio. This, in my opinion, is infinitely preferable to a basement. Not only is it not as damp as a basement storage area, but whatever is needed is right at our fingertips. Since the closet is really part of the apartment, we don't have to worry about anything being stolen. Other complexes have large storage areas inside each apartment.

If, after culling and discarding, you still come up with more treasures than you have places for, you might consider renting a space in one of the many commercial storage buildings that are becoming so popular. In most of them you, as the renter, have a key and can get to your possessions any time, night or day. The newer ones are often constructed like garages, row after row of them, and you'll have your own entrance from the outside.

Form and Function in Storage

When you have a space squeeze, make sure everything serves more than one purpose. Selecting furniture and accessories with a thought for overall use is an art that takes a little practice. End tables, for instance, can have cabinets instead of being just tables. And a flat-topped trunk used for a coffee table can hold little-used treasures that you don't want to part with. Your chair may be the kind that opens into a bed. Overstuffed furniture that has skirting reaching to the floor can hide boxes to store. There are dining tables that fit against a wall, collapse into a sideboard, or fold up out of the way altogether.

Too often halls and stairways are overlooked as storage spots. Could you put an attractive trunk or bookcase in that barren spot in the hall? Would it be possible to build a closet under the staircase? Could the back of that hinged door be put to good use with hooks or shelves?

Be creative in your quest for storage receptacles. Bicycle baskets hung on the wall of the bedroom or in the kitchen make attractive holders for many odds and ends. The old-fashioned woven straw bicycle baskets are particularly nice if you can find them. I've seen these used effectively in an entryway to hold mail. In the kitchen, you might use the wire kind to hold onions or potatoes, both of which need air in order to stay fresh. Plastic milk crates (the ones that hold twelve cartons of milk) can be turned on their sides and used to store towels, books, or toys. Since they come in different colors, you can mix or match them to compose an interesting arrangement.

A large item, such as a bicycle, can take up too much precious storage space unless you use some ingenuity. One man I know hangs his bicycle up on the wall on hooks when it's not in use. It fits in with his sporty decor and it frees his storage area for other things. You can do this with golf bags, skis and other space robbers.

When money is no object, it's fun and challenging to choose from the assortment of wall storage units that can be found in furniture stores. Some come in one piece, but most are in sections that are sold separately. You put them together in the most practical way for you. If your storage problem is acute, buy high rather than wide units, thus using the wall space to its fullest.

Some storage units feature open display space, while others only have mostly closed cabinets. Books, television sets, records, stereos, knickknacks, dishes—there's no end to what you can store in them. They even make good room dividers if you get one with a finished back instead of inexpensive plywood or pressboard. If you already have a unit without a finished back, paneling will make it attractive enough to use as a room divider.

Other wall storage units are made of cubes of hard plastic. You can arrange these in an almost infinite variety of ways and since they're small they're easy to move. The colors are bright and cheerful, and you can mix them or have them all the same hue.

The Well-Organized Kitchen

With all of the new kitchen appliances and gadgets, this room can become one of the biggest areas of confusion in the where-to-put-what department. Even the refrigerator presents a problem. Many apartments provide refrigerators that are extremely small. Unless you want to go food shopping every day or two, you have to plan to use the refrigerator space to its fullest.

Soft drinks often claim the lion's share of this precious space. Most hardware and department stores carry inexpensive bottle racks and can dispensers that hook under shelves. They make it easy to get a can or bottle, and you don't have to move everything in the refrigerator to get a drink.

When you're purchasing containers for storing food in a refrigerator, look for those that can be stacked. But measure to make sure that when you stack them, they will fit between the shelves in your refrigerator. Vinyl-coated racks will make it possible to stack irregular-shaped items that couldn't be placed on top of each other any other way. There are other shelf units for freezers that allow you to stack frozen foods over the ice cube trays without their sticking, which often occurs when you put a frozen food package on top of ice cubes.

The refrigerator is only one of the space problems to be found in the average apartment kitchen. While an increasing number of us are blessed with dishwashers, there are still those who aren't. And even if you have a dishwasher, there are times when dishes must be washed by hand. In a small kitchen, finding a place to put them while they dry is a problem.

The old standard dish drainers are awkward and take up a lot of space. There is a mini-drainer that fits onto the edges of a sink. It can be left in place without making the sink unusable, and it's so small you can hang it on a hook inside of a cabinet door. It's even versatile enough to double as a strainer when you're washing vegetables. But it doesn't hold many dishes. Another improvement on the old dish drainer is a fold-away model that will hold up to sixteen plates or saucers and eight glasses or cups along with a full silver service for eight. It doesn't take up much space when in use, since it reaches up rather than out, and it folds into even less space when you want to tuck it away in a cabinet.

I value my kitchen counter space, and I'm reluctant to sacrifice any of it to the many small appliances I don't use frequently but which I cherish nonetheless. I don't have cabinet space for them, and some take up considerable room. I solved this problem many apartments ago by getting a narrow, free-standing cabinet. In an apartment with a fairly large kitchen, this cabinet can be kept right in the kitchen. But when the kitchen isn't a big one, the cabinet should blend in well with your dining room furniture. I keep mine out of the way against a wall placed near an electrical outlet so that I can use it to keep a warming plate on when I'm serving hot hors d'oeuvres, or to plug in a fondue or a coffee pot.

It is also a good idea to have shelves around the upper part of the kitchen walls. They can be quite high—about two feet from the ceiling—and can be used for all the things that don't fit anyplace else, and that you don't use often enough to mind climbing on a chair to reach. My shelves are made of pressboard and are held up with angle irons from underneath. Making them is simple, and they're incredibly inexpensive. The cabinet and the peripheral shelving free the kitchen cabinets for dishes and other everyday utensils, which I want to have where I can get at them.

There are scores of racks and gadgets that make cabinet space go further. Some of these are stacking racks, while others attach to the insides of cabinet doors and provide compartments for endless items. The racks on the cabinet doors not only provide space, they keep things which might ordinarily be kept at the back of a cabinet in a place where you can easily reach them. Frequently-used cleaning solutions can, for example, be stored in one of these racks right inside your sink cabinet. If you store any cleaning items or other toxic substances in bottom cabinets and children reside in your apartment with you, invest in childproof locks for the cabinets. They're easy to install, inexpensive, and not difficult for an adult to operate. They provide a large amount of peace of mind for a small amount of money.

Another convenience is a large, three-section rack that keeps paper bags neat, divided by size, and waiting for you right inside a cabinet door.

One of my all-time favorite space savers is the garbage bag caddy. This little container can be attached to the inside of a sink cabinet door. You can use plastic bags or plain old paper bags as liners. Not only does it save space, it keeps the garbage out of sight. Anyone who doesn't have a garbage disposal should really like this one.

A revolving cup rack which attaches to the underside of a cabinet shelf and will hold eight cups, frees the space underneath for dishes. Another cup rack allows you to stack cups. Thus eight cups take up the space usually occupied by only one.

There are a great many revolving lazy Susan racks available for kitchen cabinets. These are made for canned goods, spices, or dishes. I prefer those with two or more shelves although the single shelf ones are convenient. Lazy Susans waste space, however, since you lose all the area around them.

Spices and herbs are a must for almost any cook these days, but they do take up room. The stores abound with spice racks in all shapes and sizes, and in varying degrees of cute. If you have an empty spot on the wall, by all means fill it with a spice rack. Don't get a small one. Get one that has enough bottles to hold all of the spices you're liable to want. And be sure that the bottles themselves are large enough to hold a full package or bottle of spice. If a bottle is too tiny to hold all of your cinnamon, you haven't solved the problem.

If your kitchen is shy of drawers, look in a hardware store for attractive, ready-made kitchen drawers which can be installed under your cabinets using just a screwdriver. These drawers are valuable additions for storage closets, too. They can be attached underneath shelves and are a convenient place to store tools.

Pots and pans cause storage problems, especially if your stove doesn't have a drawer built-in just to accomodate them. A bit of wall space or even the ceiling can save the day if you hang a pot rack on it. These handsome racks are usually made of black wrought iron and have become popular in the last few years. They can be found in kitchen shops as well as department stores. Or, if you want to be more inventive, try hanging a lattice work from the ceiling at one end of the room. Just add hooks. Or a tall, narrow bookcase can solve the pot problem for you, and it may even give you extra space in which to store other kitchen utensils.

Those necessary, bulky items which are needed to keep any home running efficiently—things like ironing boards, mops, and brooms—are usually kept near the kitchen. They can be a real storage nightmare. But the great minds of the technical world have come to the rescue again with small, inexpensive holders that keep these items handy yet out of the way. An ironing board holder not

A spice rack should have plenty of good-sized bottles and can be hung on the kitchen wall. Contact paper was used for the flower motif on the window. *Courtesy of Comark Plastics.*

only keeps the board out of sight hanging on the back of a door, it also provides a place to slip in the iron and a compartment for spray starch and other ironing helpers.

Mop and broom holders aren't new to any of us. They've been around for a long time. But they've been improved and now, instead of having to install small, ineffective clips that were forever letting the broom drop, you can get a nifty holder for the back of a door or side of the closet. It will hold securely your mop, broom, dustpan, and whisk broom.

The Well-Organized Bathroom

The tiny bathrooms offered by most apartment complexes leave a great deal to be desired in terms of storage. Even older apartment buildings, with bathrooms large enough to hold a dance in, don't usually have storage space adequate for all of today's toiletries.

In adding extra space to your bathroom, an inexpensive place to start is with a shower caddy. It hangs on the shower head—no screws or nails are needed for installation—and holds shampoo, conditioners, rinses, and other things that usually take space in a medicine cabinet.

Without breaking any but the most stringent budget, you can purchase shelving that fits over the toilet tank. The unit is installed with floor-to-ceiling tension poles so again there is no need to use even a screwdriver to put one up. And you'll leave no holes in the landlord's walls.

If your bathroom doesn't have enough towel racks, lacks holders for toothbrushes, a glass, and soap—and there isn't even a toilet paper dispenser, and you don't want to make holes in the bathroom walls, adhesive backed organizers are useful, but I've also found that you can't give them the rough treatment you can give to units that screw into something solid. The towel bars won't hold up under a child who's trying to chin himself. But for anyone with a light touch and a fussy landlord, they're an answer.

You may or may not have a medicine cabinet with a mirror, or a mirrored wall in your bathroom. One bathroom mirror is an absolute necessity and two are desirable. How can you comb your hair without seeing the back of your head? I think hand mirrors are a nui-

When space is at a premium in a bathroom, an extension mirror will give you a close look without taking up too much precious room.

sance, and the wall behind an existing mirror may not be free to take a stationary mirror. The solution is an extension mirror. These are attached to metal extension arms that open like an accordian. They have a small plate that screws into place on the wall or woodwork. The mirror, which is two-sided with a magnifying mirror on one side and a regular mirror on the other, can be pulled out and swiveled. When not in use it folds back against the wall, taking up little space.

Towels are another problem. Two towel racks just won't do it for three or four people. Vinyl-covered wire towel racks that clip over the top of a door offer a place to hang towels without making holes in the door. And those big, gorgeous, older bathrooms I mentioned earlier are wonderful places for a standing towel tree. Or if you want to improvise and get fancy, a brass clothes tree would do splendidly for this purpose.

Drying things you wash by hand becomes another problem in an apartment, especially if you don't have a patio where you can string a clothesline on a nice day. Folding clothes racks can be set up in the bathtub, and they do hold a number of garments. But they take up too much space when not in use to be practical for the average apartment. I prefer a drying apparatus that slips over a towel rack. You can buy one with ten drying hooks that will accommodate such items as lingerie, hosiery, and swimsuits. Its steel frame is coated so it won't rust and, being only 15¾″ long and 6″ wide, it tucks into a corner for storage.

I have no linen closet in my apartment. An old hump-backed trunk houses our sheets, towels, and extra pillows. We've had this trunk in various rooms in our various apartments. Right now it fits best in the bedroom, but I've had it in the living room, and no one has known it was a linen chest because it's such a lovely decorator piece.

Shelving and Closets

You will always have to store things that don't hang, so you'll need shelving. You may need a great deal of it for books, a stereo, knickknacks, magazines, and records. Just remember to make every inch of space count.

"Instant" shelving that's easy to assemble and that can be tailored to your needs is a viable and fairly inexpensive solution to many problems. Some shelves are assembled by twisting spindles into corresponding holes in the shelves. You don't even need a screwdriver to put them together. The nice part of these is that you can start with a small unit and add to it as your need grows, improvising as you go to suit the measurements of whatever you're planning to put on the shelves. Of course, they come down as quickly as they go up. On moving day you can pile up the parts and carry them out. These shelves come in smart-looking, wood-like finishes.

If money is tight and the instant shelving represents more of a cash outlay than you're ready to make, you can purchase metal utility shelves. Admittedly not very handsome, they are utilitarian.

You can assemble them with the shelves as near together or far apart as you like. If you're going to have them in the living room or some place where they'll be visible, either paint them to match the room, or cover them with adhesive-backed paper. This paper is washable and durable and comes in some attractive patterns. Study the directions before you attempt to apply it, though. I find that once it grabs a surface, it's not all that simple to move it around or change its position.

Incidentally, if you have a bookcase but need a cabinet, investigate shutters. They come in a number of styles and sizes. Use plain or fancy hinges to attach them to the bookcase. You'll have a great storage place for out-of-season clothes or, if you're short of dresser space, use this arrangement in your bedroom to hold things you're using every day. In order to conserve space, get a high rather than a wide bookcase. Long, low furniture looks good, but it eats up space.

Closets—we never have enough of them, and the ones we do have are never large enough! Not in an apartment anyway. Although many modern apartment closets have sliding doors, hinged ones are much more desirable from the point of view of space. There's nothing you can install or hang on the back of a sliding door. It's wasted space! But you can install hooks and racks and shelves, large or small, inside a hinged closet door, thus increasing its utility and your storage space. Shoes can be hung there; a hook can be installed that will hold belts and necklaces, hats or pocketbooks; over-the-door racks that accommodate hangers can be used giving you extra space for dresses (especially if they're long and your closet isn't); shelves can be put up for hats or socks.

Plan your clothes closet with care. Everyone needs to see what's in their closets. If your closets don't have lights, install them, even if they're only battery operated. It's tough to select your outfit for the day when you can't even see the colors clearly. If you have a small closet and a large wardrobe, you'll have to add a few shelves and maybe multi-level hanging rods. If the closet is large enough, divide it in half (or whatever division suits your needs). Stand a board in the closet vertically (a sturdy sheet of plywood or pressboard will do) and attach it to the back wall and the top shelf of the closet with L-shaped brackets. Use the ceiling if there isn't a shelf. On one side

The addition of shelves and multi-level rods helps a small closet do the job of a large one.

of this partition install a rod for your long garments. Measure! The longer your longest garment, the higher you're going to have to put the rod.

Some rods are held up by tension springs. They push out against the walls and stay put until you push them in and release the tension. You may want to use these as they're very simple to install and take down, or you may opt for the more permanent rod that has to be screwed or nailed into the wall. The nice thing about the tension rods is that you can move them if it turns out that you do, after all, need a rod that's higher or lower.

On the other side of the partition, install two rods—one for shirts or blouses and one for suits, skirts, or pants. Measure the longest garment you'll be hanging on that side of the closet and, adding an inch or more leeway from the floor, put up a rod on the lowest part of the closet first. Then measure from that, again allowing an inch, and install a rod in the upper part of that half of the closet.

You could also divide a closet into thirds, building floor to ceiling drawers in the middle and installing rods on either side. If the closet is wide enough you can put a dresser in the middle and work from there. Be sure the dresser is secured to the back of the closet before you attempt to attach rods to it. Using tension rods on this sort of arrangement eliminates the need to make nail or screw holes in the dresser.

You may not want to go to the trouble of installing a partition and putting in extra rods for multi-level hanging. You can buy a rod that hangs from the existing rod to provide this handy feature. This rod is adjustable. It expands lengthwise from fifteen to twenty-eight inches, and it also moves up and down.

Do you need more shelf space in your clothes closet? The vinyl-coated wire shelves that I recommend for dead storage work well in clothes closets, too. They come in a variety of sizes and are easily installed with brackets. First, measure how much room you have left above the clothes in the closet where you want the shelving. You may only be able to fit one shelf, or perhaps you can put in two or three. Plan what you are going to put on each shelf. Put the things you use most often on the lower shelves. Measure, allowing space for new purchases, before you install the shelves. Consider making them adjustable. Then it's easy to adapt as your needs change.

Shoes look neat when they're stored on a shelf, if you have room. Wire shelves aren't good for this purpose, though, as a thin high heel is apt to drop down between the wires. A good wooden shelf is best. If you don't have shelf room, use a hanging shoe bag or a shoe rack that sits on the closet floor. Lining shoes up on the floor doesn't work for me. They always end up in a disorderly heap. I've found that if the floor is the only available place, and there isn't any shoe rack, my shoes stay nicer longer if they're stored in their original boxes.

Boots are wonderful and necessary in season, but they're a problem to store out of season. If you throw them in the back of the closet, they slump over and get all misshapen. Boot trees are fine, but the boots still lie around and collect dust. I've found they store best hung on a skirt hanger. I pad the little clips so that they don't mark up the boots. Clip type clothespins over wire hangers will work for boots, too, provided that the springs on the clothespins are strong.

A piece of pegboard nailed to a closet wall or door is a swell place to hang any number of little items you want to put out of the way but not out of reach. Belts, jewelry, pocketbooks, and many other accessories can be tidily kept with this type of arrangement. You may prefer it to shelving or hooks.

A child's closet presents a special kind of problem. Little arms aren't long enough to reach the standard racks. Pegboard works wonders in closets for youngsters, allowing them to hang their treasures on hooks that are well within their reach. Multi-level hanging helps, too, but children need to reach the upper clothes. A friend of mine built an uncomplicated set of three stairs in the middle of the children's closet. The stairs are deep, safe, and not too high. Children can climb up and easily reach the clothes on the top rack. A bonus comes with this arrangement. The steps are deep enough to provide storage underneath for toys.

WHEN YOUR BEST ISN'T GOOD ENOUGH

You may find that no matter what you do your clothes closets are still inadequate. An armoire could offer a solution. The old ones aren't cheap, but they are gorgeous and make an attractive living room piece should you move and no longer have the same storage problems. An armoire also is a spectacular piece of furniture in which to house a stereo or television should you prefer to keep these out of sight.

If an armoire is out of your price range, inexpensive wardrobes can be found in most department stores. You can paint, paper, or otherwise decorate them to match your decor.

Another answer is to build a closet, from a few panels of dry wall, into a corner of the bedroom. I know several people who have done this, but it's a bit extreme for an apartment dweller unless you plan

A set of sturdy steps makes it easy for small hands to reach high places safely.

to stay in that apartment for a long time. If you are thinking of doing something like this which alters the apartment structurally, discuss it with your landlord first. He may not think your closet is the great addition you think it is. Probably the least complicated and cheapest way to get a closet is to hang a sheet on a rod across one end or in a corner of the bedroom.

The out-of-season wardrobe is always a nuisance for those who live in sections of the country that require seasonal changes of clothing. The storage of clothes not in use is a real problem. Five and dime stores carry cardboard storage boxes that fit under the average bed and will hold a number of items that you can fold. I find that this system doesn't provide enough space for two persons' clothes. So I also store foldable, out-of-season things in idle suitcases. If you do this, don't put the suitcases in a damp place, or you're apt to find your clothes the worse for wear if not actually mildewed. Put clothes that can't be folded in garment bags in the backs of closets.

Space-Saving Beds

It's a rare apartment that offers so much space that its occupants can afford the luxury of a full-time guest room. And sometimes an apartment is so tiny that even the person who lives in it must have a bed that also serves as a sofa. Fortunately, there are many ways to have a bed that isn't just a bed. A sofa bed is the most obvious alternative. Some new models are very attractive and hide the fact there is a bed folded inside. Most are adequately comfortable for sleeping, although they don't usually have box springs, just a thin mattress on a metal spring. This isn't the ultimate in comfort if you're going to use it as your bed every night, but is fine for an occasional guest.

There are many grades of sofa beds available. Look for one that has a tubular bar handgrip so that it's not difficult to open. A well-constructed model will have at least four legs supporting the mattress when it's open. A metal frame is best, and this frame should be reinforced in all the stress spots. Counterbalanced tension springs comprise the best operating mechanisms. For silence and ease of operation, nylon bearings are desirable.

Operate the bed you're considering before you purchase it to see if it is difficult to open and close. Take the measurements both open

This is not simply a handsome wall storage unit. The cabinet conceals a Murphy bed for comfortable sleeping at night. *Courtesy of Lew Raynes, Inc.*

and closed so you'll know it will fit into the space for which you're buying it before you have it delivered.

The Murphy bed is alive and well and living in the apartments of many smart people. This old-fashioned bed, which dates back to 1900, folds into a closet or cabinet. Murphy beds come in any size from twin to king and can be purchased alone or in company with a cabinet.

If you have a closet you're not in need of, you can store a Murphy bed there, fully made up and ready for use. Those who are handy with hammer and nails may want to buy the bed and the mechanism that propels it and build a cabinet to house it. If not, you can have the whole apparatus—bed, mechanism, cabinet and all for about the price you'd pay for a really good sofa bed.

The Murphy bed cabinet can be used as a room divider or placed against a wall. There's a design to fit almost any room. I've even seen one in a dining room. The people who lived in that apartment used the cabinet to display dishes, When they had company, they just moved the dining room table to one side. Not an arrangement you'd want for everyday but perfectly acceptable for guests.

Most Murphy beds are much more comfortable than the conventional sleep sofa. So if you're purchasing an all-the-time bed, you'll be happier with this setup. If opening up a Murphy bed presents a problem because of the length, you can buy a sidebed. These have the folding mechanism on the sides of the bed frames rather than on the end or top.

Some rooms lend themselves to an arrangement of two sofas that meet at a corner with an end table between them. This makes for an ideal guest room setting, providing separate beds for two people. You can purchase these daybeds complete with the end table under which part of one of the beds slides when not in use as a bed. And they're relatively inexpensive.

Room Dividers

A room divider can turn one large room into two smaller ones, or it can section off a corner of a room for privacy. You may need an area for dining, for an office, a sewing space, or a closet. The most useful divider is one that offers more than just a wall. Like so many apartment furnishings, it can serve a double purpose. For instance, a

This cozy corner seating plan offers an alternative to an apartment guest room, without sacrificing precious space. *Courtesy of the Kirsch Company.*

double-thick divider with room between the partitions can be used for storage. Or a double divider can house a fold-up bed (simply a single mattress on a steel frame) on the bottom and have shelves on the top. A room divider can also provide a bookcase, a built-in desk, or a bar.

Your room divider need not extend from floor to ceiling, although this type does offer the maximum in privacy. Hollow core doors can be attached together to form a three-sided wall. Take four or more doors and attach the middle ones together with metal mending pins (available at the hardware store), so they remain straight. Attach the end doors to these with angle irons. You may also want to attach everything to the floor with angle irons, making the room divider more secure. Folding screens serve the same purpose. And you can hide a washer and dryer or other unsightly necessities with folding doors that are handsome enough to enhance your decor.

Everyone's storage and space needs are peculiar to them and to their apartments, so my tips are general. But by using them as a springboard, you should be able to come up with just the right combination of ideas to enable you to get full use from every inch of your apartment.

Chapter 7

Insulation, Tools, and Appliances

An apartment can be both cozy and well-equipped. Insulation can make the difference between that temporary apartment atmosphere and the settled feeling of home, sweet home. In addition to the basic hand tools anyone needs, there are power tools for those of us with limited space and appliances that are designed for apartment living.

Economical Insulation

Keeping warm in winter and cool in summer has become a major expense and concern not only for the homeowner but for the apartment dweller as well. You might not pay for the heat in your apartment (although more and more ads for apartments read "plus utilities" as landlords become wary of escalating fuel costs) but you'll still want to be insulated against the cold or hot drafts of air that can invade your home.

The most luxurious apartment that I ever lived in had a northern exposure which was so poorly insulated the windows froze on the inside during really cold weather. I was new to apartment living and knew no way to alleviate the situation. It was a miserable winter, and I moved in the spring when the lease expired. If I'd known then what I know now, I'd have been much more comfortable and might have stayed in that apartment longer.

START WITH WINDOW SHADES

The proper use of window shades is more important than you might think. An Illinois Institute of Technology study concluded that lowering shades against summer sun would keep out 54 percent of the hot air that normally invades a home through the windows, while in winter shades would keep in about 31 percent of the heat that is usually lost through windows. Of course, the material that the shades are made of influences the amount of savings. And you can add another 5 to 10 percent to these figures if you install runners along the window frames so that no air will pass either in or out between the edges of the window shades and the window. But, in order to achieve these savings, you must keep your shades pulled most of the time.

Window Quilt ®, an energy-saving window shade, seals off drafts around large windows and sliding glass doors. The decorative quilted shade saves over 39 percent on heating bills and, in summer, greatly reduces air conditioning costs. *Courtesy of Appropriate Technology Corporation.*

The energy crunch brought many new products to the market. One of the most worthwhile is the Window Quilt,™ which is a thin layer of foil sandwiched between four layers of an insulating material consisting of a polyester batting and a decorative polyester cotton. These quilts, made by Appropriate Technology, are stitched with an ultrasonic bonding process which eliminates the needle holes that would occur with a more conventional method of stitching. They move on plastic tracks that keep them snug inside the window frame.

All insulating materials must now bear an R rating value, which is a gauge of heat resistance and insulating efficiency. Most storm windows have a rating of R 1.8. These window quilts are R 4.25, so they are rated as being almost two and a half times more effective than storm windows.

Apartments lose up to 50 percent of their heat through windows. In other words, if you had no windows, your fuel bill would be cut in half. Installing Window Quilts™ in all of your windows can save you up to 79 percent of that 50 percent, or over 39 percent of your total fuel bill. Unfortunately, it will cost several hundred dollars to outfit the average apartment. Whether you're prepared to make this investment may depend largely on how long you plan to stay put. On the positive side, about 75 percent of heat loss through windows occurs at night so the use of window quilts need not mean you won't see the light of day until spring.

WEATHER STRIPPING

Strips of newspaper or cloth can be used on a temporary basis to stop cold or hot air from leaking in around windows and doors. A better answer to the problem is weather stripping. There are many kinds from which to choose. Felt is fairly inexpensive but lasts for only a couple of years, and it's not as attractive as some of the other weather strippings that blend in with your decor. But if you don't plan to stay in your apartment for a long time, it may suit your needs.

Double-hung windows are a notorious source of cold drafts. Give your windows the hand test. If you can feel a draft when you hold your hand above the place where the upper and lower windows join together and overlap, the window needs to be weather-stripped. Sometimes a window needs attention even when you can't feel the draft with your hand. If you can pull a piece of paper through the place windows meet, you are losing heat. That may seem minor. But if you multiply it by all your windows, you may have a major, unnecessary expense.

Many modern windows have metal frames, making it inadvisable or impossible to use any weather stripping that must be attached with brads, tacks, staples, or nails. For these windows, use tapes that have adhesive backing and are easily applied. An impressive adhesive weather strip made of a narrow band of polypropylene is manufactured by 3M. The company claims it will outlast even brass weather stripping. Guaranteed to last for five years, it comes in either white or brown to fit in with your decorating scheme.

Weather stripping your door is important, too. Even if your apartment door opens onto a common hallway, you could be donating part of your heat to keeping the hall warm. The bottoms of doors are the area from which the most heat escapes because this is the place where most doors are ill-fitting. There are many simple ways to install weather stripping that can swiftly remedy this problem. One of the best products for an apartment door is the self-sticking door bottom which retails for around two dollars and can be applied in a jiffy. Since it's self-adhesive, it won't damage the door—a fact that's bound to please the landlord.

If your door has been cut short so that it can open over a carpet, you can purchase an automatic door bottom that lowers tightly against the floor when the door is closed and rises automatically to clear rugs when the door is opened.

Patio doors are a prime source of heat loss. Although most patio doors have double, or even triple, thermal glass, that glass is usually mounted in a hollow metal frame. Of course, metal is a grand conductor of heat, conducts it out of your apartment in winter and into it in summer. Just put your hand on the metal frame of your patio door on a cold day and you'll feel what I mean. Dalmor Corporation markets a Patio Door Insulation Kit that solves the problem. The insulating strips are a material much like that used to make foam cups—the kind you can hold while they're full of coffee without feeling the heat. This stripping is available in an attractive wood grain finish that is, I think, much more pleasing than the metal it

It takes only fifteen minutes to apply this attractive, foam-backed insulation to a patio door. It will help keep heat in during the winter and out during the summer. *Courtesy of Dalmor Corporation.*

covers. The manufacturer claims it only takes fifteen minutes to apply to a patio door. It will help keep heat out during the hot months as well.

SEASONAL WINDOW PROTECTION

Storm windows are great. So are thermal panes, which so many apartment complexes now have in place of storm windows. But they don't always answer all the problems. For instance, you may have leaks around the window frames that should be caulked.

Plastic storm windows are a good investment for the apartment dweller who finds that the landlord doesn't provide storm windows. Spend a little extra money and get plastic that's really clear. Less expensive plastic is so cloudy that you could be in for a cheerless winter.

Plastic storm windows can be installed either outside or inside. Some landlords, especially in complexes, won't allow you to put anything outside, and if you live above the first floor, you may not want to try. Most kits come complete with tape for installation. Some have vinyl frames to fit around the inside of the window. The plastic storm window then snaps easily into this frame. These snap-in windows are simple to take down, and you can store them during the summer months and put them back into place in the fall. They cost under ten dollars per window.

Keeping sun out during the summer can be as much of a problem as keeping heat in during the winter. Few apartment dwellers are going to invest in tinted glass as many homeowners do, but there is an alternative. Scotchtint Sun-Control Film made by 3M will block out up to 75 percent of the sun's heat. This film is easily applied directly to the window glass with the use of a squeegee. In winter it can be peeled off and stored for reuse.

OTHER HEAT-LOSS AREAS

Do the cold-air hand test (the one for windows) to search out air leaks around baseboards, and holes that have been made to facilitate plumbing or wiring coming into your apartment from outside. If you can feel cold air in these places, caulking is one answer. This is easily done with a caulking gun.

In some apartments more heat is lost through poorly installed electrical outlets than through windows. There's a nonflammable foam draft sealer on the market that fits snugly behind outlet and switch plates to insulate against this type of heat loss. It is installed in minutes.

The Care and Feeding of Your Heating System

We've all heard the message loud and clear: fuel costs are skyrocketing, natural resources are becoming scarcer, and we should be lowering our thermostats. Heating experts say that for each degree we lower our thermostats, we will cut our fuel bills by 3 percent. The old myth that it costs more to get heat back up to a comfort range than it does to leave it there in the first place has been disproven.

A fuel saver thermostat is available to automatically turn your heat up or down, and on or off at the times you set. This unit can be used on gas or oil systems, and it's good for either heating or air conditioning. A good one should cost less than 75 dollars so it's not a major investment. Honeywell puts out a fuel saver they claim will save up to 28 percent of your heating and cooling costs per year.

Many people, myself included, like to sleep in a cool room, so they open the bedroom windows wide at night. Naturally, precious heat escapes. Instead of doing this, turn the heat down, or close the heat vent in the bedroom about an hour before retiring. Keep the bedroom closed so the cold won't permeate the rest of the apartment. By the time you're ready for bed, the room will be a nice temperature for sleeping. We block the heat from our bedroom all winter, since we don't use the room except at night. We believe this saves a good 15 percent on our fuel bill. I also keep the heat turned down in my rather small kitchen. When I'm there, I'm usually cooking, the heat from the stove compensates for the lowered setting. In fact, I think the kitchen is probably more comfortable than it was when I kept it heated all the time. There's nothing like being a cool cook.

Allowing heat to circulate through your apartment is important. Make sure none of your furniture or drapes are blocking a heat source, even a little bit. A heat register whose air flow is hitting the arm of a sofa two feet away isn't really doing its maximum for the room.

Many landlords are careful to change furnace and air conditioner filters on a regular basis, but many others are not, especially if they aren't paying for heat. Some heating experts say these filters should be changed once a month. I have yet to find the landlord who changes filters that often, nor do I believe it necessary. But you probably should change filters every two months. Increasing accumulations of dust will tell you you've waited too long. A clean filter keeps your furnace or air conditioner from having to work overtime to push air through dirt. The system will operate more efficiently, saving you money, if this is attended to regularly. Filters are inexpensive (usually less than a dollar,) and you can easily change them yourself in about 60 seconds.

Keeping vents and radiators clean is another small but important way to minimize fuel costs by not making your heating system work harder than necessary. Dust and grease act as insulation, holding heat in.

Radiator covers, attractive as they are, also keep the heat in rather than letting it circulate freely throughout the room. If possible, remove and store them during the colder months. You can reclaim them for the summer.

Many people erroneously think that painting radiators with a metallic paint somehow enables them to reflect the heat better. Nothing could be further from the truth. Metallic paint actually keeps the heat in. But flat paint will help them function at peak efficiency. Painted to match your walls, they'll blend in, and you won't miss the radiator covers as much.

Hot water radiators must be bled from time to time. If your landlord doesn't do this, you should. Generally, it's wise to bleed them before each heating season. And you also should check your radiators occasionally during the season to see that the heat is even. Even if you're not paying for the heat, you still want to be comfortable, and a radiator or baseboard unit that has air pockets isn't giving off the amount of heat it should. When there's air in the system, one part of the radiator will feel cooler to the touch than the rest of it. *Caution:* Don't bleed radiators while the system is on. Turn it off, and let it cool down first. The water in the system is extremely hot.

The procedure for bleeding is simple. Turn the small valve on the side of the radiator. (Some radiators need a key for this.) Opening this valve lets the air out. When all the air has been released, the valve will start to squirt water so hold a basin or pail under the valve before opening it.

Tools for the Apartment

Every apartment dweller should own a toolbox that contains all the tools essential to maintaining any household. Here is a suggested list.

1. A good, substantial hammer. The type with a claw for pulling nails is the best choice.
2. A rugged screwdriver. In fact, you should have four sturdy screwdrivers: a small and a large standard type, and a small and a large Phillips (it has a cross on the end). There's a handy 4-in-1 screwdriver with four different bits that store in the handle when not in use. These are magnetized so screws won't drop while you're trying to put them into position.
3. A level. Almost a necessity if you want to hang pictures or anything else straight. A six-inch level should be adequate.
4. Pliers. Needed for a variety of chores that require a firm grip.
5. A measuring tape—preferably a metal one that retracts into a case. The hook at the end of this will slip over one end of whatever you're measuring so you can take on solo measuring jobs.
6. A putty knife. Useful for fill-in jobs on walls, or if your windows need attention. It is also invaluable if you're refinishing furniture.
7. A small push drill. This is handy for those little drilling tasks.
8. A handsaw. Get one of those with a more or less all-purpose blade.

If you love to putter, to build and repair things, you will need additional tools.

Living in an apartment doesn't preclude the possession of a workshop complete with power tools, but you have to think small. Dremel has designed a set of creative tools specifically for apartment people. Although they are small, they will tackle those big jobs for you, and they have many attachments and accessories. One of their tools can be set up on a surface as small as a card table. The power saw, for example, measures only 13″ by 12″ by 9″. It can be used for perpendicular cuts up to 1″, and it's fully adjustable for mitered cuts up to ¾″. The saw cuts plastic as well as wood. A convenient sawdust chute at the back of the motorized saw can be attached to a bag or vacuum cleaner so you won't make a mess. Dremel also makes a disc belt sander that fits into the corner of an apartment

This power tool is almost a whole workshop in one small case. It carves, grinds, shapes, saws, polishes, sharpens, routs, and it can be stored in a drawer. *Courtesy of Dremel.*

closet, and it works efficiently on wood, metal, and plastic. This sander weights about 11 pounds and stands only 15″ high.

Moto-Tool is a work shop that can be kept in a drawer. It will take care of all sorts of household projects and is a good choice when you're not going to have many tools. Moto-Tool grinds, shapes, carves, saws, polishes, sharpens, and routs, and it performs well on wood, metal, and other materials. It comes in a compact case for easy storage.

Even smaller in size are Mini-tron tools. These tools are approximately one-quarter the size and weight of their standard counterparts. The entire Mini-tron workshop, consisting of a drill, sabre/jigsaw, circular saw, and vibrating sander, fits into a case no larger than an attache case. You need to have an AC adapter for these tools.

If you're going to be doing big jobs like putting up ceiling tiles, upholstering furniture, attaching sheets or fabric on the walls, weather-stripping, or installing plastic storm windows, it will pay you to purchase a staple gun. These guns are fast, small, and convenient. You can shoot six to ten staples into place in the time it would take to hammer one nail. There is an electric variety but, unless you're going to be using one a great deal, and for heavy jobs, you'll probably be just as satisfied with the manual model.

Apartment Appliances

Your apartment may come with all the appliances you need, or it may provide none at all. Perhaps you're not satisfied with the appliances provided by your landlord and wish to purchase your own. In recent years, many appliances have been designed with the apartment dweller in mind—that is, they don't take up as much valuable space as those made for general use.

Refrigerators for apartments come in all shapes and sizes. Some are short and squat, made to fit under a cabinet or shelf, while others are tall and skinny so they can be tucked into the narrow space at the end of a kitchen or between two cabinets. Look for a model with a separate freezer door and shelves on the inside of the refrigerator door.

The freezer in your refrigerator may not provide enough space to stock up on meat and other items when they're on sale. Small, compact freezers of four or five cubic feet are available in many shapes and sizes. Some have handsome wood-grain finishes, and can be placed strategically so the top provides extra work space. If you don't have room for a freezer in your apartment kitchen, you may still be able to store frozen food by putting a freezer in a basement storage bin or closet. If you plan to do this, purchase a freezer that has a lock so you won't run the risk of sharing your food with other tenants.

Most small freezers aren't self-defrosting, and they don't always have some of the other advantages of larger models. But they do the job. If you're buying a chest-type freezer, insist on a removable storage basket. It will be much easier for you to get at the food. And make sure any freezer you buy has an adjustable temperature control. Not all small units have these desirable features.

There are clothes washers and dryers made expressly for apartment living, too. Some fit one on top of the other saving floor space. Some units are portable; the washer can be quickly attached to a sink, and the dryer plugs into a standard outlet. There are small stationary units, too, and dryers that must be plugged into a 220 outlet. These dry clothes more rapidly than the others, but if you get used to waiting an extra half hour or so for your clothes to dry, the smaller voltage dryer seems adequate. The apartment dweller who anticipates moving is better off purchasing a washer and dryer that can be plugged into any wall socket. The next place you live may not be equipped with 220 service.

If your apartment doesn't have a dishwasher, consider one of the many portable models. They hook up to the kitchen sink and can be wheeled out of the way when not in use. There are also small countertop dishwashers that sell for well under fifty dollars. However, they don't hold much, and it is time-consuming to load them properly.

The city apartment dweller has a special set of problems, not the least of which is getting groceries from the store to the apartment. Folding wire carts are the remedy. They are not difficult to take up stairs and, folded up, don't take up much room. If you have to walk to a laundromat, one of these carts is a real convenience. Most are large enough to carry several loads of wash or up to four bags of groceries.

As apartment living is getting into full swing, more and more things are being scaled down for our way of living. Apartment life no longer means going without comforts and conveniences, but it does mean thinking small.

Chapter 8

Soundproofing and Noise Control

The former U.S. Surgeon General, Dr. William H. Stewart, said, "Calling noise a nuisance is like calling smog an inconvenience. Noise must be considered a hazard to the health of people everywhere." Being assaulted by noise on all sides may not be as devastating as being physically assaulted. But if you're subjected to it for any length of time, it will affect your health, your nerves, and your disposition. And it has been proven that work efficiency drops markedly when sleep is disturbed by noise. Have you ever tried to do your best at work the day after the neighbors had a noisy party that lasted all night?

Noise is one of the worst problems we apartment dwellers face. In addition to the noise from our own washing machines, stereos, televisions, and parties, all of which are magnified by the lack of spaciousness in most apartments, we are also faced with noise from other apartments. This is especially true if the soundproofing isn't all it should be, and few apartment buildings are 100 percent soundproof.

There are three places at which you can attack the problem: the source of the noise (the offending person or machine); the path it travels (an air duct, an open window, or a corridor); and the receiver (the person it affects). And the noise can be either stopped, blocked, or muffled.

The first thing to do is find the source of the intruding sound. Sometimes the solution is as simple as requesting that someone turn down a television or stereo. People who are new to apartment living often have adjustments to make. Your neighbors may not be aware their noise is bothersome to anyone else.

If this doesn't solve the problem, find out how the noise is reaching you. Once you know this, you may be able to ease the situation considerably by applying weather stripping to a window or by cushioning a piece of duct work.

When noise can't be stopped or blocked, you have to muffle it. This can be done by hanging drapes and adding rugs, or, in extreme cases, by using earplugs.

Noise from Outside Your Apartment

It's unfortunate to have an apartment near a centralized source of noise such as an elevator or a laundry room. You may think you're stuck with the problem and the resulting noise. You may not even know where most of the noise is coming from. But before you give up your peace and quiet, investigate the sources and look for solutions.

Inspect your apartment building or complex and note all the possible sources of the noise which is affecting you. Investigate the machinery. Some machines, for example, may be noisy because they're incorrectly mounted or connected. Vibration is a major cause of noise, and it can be taken care of easily in many instances.

The owner of your building or complex may be quite willing to help you conduct an inspection of this type, particularly if he has had several complaints about noise from other tenants, and if he's convinced that remedying the situation isn't going to be costly to him. For instance, an elevator vibration, which is often a major noise annoyance, generally can be remedied by inserting vibration insulators under the elevator motor. This is a minor repair in terms of cost. Or, the noise from your neighbor's washing machine may be transmitted to your apartment through the duct work in the building. The solution to this might be to have the landlord insulate the duct work that's near each machine, thus absorbing the sound at its source. An appliance may be vibrating near a common wall between your apartment and your neighbor's place. In this case, insulation placed behind the machine should accomplish the desired noise abatement.

If your landlord is not helpful, don't just live in misery until the

One of the worst problems apartment dwellers face is noise pollution. If it is not adequately dealt with, it can affect your health.

lease has expired. Fight! There's strength in numbers. You're being bothered by an elevator, vibrating pipes, or noisy duct work. Chances are, other tenants are being bothered too. Enlist their aid.

The landlord may not be willing to invest a few dollars to fix that noisy elevator just because you complain. But when he's faced with a petition signed by a large group of his tenants, he will probably reconsider and do something to alleviate the situation. His business is renting apartments. And a group of discontented tenants verbalizing their complaints isn't good for that business.

Your group can circulate a petition protesting the noisy conditions and requesting the landlord to rectify them. Or you can encourage the other tenants who are being bothered to write notes to the landlord and include them with their rent payments. Something in writing is always more impressive and should get better results than verbal complaints.

AIRBORNE NOISE

While structureborne noise probably creates a problem common to all tenants, airborne noise, which is generally weaker, may be a nuisance only to those in the immediate area. If that's you, you'll likely have to solve the problem yourself. You could have airborne noise from your neighbor's stereo or television. In a relatively well-constructed building, this will only occur when the room you're in is adjacent to the one containing the offending machine. Rarely does a noise of this sort bother anyone if they are removed from it by one room. So the solution can be as easy as getting your neighbor to house his stereo equipment in another room away from your common wall.

Sound can also carry from apartment to apartment in the flanking paths that occur when an attic area, a crawl space, or even a basement is left open between units. Walls dividing apartments should go all the way from the ground to the roof. In many areas they are required to do so, not for the noise factor involved, but because of the fire regulations in the area.

If the noise that's bothering you is from airplanes or traffic, there's not much you can do to stop it. But you can check your windows to see if they are tightly fitted. If they aren't, caulk them or use weather stripping to block the noise; you can install heavy drapes to absorb some of the sound; You can keep your radio or television going in an effort to drown out the noise; and you can move when your lease is up. Next time, to avoid noise from aircraft, the apartment you select should be at least three to four miles from the nearest large air terminal, and that's only if the apartment building is not in a direct line with the runways. A building that is in this line needs to be fifteen to twenty miles away from the airport to insure that you will not be bothered by aircraft.

If the noise that's making your life miserable comes from a barking dog or from a noisy construction company in the neighborhood, find out if there's a noise ordinance in your city or town. As the world gets smaller and we live closer to each other, the detrimental effects of noise are slowly becoming recognized. An increasing number of areas are passing legislation that deals with noise abatement. In a northeastern city near us, the law now states that a dog is not permitted to bark continuously for more than thirty minutes nor off and on for a period of more than ninety minutes. Residents of this city who have had to deal with barking dogs every night now only need to call the police and the owners of the noisy animals will be ordered to control them. The name of the person who complains is not given to the dog's owner, so there is no fear of reprisal.

If your city or town doesn't have such an ordinance, you can go directly to the dog's owner and ask him to keep the animal quiet. The direct approach often works. People don't always realize that a noise they're accustomed to is offensive to someone else, and they are usually cooperative in doing their part to rectify the situation when they're made aware of it.

To help cut down or eliminate noise coming from outside your apartment, you can try insulating against it. Large bookcases (the ceiling to floor variety are best) filled with books will give your apartment a sophisticated, intellectual look, and act as wonderful noise barriers when placed on the wall through which the noise is coming. A stylish rug or a drape across an entire wall can also serve to deaden sound while adding an artistic touch. These measures will absorb about 25 percent of the sound. So they can't really be considered acoustical. A product must be 50 percent sound absorbing to legitimately have this rating.

Acoustical paneling is a more drastic approach to the problem that you may want to take if you like your apartment well enough to make the investment. Some panels are truly good looking, and their use can make for a handsome room. Acoustical paneling comes with ratings of from 50 percent to 85 percent. Cork panels add a warm touch while aiding in the control of sound. Panels of gypsum board ½ inch thick installed over a wall are cheaper, though not as effective in combating the noise. (The price goes up along with the percentage of noise a panel will absorb.) Armstrong makes an excellent panel called Soundsoak in an array of colors. Though this paneling was originally designed for use in offices and public buildings, there's no reason it can't be installed in an apartment. It comes in two grades or sound absorption ratings (60 and 85). Since it's made of fiberboard, you can attach pictures and other wall hangings. It's easy to clean and flame retardant.

Noise also may be sneaking into your apartment through or around the door. A hollow core or an extremely thin door can be made more sound resistant by applying a piece of plywood about 1/4 inch thick. This need not be unsightly. You can paint it, varnish it, or stain it the color of the door you're covering. Your door should also be weather-stripped if it isn't fitting tightly. This will help keep out hall noise.

Noise from Your Own Apartment

There are many reasons why noise originating within your own apartment may be bothersome. The limited amount of space found in most apartments is a major one. And, as modern technology equips us with more and more appliances, their noisy presence invades almost every area of an apartment. Many apartments are shy on inside doors and room dividers. Often the living room and dining room are one and separated from the kitchen by only a partial partition. Bedrooms usually share common walls.

The installation of a couple of doors in your apartment can greatly alleviate a noisy situation. A kitchen door is the most important. This can make a tremendous contribution to peace and quiet. And a door on the hall leading from the general living area to the bedrooms will help, too, especially if some of the family are up while others are trying to sleep. Solid doors are best. But folding doors, which are less costly and easier to install, will also serve the purpose.

The doors in your apartment should fit snugly to keep noise in the room where it's originating. But don't put weather stripping on, or in any other way block, the bottoms of doors within your apartment if there's only one central air return for your heater or air conditioner. That gap at the door bottom is there intentionally to permit the proper flow of air. If you eliminate it, you'll raise havoc with the heating system.

NOISY APPLIANCES

When you're selecting appliances for your apartment, there are several things to look for that will insure the maximum in noise-free living. For instance, when you're buying a fan, or any appliance with a fan-type operation, bear in mind that the slower an appliance runs the quieter it usually is. Speed, not size, makes noise. A large, slow-revolving fan is quieter than a small one that moves rapidly, and it is usually as effective, or even more so.

Some appliances come with a low-noise certification. Look for this when you're shopping. But don't be misled by the use of coined names like "comfy quiet" or "soothing silent." They are just names, not guarantees that the machines are any quieter than their competitors. Look for an actual certification.

Although there isn't a great deal of noise-tested machinery on the market as yet, some does have this low-noise certification. The machine should be accompanied by a copy of the certifying laboratory's test report. These noise-tested appliances generally are advertised as being "Acoustically Tested," "Sound Conditioned," or as having "Quiet Operation." As noise becomes an ever-increasing problem, more and more manufacturers are striving for quieter appliances. Perhaps sometime in the near future, noise testing will become standard practice.

If you don't have central air conditioning and are supplying your own window units to see you through the hot summer, select carefully. Be sure the unit you buy has sufficient power to cool the area you want it for. An air conditioner straining to do a job for which it was never intended is going to be a noisy as well as inefficient air conditioner. If possible, get one with a large-diameter, squirrel-cage, belt-driven fan. This is also the best kind of fan to have over your kitchen stove, but you will probably not be selecting that.

Although it's really a joyless task, you should clean the filter in a window air conditioner once a week during the hot months. The filter can get full of dust, and this may cause the condensate to freeze on the expander tubing thus restricting the air flow and causing a whistling sound.

Before you buy, insist on a demonstration in the showroom. Compare the air conditioner, fan, or whatever appliance you're considering, with competitive products to evaluate the differences in noise levels.

Because of the space problem in most apartments, the noise from the appliances, even if they are low-noise certified, is difficult to escape. Your dishwasher may make it difficult to hear the television. An obvious solution is to run the dishwasher when nobody is watching television, or when you're going to work. Always make sure the dishwasher is loaded correctly. A dishwasher full of dishes which have been loaded in a haphazard manner is going to make more noise than one that's properly filled. Pot covers clanging against the sides or door of the washer make a noisy beat.

Any unbalanced piece of machinery will cause an enormous amount of vibration. A clothes dryer is a classic example. When it is incorrectly loaded or when the load shifts, the machine becomes unbalanced and sounds like a cement mixer. When the load is evenly distributed, the dryer will operate reasonably quietly.

The same principle applies to an air conditioner fan. In fact, any machine that vibrates (and they all do to some extent) will make a great racket in your apartment because the vibrating motion from the motor causes a structureborne noise when it strikes the walls, floor, and other surfaces surrounding it. The structureborne sound then hits space around it, and it is transmitted as airborne sound. The solution is to cushion the vibrating machine with rubber or cork padding.

Put the legs of refrigerators, washing machines, dryers or other machines on rubber padding. Put padding behind the machines. Adjust the legs to balance the appliances. Most appliances have legs that will screw up or down. Be sure your appliances have no loose screws or panels. If you do find any, tighten them. If the joints don't fit together snugly, caulk them.

Any appliance that has a loose-fitting lid or cover is going to rattle and provide leaks for noise. Such lids should be fitted (or refitted) with rubber gaskets. These will absorb some of the sound from a washing machine agitator, or a spinning drum of a dryer. Plain strips of rubber can be used instead of a conventional gasket.

If your washer and dryer are still noisy, apply a layer of fireproof damping material (a material that will absorb sound) to the inside of the cabinet. BE SURE TO UNPLUG THE APPLIANCE FIRST! Glue the material you have selected to the inside of the cabinet. To be effective, the damping material should be two to three times as thick as the cabinet so it will absorb the maximum amount of vibrational noise.

You may not want to spend the money for a large amount of damping material. In this case, do a "finger test" on your appliances when they are running. To do this, lightly run your fingers over all the outside surfaces of the appliances. Lightly mark each area where you feel vibration, and when the machine has stopped and you have unplugged it, glue damping material just to these spots.

Heaters and air conditioners are big noise offenders in apartments. Sometimes this is inherent to the system and must be lived with. But in other instances, the fault lies with an unbalanced blade. To find out if this is the problem with your system, TURN OFF the system and spin the fan by hand. When the fan stops, mark the blade that's at the bottom. Spin the fan several more times. If the marked blade consistently ends up at the bottom, your fan isn't balanced. To remedy this, attach strips of adhesive tape to the blade which is opposite the one you have marked. Spin the fan a few more times. If it still isn't balanced, add more tape (or take off a little) until it is. If the noise is still too much for you, reduce the speed of the blowers if possible. Keep the blades clean, and they will operate more efficiently and with less sound.

Duct work within your apartment can cause a lot of vibrational noise. You can cut down on this annoyance by installing sound-absorbing lining material in the duct work. If the problem is with a heater, this material should be installed in both the supply and return branches of the ducts, close to the open or grille end. You should line each piece of duct work for a distance of ten feet, if that's possible. This easy step should reduce the noise from this source considerably. If the material is installed correctly, you could get a 50 percent reduction in sound. And that's well worth the trouble.

THE KITCHEN

Noisiest room in the apartment, the average kitchen can register noise readings above 100 decibels, which is considered deafening. Yes, deafening! Prolonged exposure to sounds in the 100 to 140 decibel range can impair hearing. In well-planned apartment buildings where cost is secondary to comfort, kitchens don't share common walls with other kitchens. However, since plumbing installation is easier and cheaper, back-to-back kitchens are common.

You can minimize cabinet noise—your own and the noise from next door—by installing a cork tile or soft rubber padding on the backs and shelves of all your kitchen cabinets. This helps mute the crash of dishes, canned goods, and utensils on shelves and lessens the rattle when appliances cause dishes to vibrate. Glue small rubber or felt pieces on the inside tops and bottoms of cabinet doors so that they won't make a jarring sound when you close them.

The cabinet under the kitchen sink, which houses piping, is a source of reverberating sound. To keep this noise from spreading throughout the apartment, install acoustical tiles on the inside walls.

If you use a counter-top dish drainer, place it on a rubber pad to absorb the sound of clattering dishes.

You can do a lot to reduce the sounds made by your appliances. If your refrigerator requires defrosting, do it regularly. An ice-laden refrigerator has to run longer and harder than one free of ice buildup. The harder the motor works, the noisier it runs. Vacuum the dust from the coils on the back of your refrigerator at regular intervals, too. Dirt buildup also makes the motor work overtime.

While you don't usually run a garbage disposal for any length of time, it sure is noisy when it is running. Installing a sleeve-type gasket of soft rubber between the sink and the mounting flange helps to reduce noisy vibrations.

None of your appliances, large of small, should be touching a wall when in operation. They'll make the wall vibrate causing structural noise. When you're going to run a small appliance, move it at least two inches from the wall before you turn it on. If possible, position your refrigerator and other large appliances at least two inches from the wall.

The kitchen plays its own discordant symphony against its many hard surfaces. Few kitchens have the softness that drapes or upholstered furniture provided in other rooms, although some newer kitchens come with carpeting. You might consider laying carpet squares. Not only do they alleviate the sound problem, they are immeasurable comfort to tired feet. There's definitely a difference between standing on carpeting and standing on even the best cushioned tile. If you don't want to undertake the expense of carpeting, try placing small rugs at the work areas where you spend the most time—in front of the sink, the stove, and the counter where you prepare meals.

You may think that living in an apartment automatically precludes an acoustical ceiling unless provided by the landlord. But they are neither very expensive nor hard to install, and a good one can absorb

55 to 75 percent of the kitchen noise that you and your appliances bounce against it. The panel form is a little easier to install than the individual squares. The denser or thicker the material, the more noise resistant. The best acoustical ceilings are made of mineral fiber, wood fiber, or a blend of natural and man-made fibers. Fiber glass is a poor choice because of the porosity of the material, but it is still a big improvement over regular hard ceilings. Surprisingly, you can install a good acoustical ceiling in a large kitchen for well under a hundred dollars.

BANG, BANG, BANG GOES THE PLUMBING

There are simple ways of eliminating a number of the causes of plumbing noise.

Although many faucets installed today don't have the rubber type washer that requires changing from time to time, there are still a number of older systems in operation that require new washers frequently. When a faucet drips, chatters, or seems to be singing songs, the washer is likely to be the culprit.

If the faucet has defective parts, you will notice that the noise it gives off decreases when the faucet is turned on full force, and increases when you turn the water flow down lower. This is commonly the result of a worn valve stem.

A faucet that's dripping in the middle of the night can drive you mad. You may not want to get up and start tearing the plumbing apart at that hour even if you have the proper replacement part. There is another solution. Attach a string to the faucet, running the other end down the drain. The water will follow the string silently, allowing you to finish your night's sleep. When the drip is more of a trickle and the string won't do the trick, try doing the same thing with a washcloth.

Water pressure that's been set too high will cause a great jangling and chattering of pipes. Thirty-five pounds per square inch is the maximum for an apartment's water system, and the flow velocity shouldn't exceed 6 feet per second. Fast-moving water is not only noisy, it's destructive to the plumbing. The noise it makes is called "water hammer." If you suspect that the water pressure in your apartment is set higher than it should be, advise your landlord that you want an adjustment made. If he is not willing to take care of it, either call a plumber to do it for you, or install a shock absorber called "Mini-Trol Water Hammer Arrestor." This baseball-sized device has a flexible diaphragm that compresses a sealed air cushion and absorbs the shock from water that's moving too fast. It's easily installed and costs under fifteen dollars complete with brass T-fitting.

PADDING THE BATHROOM

Next to the kitchen, the bathroom is the noisiest room in an apartment because of all the tile, which reflects noise. Pad it as much as possible. Hang luxuriously thick absorbent towels. If you have a window, use a soft, plushy material for curtains rather than a harsh plastic. Put a lush pile rug on the floor.

Medicine cabinets frequently are mounted back to back within a common wall between bathrooms in adjoining apartments or between bathrooms within the same apartment. This creates a channel through which noise can travel easily. The remedy is not difficult. Remove the cabinet. Then caulk the area around the back of the medicine cabinet of the other bathroom. If there is enough space (you only need ¼ inch or so), insert a piece of plywood or gypsum board. Then replace your medicine cabinet, caulking around its outer edges.

Ceiling exhaust fans, which in many places are required by law to be installed in bathrooms without any windows, can make a fearsome noise. There are several ways to reduce the sound. Sometimes it's possible to mount the fan on rubber grommets which will keep it away from the duct work. When this isn't feasible, insert a soft, sponge rubber gasket between the ceiling and the grille. As with all appliances, the ceiling fan will run more quietly when it's set on low speed than it will when set on high. Unfortunately, you don't always have a choice of speeds with these fans. Of course, keeping the fan clean is also important to good, quiet performance.

MUSIC—MUSIC—MUSIC

Music is said to soothe the savage beast, but in an apartment setting it can turn a peace-loving person into a savage beast. People like to listen to different kinds of music at different times of day. And in an apartment you have to cope with your next door neighbor's musical preferences as well as those of your own apartment mates.

The first rule is: never place a stereo or television against a wall to another apartment. Frequently, noise from the vibration of a stereo set makes the sound problem worse than it needs to be. Don't mount your speakers rigidly into an enclosure. Pad them so that when they vibrate, they won't shake the whole wall or the cabinet in which they're set. Use earphones. If you're concerned your children may set the volume too high, have an attenuation pad inserted into the earphone outlet. It governs the volume of sound that goes through the earphones, and you can have it set at a level that you know is safe. Most amplifiers and many television sets have earphone jacks.

This type of earphone allows you to play your stereo at any volume that suits you without bothering your neighbors. But be careful: if the sound is too loud, it can damage your hearing.

A television set can create a special noise problem. There's a pulse transformer in the back that may cause the set to emit a high-pitched noise. If this persists, installing a square of acoustical tile on the wall directly behind the set will probably eliminate the problem or reduce it significantly.

FLOORS THAT SQUEAK AND MOAN

Anyone who has ever tried to tip-toe into an apartment quietly at night is aware of how noisy a squeaking floor can be. Many wooden floors actually groan when they're walked on. This can be a major project to correct if it entails taking up the floor boards to get at the subflooring. More often it's a minor repair that any tenant can make without even checking with the landlord.

All you need is a flashlight and a helper. Ask the other person to walk slowly over the floor in the area from which you think the noise is coming. Holding the flashlight's beam on the surface of the floor examine it closely as your helper walks over it. You probably will be able to see the floor moving. This will pinpoint the problem spot. The movement may be due to a slippage between the tongues and grooves of the flooring, which allows them to rub on each other. The solution is usually a simple one. Work either mineral oil or Vaseline in between the floorboards. Apply the lubricant with a light touch. It doesn't take a lot to quiet a squeaking floor, and you don't want to create an oily mess.

SMALL NOISES

A lot of small noises add up to a big noise, so here are a few improvements worth making. Telephones placed on rubber or cork padding don't ring as shrilly as those placed on a wooden surface. Wall-mounted phones are much noisier than the desk type. But if you do opt for a wall-mounted phone, don't have it placed on a wall which you share with the next apartment. Of course, modern phones have a volume control that you can set at the level most suitable to you and your family.

Select alarm clocks that chime or make music rather than those that have ear-splitting bells. The sound from these, too, will be softened if they're placed on padding rather than on the hard surface of your dresser or night table.

Light switches can be a noise nuisance if they're turned on or off in the dead of night when people are sleeping. These switches are easily replaced, given any but the most antiquated wiring, by silent mercury switches. If you're not familiar with electrical wiring, have an electrician or the maintenance man in your apartment building do this. If you attempt it yourself, TURN OFF THE POWER FIRST!

Electrical outlets are little areas where big noises can sneak in. When they are installed back to back with your neighbor's electrical outlets, as is so often the case, you have the potential for a real noise problem. But it can be handled. AFTER TURNING OFF THE ELECTRICITY, remove the cover plate from the outlet. Then remove your outlet box. Insert fiber glass wadding around the outlet on your neighbor's side of the wall. Then put a piece of lead sheeting, 1 mm thick, against this wadding. This will form an airtight barrier. Put the box back in place, filling any obvious leaks with fiber glass. Then caulk around the edges before replacing the cover plate. It's surprising how much this can help to make an apartment sound resistant.

All buildings settle. This results in cracking of the walls, usually around the areas where the ceilings and walls join. Use a caulking gun to seal these noise inviting crevices. To do a thorough job, remove the baseboards and caulk where the floor joins the walls, too.

A rattling window on a windy night can be mighty spooky. If your apartment has this problem, examine the putty in the windows to see if it's intact or broken. If there's a break, apply new putty or ask your landlord to do so. The entire window frame may be loose. To eliminate this problem, install weather stripping.

Sound Absorption

A brick building, a weather-stripped window, or a clump of trees will block an offending noise, but won't absorb it, while soft porous materials will absorb but won't block noise.

In a small room with no sound absorbing material, any noise you hear has actually been amplified. Each absorbent item you add diminishes reverberations. A thick carpet, with a good padding under it, will absorb up to 50 percent of the airborne noise in a room. The noise gets into the fibers and is battered back and forth until it's spent. The more fibers you have, the more sound is dissipated. If the noise that's bothering you comes from the apartment that's immediately over yours, padding your room isn't going to help a great deal. But perhaps you, or the landlord, can persuade that upstairs neighbor to install good padded carpeting on his floors.

Closets provide insulation from noise because clothing is sound-absorbing. If your closet shares a common wall, you can further reduce sound by nailing empty Styrofoam egg cartons on the closet walls.

How do you know whether you've achieved a good level of sound absorption in your apartment? Follow the rule used by experts in the field of sound: If you can hear the lingering sound of a handclap or shout for more than two seconds, your room needs further work. Add more upholstered furniture, a thicker rug, another drape, liners for existing drapes, or a porous wall-hanging. Or, you can even hang some sound-absorbing material in the upper corners of a noisy room where the walls meet the ceiling. Any acoustical material will give maximum benefits when there. You can either use the least conspicuous materials available, or you can make them a part of your decor. Squares of carpeting placed in the corners will make the room design more original, while an acoustical tiling painted the color of the walls will be unobtrusive.

When all else fails, you can try inserting your own sounds in the hope they'll cover up the noises you find offensive. This is known as "acoustical perfume." (Unfortunately, this method meets with failure more often than with success.)

Background music might block out a sound you find offensive, such as your neighbor's rock concert. But the catch is that if your noise is loud enough to block an offensive sound, it's no longer "background." Instead of being the offended party, you may become the offending party.

An absolute last resort is ear plugs. I'd rather move than have to wear them. But if you sleep during the day, or if you're in an apartment with a binding lease, you may find their use necessary. These plugs can reduce the noise by as much as 35 decibels. It's best to have them fitted by an ear specialist so that you will get the type suited for you, and will have maximum comfort. Some are made of hard rubber, some of pliable wax (which molds itself to the configuration of your ear when it gets warm), and others are tampon shaped. Large earmuffs made of an acoustical material are also available.

Remember, these devices that block out noise you don't want to hear, also block out noise you do want to hear. You may not hear your doorbell chime, your phone ring, or your baby cry. Do try everything else first!

Chapter 9

Being Safe

Not many people can enjoy their homes, whether they live in apartments or houses, if they can't feel safe—safe from burglaries, safe from robberies, and safe from fires. With crime on the rise, and with examples of these dangers facing us every time we unfold a newspaper, feeling safe isn't always that simple.

To apartment dwellers, being safe presents a special set of problems. We have common halls and elevators; our apartment doors aren't always as strong as we would like them to be; maybe we feel uneasy about the fellow in the next apartment who drinks too much and may smoke in bed. But there are steps we can take to protect ourselves and our apartment homes—steps that will help us to feel, if not totally safe, at least a good deal safer.

Foiling the Burglar

Burglars are nervous while plying their chosen trade. They don't linger any longer than they have to, and the apartment that is hardest to break into is apt to be the one that goes untouched. Statistics show that most burglars will abandon a break-in and seek easier prey if they can't get in within four minutes.

DOORS

The favorite entry point for burglars is a door. In fact, a U.S. Department of Justice study claims that more than 63 percent of home burglaries are committed by thieves who enter through doors. If you're going to protect your apartment, the door is the best place to start. In many high-rise apartments, the door is the only possible entrance or exit for a burglar or anyone else. This simplifies your protection plan and reduces your worries.

A strong, solid, well-fitting door with hinges on the inside is not very inviting to the average burglar. But a door with outside hinges from which the pins are easily removed, or a door frame that has rotted and is easily broken away makes a burglar's work easy. The door to your apartment should fit its frame tightly to make it difficult to impossible for the would-be culprit to slide tools in between the door and its frame.

If your door doesn't fit snugly and you have a penurious landlord who is not willing to replace it, mount an angle iron around the bolt on the door frame so that the intruder can't insert a tool into the existing space.

LOCKS

While it is true that your apartment is more secure if it has a solid rather than a thin hollow, door, I disagree with those who say that a lock is only as good as the door that it's on. If you are unable to replace an inadequate apartment door, it is still worthwhile to install a good solid lock. In truth, while most burglars will attempt to jimmy a lock, only a few will knock down a door, especially one in an apartment building where another tenant is apt to see or hear them. And, while you may not be able to convince your landlord that he should replace the door to your apartment, you can replace or supplement the lock yourself. If the lock isn't a double one and doesn't have a deadlock bolt, replace it. Any locks that you install should have at least a one-inch bolt and be installed with nonstrippable, one-way screws to be effective.

Even if the existing locks seem adequate, it's wise to change them as soon as you take possession of your apartment. If you're moving belongings in before moving day, be sure the locks are changed first. You have no way of knowing how many keys were dispersed and to how many people during prior tenancies. While the former tenants themselves may be completely trustworthy, they may have given a key to someone who is not quite so honorable. How easy it would be for a robber to simply unlock the door (especially before you move in and are known to the neighbors) and make off with your possessions. This can happen when a key is given to a repairman, or left with your car when it is being fixed. It's easy to have a duplicate made. Some repairmen sell them although they would not think of being part of an actual burglary. When it comes to handing out the key to your new locks be extremely selective. An automobile mechanic needs only the keys to the car, not your whole set. The repairman can be let in by a neighbor or the maintenance man.

BACKUP LOCKS

Drop bolt locks are locks that grab the door frame. These are not primary locking systems, but they are excellent backups. Originally made exclusively by Segal, they're now being manufactured by other leaders in the field, such as Yale and Ilco. Some experts advise using duplicate cylinders on primary and backup locking cylinders. While this does have the advantage of requiring only one key, this can quickly become a disadvantage. There's a certain security in having different locks and knowing that no one else has both keys. On a day when you expect someone to repair something, you can lock only one lock and give that key to your manager or whoever is going to let in the repairman.

Chain locks are considered useless by most people. While I prefer a peephole (which can be installed in most doors), a properly installed chain lock is certainly better than nothing. It allows you a bit of time before a stranger can push his way in, and it may make it impossible for him to get in at all. Install your chain lock so that the door doesn't open more than a crack with the chain in place, and chances are you will be able to close it again if the person on the other side is unwelcome. Don't install a chain lock that leaves enough room for someone to get a foot in the door or slide an object in between the door and the jamb. Chain locks are useless, however, against burglars who are intent on breaking into your apartment during your absence. Although some of these locks do lock with a key, they are easily broken or cut.

The successful modern burglar has several methods of entering an apartment through the door. "Jamb peeling" is one of them. This method entails tearing away the frame of an outswinging door with a crowbar, leaving no material around the lock to protect it. A steel-reinforced strike plate installed in the hollow jamb should stop the thief from going any further with this operation after he has ripped out the frame.

Standard lock cylinders are made of brass, which is a soft metal. This makes it relatively easy to strip the threads. These standard cylinders generally offer a sturdy shoulder piece on which to pry. But there are cylinder guards available to protect most brass cylinders. This two-piece guard does double duty. Since the outer ring is beveled, case-hardened, and free to swivel, there is no place for a tool to grip. Should a burglar be successful in breaking the stile by bashing it in, he still will be thwarted because he now must pull the entire inner flange through a round hole. This is virtually impossible to do with the portable tools upon which he must rely.

Brass cylinders can be melted easily with small, compact torches that are in vogue with the more professional thief. Since these torches are used by the home hobbiest, they are readily available, with no suspicious glances cast at the buyer. If you're lucky enough to have an apartment that locks with a sunken lock, you can protect it against torching by installing an inexpensive carbon steel plate. While a thief may still succeed in melting the cylinder, he will be unable to extract the lock through the small hole in the plate.

Glass patio doors have been a boon to the burglary business since they have become so popular with apartment dwellers. While these sliding glass doors add light to a dreary apartment, they also increase the chance that the apartment will be burglarized because they generally have extremely narrow stiles or frames. The locks are quite easy to melt or break since they can't have long or thick bolts. Some of these locks aren't even key operated.

However, there are now locks on the market that will work on these doors and are rated MS (maximum security). Adams Rite, markets one they claim is "designed specifically for narrow-stile glass entrance doors." Because the bolt is housed vertically when retracted, its length is not restricted by the narrow width of the door stile. When locked, the laminated steel bolt swings upward into a horizontal position, and much of the 3-inch bolt is retained in the opposite door jamb. This pivotal feature allows the bolt to be in two places at one time. The company boasts that "a burglar using a hammer and bar to knock the bolt down will only succeed in locking it more tightly." This lock is generally put in doors before they're installed. It is available from locksmiths, but it requires professional installation. Since the bolt is made of 5-ply laminated steel, even tungsten-carbide hacksaw blades are ineffective against it.

WINDOWS

A burglar who can't get into your apartment through a door may try a window. Breaking glass is too noisy for the average burglar, and he will usually only chance that shattering sound if the place he wants to get into is in a secluded area (not too likely with an apartment); if there's something inside that he wants badly, which he will be unable to get at the next apartment; or if the neighborhood is such that he feels confident no one will interfere.

Those who live in a basement or first floor apartment in a high-crime area may want to replace the ordinary window glass with stronger glass. A triple-layer windowpane, made by the Amerada Glass Company, has two layers of strong glass with a sandwich filling of an extremely durable vinyl. It takes a determined person to break through these three layers and most won't even try. Windowpanes can also be made of Lexan. Although it is plastic, Lexan is scratch and mar-resistant. Both these alternatives will cost you about three times what a regular piece of window glass of comparable size would cost, but they're worth the expense if it means being able to sleep at night.

Window locks are the best method of preventing thieves from entering. However, the standard lock that comes on most double-hung apartment windows is worthless. In a matter of minutes, any thief with the appropriate tool, often only a screwdriver, can insert the tool between the windowsill and the lower window, and, using the windowsill as a fulcrum, force the window up so that the screws securing the lock are stripped and come out of the window sash. Knowing this, many people have tried to make their apartment windows burglarproof by installing one of the many new window locks now on the market. *Consumer Reports* (March, 1979) did an extensive study of these, and they all came up wanting. Whether pin-type, wedge-type ventilating, stop-type ventilating, friction-type, or key-operated cam latch devices, they can all be broken into with relative ease—some as easily as the conventional window locks.

However, in a series of other tests with a variety of homemade devices, *Consumer Reports* found that a window can be made less vulnerable by drilling holes from the inside of the sash three-quarters of the way through to the outside. These holes should slant downward just slightly. Into the holes, insert eyebolts which are about 5/16 inch in diameter. The bolts, of course, should fit snugly in the holes. More than one set of holes can be made on the inside sash so that you can lock the window in an open as well as closed position.

If you have sliding windows, shut the window and place a strong, wooden stick in the track on which the window rides. Then, so that an unwelcome visitor can't get in by jumping the window over the stick, insert two screws into the window track just over the end of the stick. Turn these screws until the heads are close enough to the track that when the stick isn't in the track, you can open the window just clearing the screws. This method can also be used with sliding glass doors, but it's still wise to have good locks on them, too.

A casement window can be made safer too. If you have this type of window, you should replace the simple pull latches because they are a cinch to break open. Their substitutes should be the type that must be turned in two directions before allowing the window to open. These are easily and inexpensively obtained at most hardware stores, and they are simple to install. Most will screw right into the holes left by the pull latch you've removed.

If you're in a high-crime area, you may want to protect your basement or first-floor apartment windows with grilles. These admittedly are not too handsome, although some companies offer them in a choice of colors. But if you work and are only home during the night, you can cover the grilles with draw drapes and feel cozy as well as safe. Grilles can be a danger in case of fire because most are secured with key-operated locks. You should never have a grille on your only exit point.

BURGLAR ALARMS

Since the crime rate has risen so dramatically and home protection has become big business, the home burglar alarm has jumped in popularity. You can get a very simple device or a super-sophisticated system. Some alarms are so elementary that you can carry one with you and install it on a door wherever you happen to

Window grilles may be necessary to your peace of mind, if your apartment is on a lower floor in a high-crime area.

be. And there are systems so elaborate they will turn on your appliances, allow you to monitor all entry points from one position, and let you know if there's a fire.

The trouble with many elaborate systems is that they're expensive, often over-sensitive, and usually difficult to install. If you get all possible attachments, and protect all available entry points with some of these systems, you may find the cost of the protection is more than the value of the things you're protecting.

There's a good possibility that when the alarm goes off no one will do anything about it unless you're home. After the first few times an overly-sensitive alarm goes off when nothing is wrong, your neighbors will probably ignore the noise. And if you're having a bona fide burglary, they're apt to say, "Oh, that's only so-and-so's alarm system, it goes off all the time." The noise may even serve to cover up the sounds of the burglary in progress.

Because of these drawbacks, I'm against making the large investment in a sophisticated security system. But a less costly system may provide some peace of mind.

Radio Shack markets a small 4½″ × 2¾″ × 2″ alarm which hangs on a doorknob. You can adjust the amount of movement it takes to activate the alarm which gives off a shrill sound, over 110 decibels, which lasts one minute. This battery-operated device can be hung on the door of your apartment at night and will detect any attempt to turn your doorknob. Besides warning you, it should scare away a burglar before he even gets started. It costs under $30.

A wedge-shaped doorstop siren alarm is available for under $10. However, this doesn't sound until the door has actually been opened. As it opens it pushes the face plate of the alarm, thus activating it, and it continues to sound until it is shut off.

Sunbeam makes a cylindrical alarm that can be screwed to the bottom of the door. It will sound a piercing 90 decibel alarm when the door is opened. You can deactivate it by simply swinging it up into a nonoperating position during the day. This alarm sells for around $10. There are many other simple alarm systems which can be purchased at $10 to $50.

U.S. Department of Justice figures show that in over 90 percent of all burglaries the point of entry is on the first floor or in the basement. If your apartment is on the second floor or above, you're probably safe protecting just the entrance doors with alarms. But if you live below the second floor, you may want an alarm system for your windows. For $90 to about $185 you can purchase a system that will sound an alarm if an attempt to burglarize your apartment is in progress from any point of entry. Some of these systems operate on batteries and some of them connect with your electrical current. Panic buttons that allow the occupant to sound an alarm by pushing a button, antitamper switches that make it impossible for a would-be

Ultrasonic alarm systems are *not* a good choice for pet owners. The sound waves will hurt an animal's sensitive ears, even though the alarm is *not* sounding.

thief to deactivate an alarm, and pull-traps that consist of an almost invisible wire that activates the alarm when disturbed are features of many of these alarm systems.

If you want a substantial system that will detect an intruder once he has entered your apartment, I would opt for an ultrasonic detector that operates when plugged into any electric outlet. These sell in the $75 to $175 range for the basic unit, but the alarm system generally must be purchased separately. General Electric makes an ultrasonic system called Zonar Intrusion Alarm. It is battery-operated and is supposed to monitor an area 30 feet in front of it. The alarm sounds for a full four minutes before turning off. This small (only 7″ × 4″) alarm can be set to go off immediately when the beam is broken, or you can use its ten-second delaying timer so you have a chance to turn it off if you're the one who has walked through the beam.

If you have pets, or if anyone in your family has extra-sensitive hearing, the ultrasonic alarm systems may not work for you. They operate with sound waves that, when interrupted, trigger the alarms. These waves can be acutely bothersome to animals or the few people who can detect them. There are microwave units that do the same job, although they cost a bit more. The microwave units also have the advantage of penetrating walls, so one unit can monitor more than one room.

A less expensive means of being alerted to the presence of an intruder is the use of pressure-sensitive mats. These fit under rugs and cost about $25. You can place one under the mat at your door, if you don't mind the noise whenever someone enters or exits, and place others under throw rugs by your windows. I like these mats because you can cut them to size without hurting the alarm system.

Of course, any alarm system you purchase should bear the Underwriters Laboratories (UL) tag. And no burglar alarm should be entirely relied upon. Not one of them makes your apartment 100 percent safe, only safer than it would be without one. It doesn't catch the thief—it only warns you of his presence, and may scare him off.

COMMON SENSE PROTECTION

There are a number of ways to lessen the chances that your apartment will be the successful target of a burglar without resorting to alarms. Many of these measures involve just the use of common sense.

Most home entries occur when the resident is away. Unless the intruder is intent on doing bodily harm, it stands to reason that he will prefer entering a home with nobody in it. The real pro will have cased an apartment, watching it for some length of time to ascertain the habits of the occupants. Your job is to fool him into thinking you're home when you're not.

Automatic timers are a big help in accomplishing this deception. But it doesn't do to only have one light turned on by a timer at five o'clock every night. Even a not-too-clever criminal can figure that out in a short time. Ideally, you should have several timers and put them into operation on different nights. For instance, on Monday night when you're out, have a timer on the living room light by the window set for five o'clock. On the same night have the bedroom light set to go on at six o'clock. If you're out the next night, have a timer on the light in the den set for five o'clock and have another timer turn on the radio, the one near the door, at about five thirty. I recommend having four timers in an average-sized apartment and rotating them to confuse anyone who may be watching.

Don't leave all your window shades down when you're away from home unless it's your habit to have them all down when you're home. You should strive to make the outside appearance of your apartment the same whether you're in or out.

Be circumspect about what you discuss in public places, such as on the bus, in the market, or even in the laundry room of your apartment building. Excitedly telling a neighbor or friend that you're going to be out of town for a week or week-end might be overheard by someone listening for just that sort of information.

If you're going to be out of town, either cancel delivery of your mail and paper, or, if you don't know your paper or mail person well enough to trust them, ask a neighbor whom you do trust to take your mail and paper in for you.

When you're going to leave your apartment briefly and want to leave a message for a friend or workman, think twice. A note pinned to your door is a sure giveaway that you're not in. What it says may also suggest how long you'll be gone so the burglar knows whether he must hurry or can take his time.

Gala social events such as wedding or anniversary parties, as well as other events such as funerals are often announced in the local papers. Many professional burglars are avid followers of the society and obituary pages, using these listings to select their victims. They not only find out when an apartment will be empty but can pretty well guess how long the occupants will be gone. The wisest thing to do when attending functions that have been announced in the paper, especially if you are mentioned, is to hire an apartment sitter for the occasion. That person should make his presence known by rolling shades up and down and doing other visible things. Remember, the professional burglar wants no surprises. He's out to make money, not to assault people.

The thing that may make your apartment most vulnerable is you! Many people who live in apartments leave them, if only briefly, to get the mail or run to the laundry room or the corner grocery store without locking up. That's a treat for the would-be thief who may be lurking in a corridor waiting for someone to make this common mistake. Don't just lock your door when you're leaving—double-lock it. Even though you're planning to be back in five minutes, lock it just as you would if you were going to be away for a week. One experiment done in Pittsburgh uncovered the fact that 19 of 60 apartment doors tried by the police in one apartment building were found to be unlocked. And this was in an area where there had been several recent burglaries.

MAKE YOUR APARTMENT A POOR TARGET

Identifax, a simple marking system, is proving to be a deterrent to the professional thief. He's in the business of selling what he steals, and he wants merchandise that's going to be untraceable. With an easy-to-use tool, which can often be borrowed from a local authority, you engrave numbers on valuable items such as stereos, television sets, and cameras.

Identifax started in the late sixties in a high-crime area in California. Out of a possible 11,000 families, 5,000 joined the program, and the results were startling. These 5,000 families engraved their valued possessions with numbers based on their telephone numbers and driver's licenses. The numbers were recorded by the local police. Each residence using the system prominently displayed a sticker announcing that the valuables within were so marked and registered. During the following ten years, the 5,000 families who were in the program reported a total of 20 burglaries. The remaining 6,000 families, reported over 2,000 burglaries.

This experiment impressed the nation's law enforcement agencies so much that the program was initiated on a nationwide basis. Now

Identifax numbers are registered in a national computer bank which is on call 24 hours a day and takes only a few seconds to check.

The knowledgeable burglar knows about the system and generally will not enter an apartment displaying the Identifax sticker on a door or window. If caught with marked goods, he has no chance of conning a policeman into thinking that the items really aren't stolen. And a fence won't touch these marked goods.

Your local police department can provide you with the information needed to join this program. (In some towns the program is not called Identifax; the sticker shown here is for our local program.) In some areas the police will supply you with the necessary engraving pencils or pens as well as the stickers and will even send in your Identifax numbers for you. In other places you will have to send for the equipment yourself, sometimes paying a nominal fee. Whichever way it works, Identifax is one of the best methods of

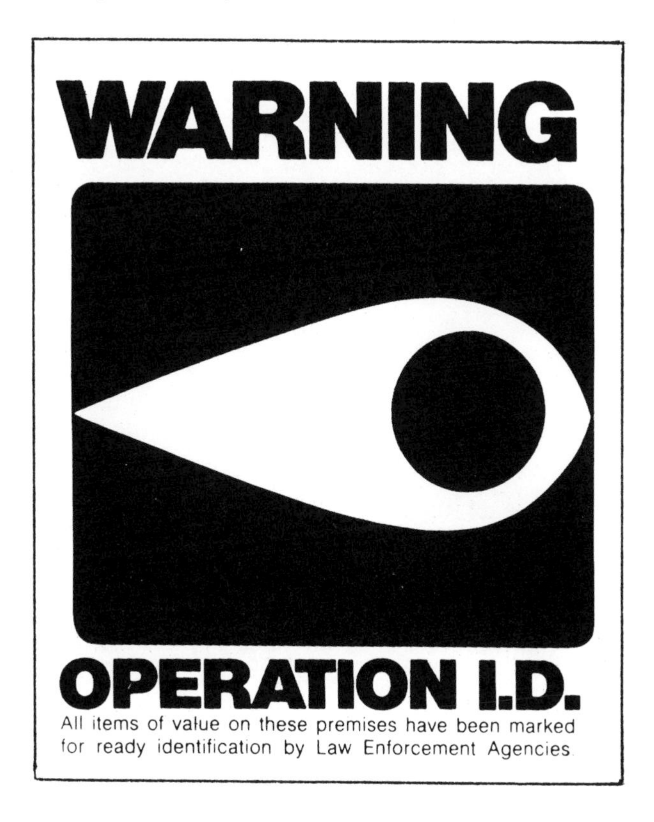

protecting yourself against coming home to find that your television, stereo, and camera have been cleaned out of your apartment. These items are popular targets for thieves because, if they're unmarked, they're easy to fence—no questions asked.

The Identifax system will protect your appliances and large valuables, but what about your jewelry or your silverware? Just because you're living in an apartment doesn't mean you can't have a safe. There are small safes available that will fit on a closet shelf or in a desk and large ones that may double as an end table and weigh up to 240 pounds. The smaller ones can be fastened or bolted to a closet shelf or locked in a desk. And it would take a very determined thief to lift a larger safe. The small safes are indispensable if you keep legal documents or valuable papers in your apartment. In fires safes and their contents have been known to survive when everything else in a building has been completely destroyed.

Protection From Fire

Fire in a home is one of the most frightening things that can happen to anyone, especially at night. The apartment dweller is particularly vulnerable because he may be the victim of a fire due to the carelessness of someone in a neighboring unit. There are things you can do to at least lessen the chances of having a fire in your apartment and to diminish the damage and danger should a fire occur.

Prevention is a good place to start. Before you plug in small kitchen appliances, find out how adequate the circuits are in your kitchen. Some older apartments are not up to snuff on their wiring and were never meant to accommodate the many appliances used today. Ask your landlord how up-to-date the wiring is and what amp service it provides. If in doubt about its adequacy, check with your local building inspector to find out if the wiring meets the current standards required in your area. If it's in violation of the code, your landlord may be forced to rewire.

Make sure that all the cords on your appliances are intact, not frayed or split, and that they are large enough to take care of the appliances on which they're being used. When the cord feels hot to the touch, something is wrong. Don't use that appliance again until it's fixed.

Keep at least one fire extinguisher in your apartment, preferably in the kitchen. And make sure that it's active. Some apartment complexes provide extinguishers for you. If not, you can purchase one for $10 to $12.

If you're in the process of remodeling your apartment, be cautious about the paint you choose. Although with the advent of water-based paints the danger greatly diminished, it's still wise to read the label on any paint you're using. The safest paint is labeled "Non-flammable" or "Non-combustible." If a can is labeled, "Caution—combustible" it is safer than one that bears a label marked "Warning—flammable" or "Danger—extremely flammable." When using paints that are not water-based, keep away from anything with an open flame, such as a gas stove. Work in a well ventilated area, and don't smoke.

IN CASE OF FIRE

Have an escape plan for you and your family in case of fire. Discuss it and practice so that if a fire does occur in your apartment or building, everyone will know where to go and what to do. Have a rendezvous point at which to meet once out of the building so you'll know when everyone is out of danger. Once out of the apartment, don't go back in to get a valued possession. Many people are killed each year returning to burning buildings. The fire may be much worse than your appraisal of it.

Many cities and towns have ordinances requiring fire escapes in apartments, but many others do not. Home fire escape ladders may be purchased inexpensively. They fold up and will fit under a bed or dresser. I recommend one for each bedroom on the second or third floor of an apartment. American LaFrance makes steel escape ladders in two lengths: 15 feet and 25 feet. The deluxe models have non-slip treads. These ladders hook over the windowsill and provide 1″ wide rungs right down to the ground. Much safer than jumping!

A bedside telephone is a great help in case of fire. Some areas have a master number to dial in case of any emergency. In other places you need to know the number of your local fire department. Keep this number next to the phone or, better yet, memorize it.

Never leave bedroom doors open while sleeping. They offer considerable protection from toxic smoke when closed, and they often act as a draft, pulling smoke and flames toward you, when left open. If you awaken to a fire in your apartment during the night, call the fire department, then roll out of bed and crawl on the floor to the exit you're going to use. If a door is hot to the touch, don't open it. If you can see no signs of heat or smoke around the door, brace yourself against it while you open it a crack. (The force of the fire can push it open once it has been unlatched.) If the fire is outside your bedroom door, seal off the crack at the bottom of the door with bedding and go out the window (if this is possible) or wait for help.

SMOKE ALARMS

One of the best devices to come along in the area of safety is the home smoke alarm. They have saved an incalculable number of lives. Every apartment should have at least one and preferably more. There are two types, the ionization or the photoelectric, from which to choose. Each has its advantages.

Woman's Day magazine conducted a test program and concluded that every home should have at least one of each type. The ionization detectors are quickest to respond to the type of smoke produced by a flaming fire, while the photoelectronic type is more sensitive to a smoldering fire which so often starts from a carelessly dropped cigarette or a faulty electric cord. Smoldering fires are responsible for most home fire fatalities.

Neither type of alarm is expensive. They range in price from $20 to less than $100. In selecting a detector (or, better yet, detectors), check for what it takes to trigger the alarm. You also need to know how loud the alarm is and what it sounds like. Are all the people living in the apartment going to be able to hear it? Battery-operated units have a softer alarm than most systems that operate on house wiring. If the alarm you're considering is battery-operated, does it have an indicator that makes a loud noise when the batteries are becoming weak? How long does that warning go on before the batteries go dead? Do you have a week, a day, or a month to get new batteries? (If your detector is UL-approved, as it should be before you consider it, the test noise must sound at least a week before the batteries will be dead.) The National Fire Protection Association recommends that you test your smoke alarm by pushing the button about once a week.

I favor battery-operated smoke alarms for apartment dwellers. Although the alarms aren't as loud, apartments aren't usually as large as single family dwellings and the chances of hearing the alarm are better. If a fire starts in your electrical system, or if for any other reason the wiring becomes nonfunctioning, your alarm is useless if it depends on electricity. If you do choose an electrically-operated alarm, be sure you don't plug it into a socket that operates from a wall switch. It's too easy to inadvertently turn off that switch and deactivate your alarm.

Where to place the alarms is always a problem. The kitchen seems a likely spot, but since the alarms are so sensitive to smoke or flame they are apt to be set off by cooking. The living room is a good place for a photoelectric detector in case of a dropped cigarette. Then there should be one outside each bedroom door. And anyone who smokes in bed should have a detector right near the bed. When one detector must suffice, put it in the hallway that leads to the bedroom.

Honeywell has a Sensitivity Calibrator on their alarms which allows you to fine tune your detector to minimize the possibility of having it go off from cooking or smoking. For instance, if you have one of these alarms near your kitchen, you would set it to be less sensitive than the one you would place near your bedroom. Honeywell's battery-operated model begins to beep at least thirty days before the battery will be dead.

If you use gas in your apartment for heat or to run appliances, a gas detector is a good investment. It can monitor either natural or LP gas. Gas detectors should be installed right in the room with the gas appliances. If you use LP gas, which is heavier than air, the detector should be placed low in the room—right near the floor. If you use natural gas, which is light and rises, place your detector high, just as you would a smoke detector.

Heat detectors will sound an alarm when the heat reaches a certain temperature. These are fine for a kitchen because it takes a temperature of about 131° F to set them off, and they are unaffected by smoke.

An emergency light is another safety feature worth having in the average apartment. These are portable lights that, when plugged into a wall outlet and set on "auto," turn on during a power failure. If you have to find your way down a long, dark corridor after leaving your apartment, you can unplug the light and carry it to show you the way. General Electric's light retails for about $18.

Tenants Insurance

While you're making your apartment safe, don't overlook insurance. Your apartment building, of course, should be insured by the landlord. That's not your worry. But insuring the contents of your apartment is your responsibility. A tenants or renters insurance policy will cover furniture, clothing, and most other personal property for fire, theft, vandalism, smoke damage, lightning, and other mishaps and catastrophes. In many cases, the insurance company won't even send an appraiser but will insure the goods for what you say they're worth. However, if there is an accident for which you want to collect, an appraiser will be Johnny-on-the-spot to tell you what your things are worth.

Liability coverage will pay costs that may arise if a visitor is injured in your apartment, or if a member of your family hurts someone in any way not involving an automobile. A liability clause is included in most renters insurance policies. This clause even provides coverage if your dog bites a guest or delivery person. If this clause doesn't appear in your policy, do invest the few dollars annually that it will take to purchase liability insurance as an extra.

A basic policy might not protect all your treasures, such as jewelry, fine arts, furs, cameras, silverware, and rare collections. To protect these, you will probably need a Scheduled Personal Property Endorsement. For this type of insurance, the items in question will be appraised by the insurance company.

The premium you pay for depends on several things. One consideration is the distance between your apartment and the nearest fire department. Another is whether that fire department is a regular, full-time one (firemen on duty 24 hours a day), or a volunteer department manned by personnel who don't go to the firehouse until there is a fire in progress.

If you live in a high-crime area, your premium may be higher than average. Conversely, a low-crime neighborhood can mean a lower premium. A relatively fireproof building with up-to-date wiring gets you a lower premium than a building that the insurance company considers a potential firetrap. And, naturally, the value of your possessions is a major consideration in determining your premium.

Chapter 10

Condominiums and Co-ops

In many ways, the pluses and minuses of condominium living parallel those of apartment living. Noise problems, inherent in living in close proximity to other people, must be dealt with; security measures should be taken; the same storage and space situations generally exist; and pets must be selected and cared for with consideration for the nearness of neighbors. The legal aspects of condominium ownership and the lack of tenant-landlord relationships are the major differences between condominium and apartment living. Some people find living in a condominium a happy medium between owning a house, with all its responsibilities, and living in an apartment with none of the benefits of home ownership. To them, the right condominium can offer the best of both worlds.

What Is a Condominium?

Condos are being developed with many faces—from high-rise buildings to one-story dwellings. They can be found in old, existing structures and in new buildings designed specifically for this purpose. Many buildings and complexes that have been used as rental apartments are being offered for sale as condominiums.

When you purchase a condominium, you're buying a unit in which to live, and you're either renting or buying a share in the common areas such as land, recreational facilities, parking lots, halls, and even roofs. (This is discussed in more detail later in this chapter.)

What Is a Cooperative?

Don't confuse condominiums with cooperative housing. As a resident in a co-op, you would not own your unit individually as you would in a condominium. It would be owned by the housing corporation of which you would be a member. You would own stock in all the units as an entirety and be given exclusive use of the unit in which you lived. Cooperative housing projects are run by boards of directors elected by members.

Although co-ops have been available in this country for many more years than condominiums, they don't enjoy the same popularity. New York City and Florida are the only places co-ops flourish. Since co-ops and condos are run in basically the same manner and offer many of the same benefits, this may seem puzzling. But the stock cooperative has one major flaw, and it appears at resale time.

Since there is one blanket mortgage on the entire property, a buyer must be able to immediately provide sufficient funds to cover whatever equity (plus property appreciation) the seller has in the premises. If the seller has owned the co-op for any length of time, this will probably be a sizable sum. The blanket mortgage cannot be disturbed for the benefit of making a sale. A buyer in effect takes over the remainder of the seller's part of the mortgage. When a co-op is sold, the buyer is purchasing stock in the total property. In some places (New York, for instance) you may be able to borrow money against the co-op stocks. But it is not common practice. If you obtain a personal loan, you are going to be repaying it at the same time you're paying off the mortgage. This means two payments instead of one.

When Your Apartment Goes Condo

Should the owner of the apartment building or complex in which you're living decide to sell his property as condominium units, you'll be faced with the decision to buy or not to buy.

There are many points to be evaluated in making this important choice which could make you the owner of your home. The laws governing condominium conversions in your community will dictate the terms of a conversion. Those laws, along with the other considerations given to any condominium purchase, should clue you in to whether purchasing your unit is a wise or risky move.

Converting existing apartments into condominiums is a relatively new scheme and one that is rapidly gaining in popularity. Because it is new, many areas do not have laws to govern these sales. Officials of townships, municipalities, and counties, faced with this situation, have scrambled to quickly pass appropriate legislation.

As conversions to condos have become more widespread, some state governments have stepped in, making things more equitable and more uniform by passing legislation that spells out the manner in which condo conversions will be dealt with throughout their state. These laws, of course, supersede any statutes already in existence in the cities, towns, and counties of that state.

But wherever you live, should your apartment go condominium, your current lease must be honored. You will be allowed to stay in your apartment until that lease expires whether or not you opt to buy. In most cases, you must buy or be gone when the lease is up, but there are exceptions to this. Senior citizens or handicapped persons are typically dealt with more kindly. In many areas, they're allowed a two- or three-year grace period, from the date conversion papers are filed by the owner, in which to either purchase the premises or find other living quarters.

In a few places, such as New York City, a percentage (usually 50 percent) of the tenants must vote in favor of conversion before the landlord is permitted to put his units up for sale. In other cases, such as under Pennsylvania state law, 100 percent of the tenants may be dead set against the conversion and it will still be allowed on the grounds that the owner has the right to sell his property in any way he wishes.

In most places, all units must be offered to the people who occupy them before they can be put up for sale on the open market. Laws governing pricing of these units differ greatly. In some municipalities, the units are offered to the tenants at a lower price than they are when offered to outsiders. In other places, the reverse is true, while in still other areas the law calls for one price, applicable for all potential buyers. In some areas where the law favors the renter, the price to the tenant is legally set at a multiple (often ten) of the annual rental. This can make the purchase extremely attractive for the tenant because it usually is less than the market price. It is often the case that once an owner has officially quoted a price to a tenant, he can't offer an outsider a lower price for at least a year.

Before you agree to buy your apartment, acquaint yourself with the real estate prices in your area so you can judge whether the price for your unit is fair. Is it worth the price for you not to move? Also study the declaration and bylaws (discussed later) just as you would if you were purchasing a unit in a new condominium.

Investigate the financing available for the condo conversion. You may be pleasantly surprised. A smart owner who is looking for a smooth transition of his property is often able to put together an attractive financing package with a local bank at an interest rate lower than the going rate in the area. Even ¼ percent adds up to a substantial savings over the life of a mortgage.

There is resistance to condominium conversions in areas where there is a shortage of available rental properties. It does present a hardship for those who, for whatever reason, prefer renting to owning, often leaving them with a slim choice of living facilities—and those at inflated prices.

Older Buildings as Condominiums

Buying into a condominium in an older building, one that has been converted from a hotel, a barn, a warehouse, or other structure, can be riskier than purchasing a unit in a new condo, or in a building you're living in and know something about. Many conversions are only superficial. The new face—shiny-bright kitchen, modern bathroom, plush wall-to-wall carpet—is usually nicely taken care of. But the wiring may be old and the plumbing about to stop functioning. Remember, when you purchase your unit, you're also buying into the common plumbing, wiring, etc. Should these utilities flounder after you take over your unit, you'll be responsible for a share of the repair bills.

Some older buildings which have been converted are good buys indeed. Any sincere attempt at turning an old building into a decent condominium should entail two steps. The first is restoration, which doesn't always show. And the second is modernization, those cosmetics that are readily apparent.

Any honest developer or owner who's interested in converting an older property into a condominium first will get a report from an engineer. This report will cover the structural condition of the building, the electrical and plumbing components, and the state of all mechanical items. It will go into detail on what must be done to put the structure in like-new condition. If the developer is on the level, he shouldn't object to discussing this report with you or even showing it to you. If he hasn't obtained a report of this type, chances are he hasn't done an adequate job of restoration either.

Deciding to Buy

If you want the pride of ownership with no lawns to cut or driveways to shovel, a condominium may be just the answer for you. But proceed with caution. Laws governing the buying and selling of condominiums vary greatly from place to place. Some states now have stringent laws protecting the condo owner, while others do not. And in any case, you must read every word of a condominium sales agreement and the other condo documents before you sign anything.

YOUR OBLIGATIONS

Anyone who is contemplating the purchase of a condo or co-op should be aware that he's not obligated to pay only for the unit itself, or for the stock if it's a co-op. There will be a charge (usually monthly) over and above the principal, interest, and taxes, which should be used to pay for maintenance of the common areas. Your principal and interest payments will remain the same unless you have a variable rate mortgage (one which may be rewritten at specified intervals to accommodate the current mortgage lending rate), but your maintenance fee could go up drastically to cover increasing costs or to purchase new equipment (which you may not be in favor of).

If the land on which your condominium is situated is owned by the condominium association, which in effect is you and the other owners, the maintenance expenses will probably stay realistic, escalating only as costs go up. But if the land is held by the developer, the maintenance costs could skyrocket once the development has been 100-percent sold. When the developer, not the condominium association, owns the land, he can charge what he sees fit for its maintenance, though it is usually contractually limited. Should he, for instance, choose to charge twice the going rate for mowing the lawns, you may be powerless to do anything but pay him. Snow removal also may become a major cost. In some areas, there are laws to protect you from exorbitant costs when the developer is in control. Other places still allow this type of bilking to go on.

If you aren't savvy when it comes to assessing what it should cost to operate the condominium, have someone who is knowledgeable take a look at the common areas. Estimate realistic operating costs, and compare them with what the developer has budgeted. In some less reliable and unsupervised condominiums, operating costs may start low and increase as soon as the development is full. If it's a "too-good-to-be-true" figure for operating costs, chances are it isn't true, or won't be for long.

Don't be lulled into a sense of security by the rhetoric spewed out by a salesman. His word that certain things will be done is not a substitute for a legal document. Don't buy a condo just on the basis of the individual unit in which you're interested. Get an overview of the entire project—what it will include, how large an area it will cover, and just what your responsibilities toward the total condominium community will be.

If you're buying a condominium before the whole development has been completed, find out if the developer has sufficient money to complete the entire project—all units and all common areas—without using your down payment as part of his operating costs. Many places require that all down payments be held in escrow accounts until the entire development is completed. This is the best protection for you. But, if this is not the case, a condominium owner may find himself living in a project with uncompleted sidewalks, no lawns, no clubhouse (if one is in the plans), and no way to get these amenities if the developer runs out of funds, which can happen even to the most well-intentioned, honest condominium developer.

You need to determine what kind of project the condominium is ultimately going to be. You should know the degree to which occupancy may be transient. While you should have the right to lease your property if you want to do so for any reason, stay away from a development with a very transient population, which lowers values. In any project with federally-insured mortgages, government regulations specify that a residential unit cannot be leased for a period of less than thirty days. This restriction is an asset to the development as a whole. But you do want the option of renting your property on a long term basis, even if it seems unlikely at the time of purchase that you'd ever be doing so.

You also want the right to sell your unit to whomever you choose and for whatever price you can get. Some condominium sales agreements state that you must give the condominium association right of first refusal. This means that before you can sell your unit, or even put it on the market, you must first offer it to the association. They have a previously stipulated length of time (usually anywhere from thirty to ninety days) in which to decide to buy or not to buy. During this time, you must wait for their decision. You can't sell to anyone else. If you're in a hurry, this can put you into real trouble.

Of course, you should have a reliable lawyer look over any agreement before you sign it. But it's a good idea to be alert on your own behalf as well. Look over the sales agreement for a "Liquidated Damage Clause." It will tell you under what conditions, if any, you could lose your down payment. It could be that if you fail to get financing after the agreement has been signed, you'll forfeit your money. There are other circumstances under which you can lose your deposit, too. Find out before you sign! In your eagerness to purchase a home, and with an anxious salesman pressuring you, it's tempting to sign before you know all the ramifications of doing so. You can pay for a hasty act for many years to come.

Take a good long look at the common areas. Determine if they're worth the fee you'll have to pay. If you don't swim, don't play tennis, and are sure that you will have no opportunity to use the facilities in a common clubhouse, you may not want to purchase a unit in a condominium that provides these things. You'll be paying for them even though you never go near them. Are the streets maintained by the municipality, or will they be the responsibility of the condominium association (meaning that their upkeep will be paid for by you and the other residents)? This can become costly.

THE TITLE

You're better off with a fee simple title to the common areas. This means that the owners of the units are also owners (collectively) of the common areas. Beware of a leasehold title. It means you are only renting the land and the common areas. The Department of Housing and Urban Development (HUD) has this to say about leased land: "Some condominium developers retain ownership of parts of a project, usually the recreational facilities and sometimes the land, and lease them back to the buyers for 99 years. It is important to be aware of the difference between full ownership (fee simple title) which gives the owners control of the common area and a leasehold which gives the lessee full control over the property under the lease.

"A developer or salesman may claim that more amenities can be provided by a leasehold arrangement and the condominium can be offered at lower prices. However, what can and does sometimes happen to the consumer is that he may be subjected to exorbitant rental charges initially and still higher rates over an extended period of time, in addition to the monthly assessment on the condominium. Failure to pay the monthly obligations could result in complete loss of your investment through foreclosure."

Another way in which a developer may keep control of the common areas is by retaining 51 percent of the units. In this way he can control the project not just as the developer, but as an owner. He alone, not a group of owners with equal or near-equal votes, will run the condominium. It becomes in essence a dictatorship.

THE ASSOCIATION

The Association, which is comprised of all the owners, is established by the Declaration (an important document which will be discussed later). It is governed by a board that's usually elected by the unit owners. As a condominium owner, you should attend all association meetings and vote on every issue. They concern you and your family. And they'll determine your lifestyle while you're living in that development. Don't become lax in this or you'll discover that a handful of people are setting the conditions under which you're allowed to live in your home.

Condominium owners are fortunate to have this opportunity to voice their opinions and have a say in the government of their development. It's a built-in asset that comes with condo ownership. Apartment dwellers aren't as fortunate in this regard. We must form our own organizations to fight for fair treatment. But we are able to move out if the situation becomes intolerable. If a condominium owner finds that the development isn't being run to his liking, he may still be stuck living there at least for the time it takes to sell the unit.

THE BYLAWS

The bylaws of a condominium are generally established by the board. It's tricky to make bylaws equitable and still retain the right degree of permissiveness. A condominium in which the laws are too lenient may have an unhappy atmosphere in which a rowdy element dominates. On the other hand, if the laws are too strict, condo owners will feel oppressed. If that happy medium isn't obtained, and the owners aren't content with the board of directors, they should be able to replace the board. But in order to do so, it must be stated in the bylaws that this is allowed. Otherwise the board will be in power for the term for which it was elected, like it or not.

Many people think that the bylaws for condominiums were created and are controlled by federal law. They are mistaken. The only condominium owners protected by federal law are those who buy in a condo where mortgages are insured by HUD-FHA (Federal Housing Administration) under the National Housing Act. But you can find out from your state real estate commission what the laws governing condominiums are in your state.

Included at the end of this chapter is a copy of the bylaws used in any condominium where the mortgage is insured by HUD-FHA. They are fair and equitable, and you might want to compare them with the bylaws of any condominium in which you're considering purchasing a unit.

THE DECLARATION

This extremely important document (also called "Covenant and Restrictions," "Plan of Condominium Ownership," "Master Deed," or "Declaration of Conditions") should be read carefully. It contains the restrictions and covenants that will be the law in your condominium. So before you buy, be sure it's something with which you can live. Changing it isn't easy. It's prepared by the person or corporation who previously held the property as a single deed estate. At the time the Declaration is recorded, the property becomes a number of condominiums each with a separate title or deed.

The Declaration addresses itself to the various characteristics of the specific condominium with which it deals. It will spell out for you just what your rights and responsibilities will be if you purchase a unit in that condo. It is in this document that you'll find not only a description of the unit you're purchasing but a listing and description of all the common areas as well. If the parking lot or recreation areas aren't listed as common areas, don't assume that the ommission was an oversight. You'll probably find they aren't part of the common property at all, and you'll be charged for their rental each month over and above your maintenance fee. Avoid this condominium. Any condo financed by HUD/FHA isn't permitted to lease areas in this way.

DEGREE OF OWNERSHIP

The Declaration will also tell you what ratio of the entire condominium project you will own or control with the purchase of any specific unit. This is important because it will govern the following:

1. The number of votes you'll have in association matters.
2. How much you'll be charged for maintenance of common grounds.
3. The percentage of common grounds you'll own.
4. The real estate tax you'll have to pay.

In some condominiums, the ownership of common property is the same for each buyer no matter how large or small his individual unit. In other condos, this degree of ownership is directly proportionate to the size or cost of the unit. If this degree of ownership is governed by law, it will be the same in any condo property within that area. In other places this percentage may be computed by the developer. Beware of fine print that says unit ratios may be changed in the future. What starts off as a good deal, percentage-wise, could end up as a very expensive proposition.

INSURANCE

Most condominium declarations provide for a master hazard insurance policy. You should receive a copy of the insurance policy when you get your master deed. But before you buy, check on this insurance. The insurance policy should name the board of directors along with each unit owner as the insured. This is an extremely important and often overlooked detail. If you're going to own and be responsible for a portion of the entire project, you should know whether the development in its entirety, including all the common areas, is adequately protected by insurance coverage. The company carrying the insurance for the condominium will be able to tell you if there is as much coverage as they recommended. And you can check out the reliability of the insurance company by writing or calling the insurance commissioner's office in your state. They'll tell you the number of complaints lodged against that company for any given year.

COMMERCIAL UNITS

Commercial properties within condominiums are described in the Declaration. There are two ways in which these commercial units are handled, and the Declaration will tell you which prevails in the condominium in which you're interested. One method is to sell commercial properties individually, just as the residential units are sold. In this event, the person who owns the property gets all of the profits from it. Another way of dealing with commercial properties is to consider them part of the common estate—that is, to assume they belong to all the unit owners. The profits from their rental should go into a fund to reduce the general assessment to all the owners. This is great as long as all the commercial units are rented. But if they are vacant, all the unit owners are responsible for them—the mortgage must still be paid.

TAXES

Currently, the condominium owner is dealt with more kindly in the matter of taxes than the average apartment dweller. He's entitled to the same income tax advantages as conventional homeowners. This means that all real estate taxes and mortgage interest paid may be deducted from his taxable income. This is one tax break that condominium owners receive but apartment dwellers don't.

Checklist for Condo Buyers

1. How old is the property?
2. Where is it located? Is it convenient for you?
3. Is the neighborhood a good one? Is it on the way up or down? (Never buy in a declining neighborhood.)

4. Are you close to public transportation?
5. How is the property managed?
6. If it's a conversion from an older building, was there an engineer's report? Were the suggestions followed?
7. How is the financing handled?
8. If this is a conversion from apartments to condominiums, are the tenants buying or moving out? (A good percentage usually buy if they like living in the building or complex.)
9. Are the common areas well maintained?
10. What is the reputation of the builder or developer who has undertaken the project? (Leopards and developers rarely change their spots.)

BYLAWS USED IN ANY CONDOMINIUM WHERE THE MORTGAGE IS INSURED BY HUD-FHA

BY-LAWS OF ______________________________ CONDOMINIUM

Article I

PLAN OF APARTMENT OWNERSHIP

Section 1. *Apartment Ownership*. The project located at ______________

Street, City of ________________, State of ________________, known

as "________________ Condominium" is submitted to the provisions of*

______________________________ .

Section 2. *By-Laws Applicability*. The provisions of these By-Laws are applicable to the project. (The term "project" as used herein shall include the land.)

Section 3. *Personal Application*. All present or future owners, tenants, future tenants, or their employees, or any other person that might use the facilities of the project in any manner, are subject to the regulations set forth in these By-Laws and to the Regulatory Agreement, attached as Exhibit "C" to the recorded Plan of Apartment Ownership.

The mere acquisition or rental of any of the family units (hereinafter referred to as "units") of the project or the mere act of occupancy of any of said units will signify that these By-Laws and the provisions of the Regulatory Agreement are accepted, ratified, and will be complied with.

Article II

VOTING, MAJORITY OF OWNERS, QUORUM, PROXIES

Section 1. *Voting*. Voting shall be on a percentage basis and the percentage of the vote to which the owner is entitled is the percentage assigned to the family unit or units in the Master Deed.

* Identify state law establishing apartment ownership.

Section 2. *Majority of Owners.* As used in these By-Laws the term "majority of owners" shall mean those owners holding 51% of the votes in accordance with the percentages assigned in the Master Deed.

Section 3. *Quorum.* Except as otherwise provided in these By-Laws, the presence in person or by proxy of a "majority of owners" as defined in Section 2 of this Article shall constitute a quorum.

Section 4. *Proxies.* Votes may be cast in person or by proxy. Proxies must be filed with the Secretary before the appointed time of each meeting.

Article III

ADMINISTRATION

Section 1. *Association Responsibilities.* The owners of the units will constitute the Association of Owners (hereinafter referred to as "Association") who will have the responsibility of administering the project, approving the annual budget, establishing and collecting monthly assessments and arranging for the management of the project pursuant to an agreement, containing provisions relating to the duties, obligations, removal and compensation of the management agent. Except as otherwise provided, decisions and resolutions of the Association shall require approval by a majority of owners.

Section 2. *Place of Meetings.* Meetings of the Association shall be held at the principal office of the project or such other suitable place convenient to the owners as may be designated by the Board of Directors.

Section 3. *Annual Meetings.* The first annual meeting of the Association shall be held on ________________ (Date)*. Thereafter, the annual meetings of the Association shall be held on the ________________ (1st, 2nd, 3rd, 4th) ________________ (Monday, Tuesday, Wednesday, etc.) of ________________ (month) each succeeding year. At such meetings there shall be elected by ballot of the owners a Board of Directors in accordance with the requirements of Section 5 of Article IV of these By-Laws. The owners may also transact such other business of the Association as may properly come before them.

Section 4. *Special Meetings.* It shall be the duty of the President to call a special meeting of the owners as directed by resolution of the Board of Directors or upon a petition signed by a majority of the owners and having been presented to the Secretary, or at the request of the Federal Housing Commissioner or his duly authorized representative. The notice of any special meeting shall state the time and place of such meeting and the purpose thereof. No business shall be transacted at a special meeting except as stated in the notice unless by consent of four-fifths of the owners present, either in person or by proxy.

Section 5. *Notice of Meetings.* It shall be the duty of the Secretary to mail a notice of each annual or special meeting, stating the purpose thereof as well as the time and place where it is to be held, to each owner of record, at least 5 but not more than 10 days prior to such meeting. The mailing of a notice in the manner provided in this Section shall be considered notice served. Notices of all meetings shall be mailed to the Director of the local insuring office of the Federal Housing Administration.

---

* This date must be approved by the FHA Insuring Office.

Section 6. *Adjourned Meetings.* If any meeting of owners cannot be organized because a quorum has not attended, the owners who are present, either in person or by proxy, may adjourn the meeting to a time not less than forty-eight (48) hours from the time the original meeting was called.

Section 7. *Order of Business.* The order of business at all meetings of the owners of units shall be as follows:

(a) Roll call.
(b) Proof of notice of meeting or waiver of notice.
(c) Reading of minutes of preceding meeting.
(d) Reports of officers.
(e) Report of Federal Housing Administration representative, if present.
(f) Report of committees.
(g) Election of inspectors of election.
(h) Election of directors.
(i) Unfinished business.
(j) New business.

Article IV
BOARD OF DIRECTORS

Section 1. *Number and Qualification.* The affairs of the Association shall be governed by a Board of Directors composed of ________________ persons,** all of whom must be owners of units in the project.

Section 2. *Powers and Duties.* The Board of Directors shall have the powers and duties necessary for the administration of the affairs of the Association and may do all such acts and things as are not by law or by these By-Laws directed to be exercised and done by the owners.

Section 3. *Other Duties.* In addition to duties imposed by these By-Laws or by resolutions of the Association, the Board of Directors shall be responsible for the following:

(a) Care, upkeep and surveillance of the project and the common areas and facilities and the restricted common areas and facilities.
(b) Collection of monthly assessments from the owners.
(c) Designation and dismissal of the personnel necessary for the maintenance and operation of the project, the common areas and facilities and the restricted common areas and facilities.

Section 4. *Management Agent.* The Board of Directors may employ for the Association a management agent at a compensation established by the Board to perform such duties and services as the Board shall authorize including, but not limited to, the duties listed in Section 3 of this Article.

Section 5. *Election and Term of Office.* At the first annual meeting of the Association the term of office of two Directors shall be fixed for three (3) years. The term of office of two Directors shall be fixed at two (2) years, and

---

** The number should be an odd number not less than five.

the term of office of one Director shall be fixed at one (1) year. At the expiration of the initial term of office of each respective Director, his successor shall be elected to serve a term of three (3) years. The Directors shall hold office until their successors have been elected and hold their first meeting. (If a larger Board of Directors is contemplated, the terms of office should be established in a similar manner so that they will expire in different years.)

Section 6. *Vacancies.* Vacancies in the Board of Directors caused by any reason other than the removal of a Director by a vote of the Association shall be filled by vote of the majority of the remaining Directors, even though they may constitute less than a quorum; and each person so elected shall be a Director until a successor is elected at the next annual meeting of the Association.

Section 7. *Removal of Directors.* At any regular or special meeting duly called, any one or more of the Directors may be removed with or without cause by a majority of the owners and a successor may then and there be elected to fill the vacancy thus created. Any Director whose removal has been proposed by the owners shall be given an opportunity to be heard at the meeting.

Section 8. *Organization Meeting.* The first meeting of a newly elected Board of Directors shall be held within ten (10) days of election at such place as shall be fixed by the Directors at the meeting at which such Directors were elected, and no notice shall be necessary to the newly elected Directors in order legally to constitute such meeting, providing a majority of the whole Board shall be present.

Section 9. *Regular Meetings.* Regular meetings of the Board of Directors may be held at such time and place as shall be determined, from time to time, by a majority of the Directors, but at least two such meetings shall be held during each fiscal year. Notice of regular meetings of the Board of Directors shall be given to each Director, personally or by mail, telephone or telegraph, at least three (3) days prior to the day named for such meeting.

Section 10. *Special Meetings.* Special meetings of the Board of Directors may be called by the President on three days notice to each Director, given personally or by mail, telephone or telegraph, which notice shall state the time, place (as hereinabove provided) and purpose of the meeting. Special meetings of the Board of Directors shall be called by the President or Secretary in like manner and on like notice on the written request of at least three Directors.

Section 11. *Waiver of Notice.* Before or at any meeting of the Board of Directors, any Director may, in writing, waive notice of such meeting and such waiver shall be deemed equivalent to the giving of such notice. Attendance by a Director at any meeting of the Board shall be a waiver of notice by him of the time and place thereof. If all the Directors are present at any meeting of the Board, no notice shall be required and any business may be transacted at such meeting.

Section 12. *Board of Directors' Quorum.* At all meetings of the Board of Directors, a majority of the Directors shall constitute a quorum for the transaction of business, and the acts of the majority of the Directors present at a meeting at which a quorum is present shall be the acts of the Board of

Directors. If, at any meeting of the Board of Directors, there be less than a quorum present, the majority of those present may adjourn the meeting from time to time. At any such adjourned meeting, any business which might have been transacted at the meeting as originally called may be transacted without further notice.

Section 13. *Fidelity Bonds.* The Board of Directors shall require that all officers and employees of the Association handling or responsible for Association funds shall furnish adequate fidelity bonds. The premiums on such bonds shall be paid by the Association.

Article V
OFFICERS

Section 1. *Designation.* The principal officers of the Association shall be a President, a Vice President, a Secretary, and a Treasurer, all of whom shall be elected by and from the Board of Directors. The Directors may appoint an assistant treasurer, and an assistant secretary, and such other officers as in their judgment may be necessary. (In the case of an Association of one hundred owners or less the offices of Treasurer and Secretary may be filled by the same person.)

Section 2. *Election of Officers.* The officers of the Association shall be elected annually by the Board of Directors at the organization meeting of each new Board and shall hold office at the pleasure of the Board.

Section 3. *Removal of Officers.* Upon an affirmative vote of a majority of the members of the Board of Directors, any officer may be removed, either with or without cause, and his successor elected at any regular meeting of the Board of Directors, or at any special meeting of the Board called for such purpose.

Section 4. *President.* The President shall be the chief executive officer of the Association. He shall preside at all meetings of the Association and of the Board of Directors. He shall have all of the general powers and duties which are usually vested in the office of president of an Association, including but not limited to the power to appoint committees from among the owners from time to time as he may in his discretion decide is appropriate to assist in the conduct of the affairs of the Association.

Section 5. *Vice President.* The Vice President shall take the place of the President and perform his duties whenever the President shall be absent or unable to act. If neither the President nor the Vice President is able to act, the Board of Directors shall appoint some other member of the Board to so do on an interim basis. The Vice President shall also perform such other duties as shall from time to time be imposed upon him by the Board of Directors.

Section 6. *Secretary.* The Secretary shall keep the minutes of all meetings of the Board of Directors and the minutes of all meetings of the Association; he shall have charge of such books and papers as the Board of Directors may direct; and he shall, in general, perform all the duties incident to the office of Secretary.

Section 7. *Treasurer.* The Treasurer shall have responsibility for Association funds and securities and shall be responsible for keeping full and accurate accounts of all receipts and disbursements in books belonging to the Association. He shall be responsible for the deposit of all moneys and other valuable effects in the name, and to the credit, of the Association in such depositaries as may from time to time be designated by the Board of Directors.

Article VI

OBLIGATIONS OF THE OWNERS

Section 1. *Assessments.* All owners are obligated to pay monthly assessments imposed by the Association to meet all project communal expenses, which may include a liability insurance policy premium and an insurance premium for a policy to cover repair and reconstruction work in case of hurricane, fire, earthquake or other hazard. The assessments shall be made pro rata according to the value of the unit owned, as stipulated in the Master Deed. Such assessments shall include monthly payments to a General Operating Reserve and a Reserve Fund for Replacements as required in the Regulatory Agreement attached as Exhibit "C" to the Plan of Apartment Ownership.

Section 2. *Maintenance and Repair.*

(a) Every owner must perform promptly all maintenance and repair work within his own unit, which if omitted would affect the project in its entirety or in a part belonging to other owners, being expressly responsible for the damages and liabilities that his failure to do so may engender.

(b) All the repairs of internal installations of the unit such as water, light, gas, power, sewage, telephones, air conditioners, sanitary installations, doors, windows, lamps and all other accessories belonging to the unit area shall be at the owner's expense.

(c) An owner shall reimburse the Association for any expenditures incurred in repairing or replacing any common area and facility damaged through his fault.

Section 3. *Use of Family Units—Internal Changes.*

(a) All units shall be utilized for residential purposes only.

(b) An owner shall not make structural modifications or alterations in his unit or installations located therein without previously notifying the Association in writing, through the Management Agent, if any, or through the President of the Board of Directors, if no management agent is employed. The Association shall have the obligation to answer within   days and failure to do so within the stipulated time shall mean that there is no objection to the proposed modification or alteration.

Section 4. *Use of Common Areas and Facilities and Restricted Common Areas and Facilities.*

(a) An owner shall not place or cause to be placed in the lobbies, vestibules, stairways, elevators and other project areas and facilities of a similar nature both common and restricted, any furniture, packages or objects of any kind. Such areas shall be used for no other purpose than for normal transit through them.

(b) The project shall have ____________ elevators, ____________ devoted to the transportation of the owners and their guests and ____________ for freight service, or auxiliary purposes. Owners and tradesmen are expressly required to utilize exclusively a freight or service elevator for transporting packages, merchandise or any other object that may affect the comfort or well-being of the passengers of the elevator dedicated to the transportation of owners, residents and guests.

Section 5. *Right of Entry.*

(a) An owner shall grant the right of entry to the management agent or to any other person authorized by the Board of Directors or the Association in case of any emergency originating in or threatening his unit, whether the owner is present at the time or not.

(b) An owner shall permit other owners, or their representatives, when so required, to enter his unit for the purpose of performing installations, alterations or repairs to the mechanical or electrical services, provided that requests for entry are made in advance and that such entry is at a time convenient to the owner. In case of an emergency, such right of entry shall be immediate.

Section 6. *Rules of Conduct.*

(a) No resident of the project shall post any advertisements, or posters of any kind in or on the project except as authorized by the Association.

(b) Residents shall exercise extreme care about making noises or the use of musical instruments, radios, television and amplifiers that may disturb other residents. Keeping domestic animals will abide by the Municipal Sanitary Regulations.

(c) It is prohibited to hang garments, rugs, etc., from the windows or from any of the facades of the project.

(d) It is prohibited to dust rugs, etc., from the windows, or to clean rugs, etc., by beating on the exterior part of the project.

(e) It is prohibited to throw garbage or trash outside the disposal installations provided for such purposes in the service areas.

(f) No owner, resident or lessee shall install wiring for electrical or telephone installation, television antenae, machines or air conditioning units, etc., on the exterior of the project or that protrude through the walls or the roof of the project except as authorized by the Association.

Article VII
Amendments to Plan of Apartment Ownership

Section 1. *By-Laws.* These By-Laws may be amended by the Association in a duly constituted meeting for such purpose and no amendment shall take effect unless approved by owners representing at least 75% of the total value of all units in the project as shown in the Master Deed.

Article VIII
Mortgagees

Section 1. *Notice to Association.* An owner who mortgages his unit, shall notify the Association through the Management Agent, if any, or the President of the Board of Directors in the event there is no Management Agent, the name and address of his mortgagee; and the Association shall maintain such information in a book entitled "Mortgagees of Units."

Section 2. *Notice of Unpaid Assessments.* The Association shall at the request of a mortgagee of a unit report any unpaid assessments due from the owner of such unit.

Article IX

COMPLIANCE

These By-Laws are set forth to comply with the requirements of* ______

____

In case any of these By-Laws conflict with the provisions of said statute, it is hereby agreed and accepted that the provisions of the statute will apply.

* Identify state law establishing apartment ownership.

Index